man is not created

Knowledge is not

MW00647334

a bad habit

teaching > teacher

Practice is watching your thoughts

ZEN-YOGA

Zen-Yoga

A Creative Psychotherapy to Self-Integration

Paramahaṁsa Jīvanmukta Mahābodhisattva

P.J. Saher

MOTILAL BANARSIDASS PUBLISHERS
PRIVATE LIMITED • DELHI

5th Reprint : Delhi, ***2015***
First Edition : Delhi, 1976

ISBN : 978-81-208-0809-6

MOTILAL BANARSIDASS
41 U.A. Bungalow Road, Jawahar Nagar, Delhi 110 007
8 Mahalaxmi Chamber, 22 Bhulabhai Desai Road, Mumbai 400 026
203 Royapettah High Road, Mylapore, Chennai 600 004
236, 9th Main III Block, Jayanagar, Bengaluru 560 011
8 Camac Street, Kolkata 700 017
Ashok Rajpath, Patna 800 004
Chowk, Varanasi 221 001

Printed in India

by RP Jain at NAB Printing Unit,
A-44, Naraina Industrial Area, Phase I, New Delhi–110028
and published by JP Jain for Motilal Banarsidass Publishers (P) Ltd,
41 U.A. Bungalow Road, Jawahar Nagar, Delhi-110007

DEDICATION

Humbly dedicated to all those holy Masters and also to the future Avatara Lord M.M. (*Rex Imperatoris lemuriana*) who helped the author to compile this book for the benefit of mankind.

Their promise is:

> *"Whoever righteously owns this book and treats it with reverence, shall, though he read it or not, receive Their blessings. Harm stays away from one who buys this book as a gift for another."*

—THE ORACLE OF LEMURIA.

TABULA GRATULATORIA

1. Shri S. N. Tavaria
2. Shri Ram and J. McCartney
3. Therese Hinterthür
4. Fam. Nonas and Dastur Framroze A. Bode
5. Arnhild Ruppert-Illguth
6. Carlo Bayer
7. Manfred K. Müller
8. Eva Brökelmann
9. Gisela, Wick
10. Fam. Manfred Ortol
11. W. Suszek
12. Fam. Bergmann, Detnold
13. Standard Kessel & Co. Ltd.
14. Fam. Helbing, Oberhausen
15. Marlies Imhoff (in memoriam)
16. Anneliese Neureiter geb. Fritsche
17. Elisabeth Vogel
18. Elisabeth Watermann
19. Prof. Dr. Stiehl & Associates
20. Staatssekretär Bergmann & Land NRW

FOREWORD

The erudite works of Dr. Saher on Zen-Yoga and allied subjects, are now known to thousands. Many books have been written on the various aspects of Yoga, so that its basic techniques are known all the world over.

It is with the greatest pleasure, therefore, that I now write a Foreword to Dr. Saher's new work "ZEN-YOGA", as it is quite unique, giving knowledge and instruction which, to the best of my knowledge, is hitherto unpublished.

The basis of this new book, Dr. Saher tells me, is a manuscript in Sanskrit which he obtained from India, and its particular value lies in the depth and detail with which this new material has been studied and presented.

Dr. Saher is to be congratulated, not only for his skilful translation from the Sanskrit, but also for the clarity with which he has applied this to western needs and western minds.

Much has been written in the past regarding the psychosomatic effects of Prāṇāyāma and Āsanas, but in his text, Dr. Saher explains clearly the mechanism by which brain and mind operate in conjunction with bodily functions, emotions and psychic experience, and also how these may be controlled and applied for our betterment.

He also shows how specific areas of the brain control similar areas of mind, how these can be applied to Self-analysis, and by means of exercises also given in the text, so control both mind and body, that Self-Realisation is possible in the highest sense, and that even before this stage is reached, Health, Harmony and Serenity will be attained, surely to be prized for themselves alone.

For those who are already students of Yoga Dr. Saher has opened new avenues of thought, new areas of knowledge which allow the student to move into Yoga in greater depth and with greater understanding.

For those to whom Yoga is a new subject, this book will provide a worthy introduction to a way of life in which the rewards become ever richer as the study proceeds.

All the Scriptures of the world throughout the ages have proclaimed to man the need to "KNOW THYSELF". In "ZEN-YOGA" Dr. Saher has provided a sure path to this knowledge.

James McCartney

PREFACE

My Encounter with an Ustad (= an Adept of Zen-Yoga who has attained cosmic-consciousness):—

Remembering the time-worn custom which requires a visitor to bring a small present when calling upon a high personage, I had brought with me a small gift. But I forgot another important custom.

"Remove your shoes?" the Chamberlain commanded sternly.

I was delighted to do so because of my sprained ankle. On entering the Master's private office, I saw, at the far end in a brightly lit enclosure, an erect and stately figure, dignified yet not aloof. I approached him, set down my offering and bowed low in salutation. There is an aesthetic dimension in this ceremony which transcends its function as an expression of respect and courtesy. I eyed him in silence. His noble face, pictured in grey and brown, had that elusive element which the French aptly term *spiritual.* His expression was modest, mild and yet strong, and the large eyes had an extraordinary tranquillity and beauty. The nose was short, straight and classically regular, and his beard made more noticeable the gravity of his mouth. Such a face might have belonged to one of the saints who graced the Church of the Middle Ages, except that his possessed the added quality of intellectuality. Although he had the eyes of a dreamer, I felt in some inexplicable way that there was something more than the visionary behind those heavy lids. For a moment it seemed that a Self much superior to my everyday ego had assumed the guise of this oracular mystic to guide and comfort me.

"Your Eminence has indeed been gracious to receive me," I stammered.

"Your arrival does not surprise me," he replied. "Our meeting was foreordained. Much more than mere chance brings you here again. A higher power ordained and then arranged our encounter, and this is the appointed hour."

The Sufferings of mankind.

His gaze rested on me. He had the eyes of a thinker, idealist and poet, and the sufferings of mankind were reflected in those pupils. He was at once an inspired dreamer, as aint possessed of great serenity, and a practical man of affairs. His smile was friendly, and he welcomed me cordially and yet with a courtly dignity.

"All you see here is yours," he said. "You have come home."

Now I felt like Dorian Grey looking at his own picture when it reflected an unblemished character. For the man (if, indeed, he was not something more) appeared as the epitome of all that was divine and noble in me; as a kind of psychic projection of all that was best, yet buried, in me. This was a splitting of my being as in the psychotic states of excessive L.S.D. addiction or in the Schizophrenia of an artificially induced insanity. Yet the discomfort was experienced as blissful pain, with the pain declining until I knew only a beautific state of being.

Within minutes, I was again my usual self. His gaze still rested kindly on me. It was then that I realized I had been looking, not at him, but through him as it were, right to the hills towering in the distance.

"You gaze at our heights." He spoke with a gentle irony. "I would that all the world should do the same. Usually our guests prefer to concentrate upon the depths. When they speak of us abroad, they mention only the low level to which this land has sunk. Our 'heights' are seldom mentioned even by those who ought to know better. All speak of our glorious past, but make little mention of our future. Our ancient days are spoken of with veneration while our youth is ignored. We have been dismissed as a 'dying' civilization for hundreds of years. Yet here we are, still very much alive. We would like to read in your journals of our hopes, our strength, our vitality. But the West accords us the respect reserved for the world's largest museum."

As we talked I became increasingly aware of the duplex power of his eyes. They were penetrative and hypnotic at the same time. They read my soul and ruled it. They extracted from my mind all its secrets and they compelled me to remain passive and receptive in his presence. He told me how the

my questions & problems disappeared

I told him all my worries

 I felt Peace

paths of men cross and criss-cross at the bidding of unseen forces, and how what appeared to be coincidences were likely to be pre-arranged links in a chain of causes destined to secure certain effects.

After I had told him of my woes and worries, he said, "The law of spiritual evolution is ever at work." Without a trace of vanity, he referred to himself as the *Fakir-ul-Fukara*, the chief of all Adepts, one who can freely function as a spiritual being while being apparently encaged in a physical body. I felt that what he said was true. Here was one of those rare gems of Eastern tradition—those almost unique Adepts who have shared the councils of the gods and are acquainted with a wisdom man is not yet able to learn. Something in this saint held my attention as steel filings are held by a magnet.

My initial perplexity slowly faded as his fascination gripped me ever more firmly. Now I was aware of an important change taking place in my mind. One by one the questions I had prepared in my hotel with such care were discarded. They no longer seemed to be of the least importance. Nor did solving the problems which had hitherto worried me seemed to matter, either. I felt a deep, steady river of serenity flowing through me. A great peace, the peace which has been described as 'passing understanding' was penetrating to the most inaccessible reaches of my being. It was for this that I had been born. Not to make films, nor to take part in revolutions. Questions which had tortured me now seemed irrelevant. Of what worth were Evas and idiots, blonde hair and pink bottoms, my poetry and my past. How petty loomed the panorama of my lost years. I surrendered to the deepening sense of restfulness. For how long I do not know, but certainly for not less than an hour. The passage of time provokes no irritations when the chains of mind-made problems have been discarded. Little by little, a new question established itself in my consciousness :

"Does the *Ustad* emanate spiritual peace as the rose emanates fragrance ?"

It was as if His Eminence were no longer contained by the room, but that the room, including myself, was contained in him. Yet, at the same time, it was as if he, and the room in him, were also contained in me. He was, I felt sure, more

I was not born for XYZ shit

than a man of spiritual power. He was Spirit itself. The fact found clear reflection in his expression, which was one of unshadowed light and joy. It said with that simplicity which carries perfect conviction, 'Your real self is bliss, and that is why I am bliss'. From his position of spiritual eminence—serene, free and possessed of an all-embracing wisdom, he seemed to have the perspective of a heavenly being. He exemplified compassion more than he embodied wisdom. This was no mere preacher of dogmas. He radiated light. Was he unique? Only to me, I felt sure. Why should there not be radiant beings? Such are not enigmatic; they are transparent, which is the highest state of mysticism. There is no mystery about them. They are in the open, perpetually on view. If we feel removed from them it is only because we cannot accept their divine simplicity. With what are these luminous beings illumined? They are aflame with life. They radiate unending bliss. They know a serenity and joy only to be experienced above the chaos of mankind. Yet they remain committed to the human family. They are the god-men, divine yet human; closer to me than my skin, closer than my ego.

His Eminence was looking straight at me. His gaze made it clear he did not fear to face the world. He had neither rejected the world nor renounced it. He appealed as being a part of it, just as the mountains, majestic and abiding, are a part of it. Microcosmically, he *was* the world. In him was all that ever could be of creation. I was flying high in metaphysical regions, but the man in front of me was beyond such stupid dreamings. He knew that man alters little; that it is dangerous to play with souls, it being trouble enough to save one's own. He informed me, and without the intervention of words, that man can do one thing only, and that is the only thing worth doing. That is to clean the windows of his soul to admit the Light, that the Heaven that is everywhere about us (could we but see it!) might establish itself in ourselves.

I was at the very heart of the transformative process; all was death and transfiguration. Facing him was spiritually exhausting, and yet I experienced a novel sort of peace—the augur of a deeper and more enduring serenity. It was the peace of a man who was somehow able to reconcile his past

Compassion > wisdom.

with his present condition. But what of the future? Has not man a *recollection* of the future. Out of misplaced caution we call this type of memory, prevision. These rare flashes include all that can be in time—the Ustad explained. Nor is this quasi-omniscience limited, impeded or baffled by our artificial division of time into past, present and future—nor, for that matter, by experiences of a dead, ill-remembered or forgotten past. Said the Ustad, "Amnesia is the reaction of a sensitive mind overtaxed. A power can be acquired for removal of the hypnotic blocks obstructing the free flow of memory in both directions, provided...."

The spell was broken at that moment by someone entering to announce that the midday meal was ready. I was surprised to see that my hand and ankle were both fully healed. I was still struggling with my grateful astonishment as I was shepherded into the majestic dining hall. When we washed our hands, I was given a napkin with my name printed on it, and this occasioned me further surprise.

P. J. SAHER

Clean the window of your Soul to admit Light.

Clean your mind & truth will appear

Domain of emotions & passions

irrational beliefs / opinions

strong attachments & aversions

CONTENTS

EXPLANATION OF ILLUSTRATIONS

1. The rising of the Kundalini in the Spinal Cord (as seen through esoteric X-Rays of Röntgen Laboratories) during deep meditation as explained in this book.
2. The anatomical brain reconstructed as a Computer kybernetically co-ordinating the Centres.
3. A Centre seen as a Mandala of anatomical re-constructs.
4. The brain as pivot of the seven channels leading to it from the Centres—Mandala of the Esoteric Sciences.
5. The ancient Temple of Aloma-Alomanaris in Lemuria where this secret science was first practised.
6. Mandala meditation practice for beginners.
7. The Centres—and how they fit inside the anatomical brain.
8. Anatomy of the First 5 Centres.
9. Psych-cybernetics of the seven Centres.
10. The principal Three Centres working in cosmic harmony with the Phases of the MOON.
11. Travels with the Astral Body to other Galaxies.
12. The three principal Centres in psycho-cybernetic Regulation with each other.
13. The "Milky Way" seen as an exact Replica of psycho-astrological Meridian Points in the brain.
14. A Centre converging with a Chakra of the Kundalini.
15. The third Chakra of the Kundalini as seen in an Astral Body.
16. The same third Chakra as seen in a Mental or Causal Body.
17. The complete astral body as seen during a Zenoga meditation as described in this book.
18. The Mental body—as above in foregoing illustration.
19. All three bodies combined—DHARMAKAYA—seen as in previous illustration.
20. The central Star as the macrocosmic Centre co-ordinating the micro-cosmic Centres.

Remove obstacles
Clean mind
Clear mind
Remove impurity
Remove film.

AUTHOR'S NOTE

> "And what was to my surprise, he became angry with me, because he had misled me!"
>
> *Khalil Gibran*

This book is written in two parts. Part I contains practical methods and formulae written in simple language, which anyone can understand. *SOME OF THE CHAPTERS ARE FOR ABSOLUTE BEGINNERS* (so advanced readers, kindly bear with me). The practices and methods are not the basic cause of the expansion of consciousness but they are instrumental in removing obstacles, just as the husbandman prepares his ground for sowing. Some ideas may appear contradictory, not that I am of two minds, but to encourage the reader not to accept what is written, but to sit back and think. Wherever there is such a contradiction, a second reading will distinctly reveal the explanation.

In Part I, guidance and practices are recommended for the important functions of eating, sleeping, sex and breathing. This is not done with a view to presenting a new theory. All that is stated in this regard has been tried out over long periods, on many persons of different constitution, sex and age, and in each case without exception, the results have been specifically good.

Part II is written from a metaphysical viewpoint and to show the underlying basis on which the recommended exercises and practices have been built; as well as to provide further practices of an advanced nature.

In conclusion we quote the famous astronomer Kepler :

"If you forgive me, I rejoice; if you are angry, I can bear it. The die is cast, the book is written. It may well wait a century for a reader, as God has waited six thousand years for an observer."

I

THE APPLICATION OF METAPHYSICAL WISDOM TO PRACTICAL LIFE

Peace thru understanding

INTRODUCTION

THE LAWS OF SPIRITUAL SUCCESS

With the help of practices explained in the following pages one can attain within a few years a stage of development for which mankind would need an illimitably long period spreading over countless incarnations on the slow spiral of evolution. The science of these systematic, psychological practices we call : Zenoga.

The dominating aim of Zenoga is concentration of the mind through a better understanding of the metaphysiology of brain-structures. To start with, we may consider the mind as a functional system of extremely subtle vibrations (called 'rotations') which for convenience we divide into four Sections.

Section 1. is the part nearest allied to the anatomical brain while Section 4. we look upon as nearest allied to the Soul (or Ātman). Between Section 1. (citta) and section 4. (Ātman) we have Section 3. (governing the realm of extra-sensory perception) and Section 2. The latter is further subdivided so that Sec. 2 alone has the peculiarity of having two Sub-Sections : Sec. 2 (*a*) and Sec. 2 (*b*).

Sub-section (*a*) of Section 2 is very closely allied to the body's (or rather the brain's) 'Reticular Activating System (=RAS, for short) situated in a cone-shaped maze of nerves in the brain-stem. Subsection (a) intercepts the flow of information, coming up from our physical body, before such impulses of 'information' enter the *Thalmus* for further distribution to the decision-making regions of the *Cortex*. It is therefore in a position to modify (=tone down) or accentuate (=tone up) the different 'message-impulses' as it chooses. It can, because it has profuse neural connections with the *Hypothalmus*, channel reports of bodily disorders (eg: indigestion, toothache) directly to the latter without consulting the conscious mind. All unconscious physiological activity of our body (eg: digestion, breathing) falls under the domain of Sub-Section (a). Thus we are not aware of its constant and complicated guiding of the work of digestion in our belly—unless and until something goes wrong. Then we become aware of the effort involved because we become conscious of it; this 'becoming conscious of it' we then call a bellyache. Without Sub-Section (a) all life would be one long stomach-und bellyache.

Sub-Section 2 (b) is that part of the mind which enables us to concentrate, meditate, receive intuitions from on high—in fact it is so utterly different from Sec. 1 and Subsection (a) of Sec. 2 that we are justified in saying that between Sec. 1 plus Sub-Section (a) of Sec. 2+ and Sections 4, 3, plus 2 (b)++ there is a very wide gulf. This 'gulf' running like a river separating two subcontinents is called in Zenoga : '*No-Man's-Land*'. Concentration of mind (in the true sense of the word) begins on the other side of No-Man's-Land, that is, in Sub-Section (b) of Sec. 2 and onwards. Spiritual discipline means, according to Zenoga, the voluntary yet purposeful development of Section 1 (Sub-Section (a) of Section 2 need no longer be counted as its functions are exclusively of a physiological nature) to *that* stage when we are capable of crossing over No-Man's-Land to Sub-Section (b) of Section 2 and thus to the Higher Sections. That stage is known in Zenoga as : the Critical-Certain-Stage (=C.C.S. for short).

Our task in Zenoga is to reach that Critical-Certain-Stage. From thereon spiritual progress is automatic and effortless, quite free of do's and dont's.

Thus we leave aside the Higher Sections for the time being and confine ourselves to the Lower Sections which in effect means Section 1. or the anatomical brain.

All the four Sections of mind are co-ordinated as one integral whole by means of psychic quartermasters in key-positions. They are known in Zenoga as Centres. There are *seven* (7) Centres distributed over the four sections of the mind. The first four of these seven are situated in Section 1., the 5th. in Sec. 2 (including both subsections), the 6th. in Sec. 3 and the 7th. in Sec. 4.

To make it more characteristic, Zenoga calls the 7th. centre the 'Senior Managing Director' (if we imagine every

+Lower Sections, Collectively speaking.
++Higher Sections, Collectively speaking.

person to be a joint-stock company complete in itself the 6th. centre 'Junior Managing Director', the 5th. centı 'General Manager' and the four centres in Sec. 1 as 'Departmental Heads' or 'Divisional Directors'.

More seriously the seven centres are :—

1. Integrity Centre
2. Emotivity Centre
3. Sensuosity Centre
4. Mobility Centre

All four of them,
centres I., E., S., and M.
are in Sec. 1.

5. Intuitional Centre
in Sec. 2
6. Paramental Centre
in Sec. 3
7. Transcendental Centre
in Sec. 4

We will here describe in short at least the first four centres before passing on.

I. or I. centre means :

I. = INTEGRITY—through—intellectual — INTROSPECTION
for short : integrity
thus

I. Centre means :
rational Reflection consciously and conscientiously done. Its aim is knowledge through a balanced mind as well as decisions arising therefrom. This 'centre' (as we call it) is known in Sanskrit as IHĀ or 'the Will-to-know', meaning the conscious and programmed analysis undertaken with a view to acquire exact or '*integer*' knowledge of a thing, problem or situation solely or predominantly by means of unbiased reasoning. This centre governs all which in Yoga/Vedānta falls under the heading of sattva. The I. centre is that (hypothetical)
spot in the brain which

consciously commands,
reasons, and guides our thinking.

E. or E. centre means :
E. = Evocative—of—Emotions;
for short : Emotivity
thus
E. centre means :
The focus—or the point to which an emotion keeps all attention riveted; ie: the ability or propensity of the emotions to corner or divert attention to themselves. It is that (hypothetical) spot in the brain which arouses all spontaneous feelings; spontaneous and even unnoticed or semi-conscious reactions (=activity) out of feelings. The domain of various emotions and passions including irrational beliefs, passionately held attachments and aversions, all forms of diverse and even contradictory feelings, fancies, whims, tendencies, sub-conscious inclinations—all decisions not carefully debated as to pro and contra in a balanced way beforehand, all 'on the spur of the moment' decisions (later regreted, and one knew that in all probability they *would* be later on regreted), all general unexplained (even unexplainable) 'likes' and 'dislikes'. This centre governs all which in Yoga/Vedānta falls under the heading of rajas (=activity, activity begun or continued on the initiative of one or more emotions). This 'centre' (as we call it) is known in Sanskrit as Ekāyana=the focus; emotions tend to focus all attention on themselves.
S. or S. centre means :
S. = Sensuo—Vitality
for short=Sensuosity
thus
S. centre means :
that spot in the brain which commands reflexes; reflex movements, sub-conscious, impulsive acts (also called 'motor' movements or 'reactions') arising

from a concealed memory of man's evolutionary past; atavistic perversities and/or reflexes conditioned therefrom. This region favours decision made not only against one's better judgement but also against one's own natural likes and dislikes; decisions (as if) forced upon one, (='driven to it'). 'Drives' born out of an insatiable thirst (eg : drugs, sex, etc.) or a seemingly irresistible impulse: 'I couldn't help it', 'I just had to', 'I *must*',—decisions made by the 'blood' as it were. (D. H. Lawrence's 'thinking with one's blood'; Aldous Huxley's explanation of a successful orator as one who 'speaks' or appeals to the stomach-thinking of his listeners). All uncontrollable urges, genuinely 'insatiable' longings—as if some strange force thrusted its decisions on one using him (or her) merely as an instrument of craving.

This centre governs all which in Yoga/Vedānta falls under the heading of Tamas (=dullness of wit, brute stupidity; intelligence made inert through inertia, inactivity of reasoning). In Sanskrit the word Sat means Being— yet also vitality as a characteristic of Being, vitality as the potential energy of being, vitality as 'asleep' or 'hidden' in every being; thus in every human being there are untold reservoirs of vitality (=vital energy) untapped. The S. centre depicts vitality divorced from reason and devoid of feelings.

M. or M. centre means :

M=Mobility of muscular and assorted movements for the mobile (ie: continuing) execution of decisions for short : Mobility
thus

M. centre = means :
that spot in the brain which combines
the aforementioned
(a) thoughts,
(b) feelings, and
(c) reflexes

to form a specific decision. It is like a mathematician. It counts or 'reads' the varying intensities in the first three centres either totaling up the sum (of rotating units of vibrations in the intensities) if they be all of *one* kind (ie : all plus or all minus) or striking a balance. It favours the side (centre or pair of centres) having the higher score of vibrations be it plus or minus. It *always* favours the winning side and that too in a most unique way: it transforms the vibrations of the losing side into those of the majority-holder (minus into plus or vice versa) and then adds even that to the majority's total figure. It has also a kind of 'casting' vote in case of a tie. Such casting vote is always thrown in the scale of the plus vibrations, for the M. centre has no minus vibrations of its own though it does possess a small force of plus vibrations to tip the balance. The M. is known in Sanskrit as Manas or in Latin mens which literally means mind; the M. centre carries out 'interdepartmental memos' of and in the mind. It signifies mobility as a cardinal characteristic of mental operations.

Now before we can proceed further to the Higher Sections we must have practical exercises for reaching that Critical-Certain-Stage. But no practical measures are of any use unless we come to terms with the cardinal problem of the spiritual life—or for that matter any kind of serious or purposeful living—which is :

> how to keep up our interest in and enthusiasm for the QUEST in spite of countless difficulties and reverses ?

Moreover, let's not forget that the severest trial comes in the form of that monotonous routine of everyday life, the aptly-called 'grauer Alltag', which drains away our strength and enthusiasm alike. For the bulk of our earthly existence is (except in very unusual cases) made up of trifling events and incidents. Even a primeminister or a Hemmingway-hero needs must spend a considerable portion of the day dressing, undressing, brushing his teeth, drinking out of a glass (primeminister)

Be at Peace.

or bottle (Hemmingway-hero)--and other less mentionable chores of daily living. Great, meaning extraordinary, events occur but rarely in the life of an average person. To bring forth enthusiasm for 'great' things is almost unavoidable; but how about maintaining such enthusiasm in midst of the daily grind of routine? The acid test for a beginner on the spiritual path lies in sustaining interest for the QUEST even in the midst of the common details of life. To maintain equipoise in spite of ceaseless provocations caused by the trifling irritants of everyday existence demands a resoluteness of which only a handful are capable. And yet the viability of the spiritual life is tested in the field of our ordinary activities (like, for instance, the patience or lack of it with which we wait for a bus) and seldom in the spheres of extraordinary achievements. Without enthusiasm even the spiritual QUEST will appear tiresome. But how to keep the fires of enthusiasm burning in the face of idiotic trifles?

More spiritual aspirants have fallen 'back to usual' because of a failure to sustain enthusiasm for the QUEST than due to any other single cause. The indispensable quality of enthusiasm is known in Zenoga as Prīti= that element of genuine joy with which we do a thing. To tasks of our delight we rise betimes and go to them with longing. Only an enthusiastic life is capable of creativity. When we live 'creatively' our actions are not stereotyped but reveal an individuality all their own. The pre-condition for enthusiasm is a condition of profound interest in any theme, thing or person. Can you imagine enthusiasm without interest? The opposite of *profound* interest is not only indifference but also 'shallow' interest which may aptly be called : sensationalism. Genuine enthusiasm is rooted in profound interest—an interest which borders on commitment and so draws sustenance from the very depths. A person who is full of such commitment to the QUEST is too enthusiastic to experience dullness even in routine or to be deterred by trifles however frequent or obstacles however great.

The reason why most people do not possess such undiminishing enthusiasm for the QUEST (or for anything else except perhaps the fondling of their grand children) is that modern man lives his life at a rather superficial level. This cannot be devotion not dogma

helped in modern techno-civilizations because of the topheavy emphasis put on speed and efficiency.

We are all in a terrific hurry; to go from where we are to where we are no better. Such a 'fast' or superficial life needs a constant supply of sensations to keep it going. Without kicks or titilations the danger of depression arising from drudgery cannot be avoided. The modern world may be described as one keen on being 'high' by constant kicks of some kind or another. Alcohol is a kick, sex is a kick, sleeping-pills are a kick, murder mysteries are a kick—even the 'guru thing' can become a kick. Now true spirituality is essentially a matter of deep experience and not of kicks. So long as we allow our mind to function at superficial levels we can gather no deep experiences. Without deep experience we get sex-orgies instead of love, partys instead of friendship, dogma instead of devotion, respectability instead of ethics, theology instead of religion; a mind content to dissect a dogma but incapable of comprehending the indwelling spirit. Depth of experience alone is the yardstick of spirituality and, that too, irrespective of the sphere of activity. One can be intensely spiritual while working in the Stock- Exchange or in a brothel—or one may be anything but spiritual in a church or in an Ashram. There is no penumbra of approbation around any activity sui generis.

And that is why most men are dissatisfied with the objective conditions of their life. For a superficially led life is always complaining about its destiny just as a bad workman quarrels with his tools. The discontent of these malcontents is chronic because of the perpetual sense of injustice with which they colour all incidents; instead of counting their blessings. Such a person carries on a feud against, what he calls his 'fate'. How acutely we feel thwarted by the circumstances in which we have been placed when we ignore the spiritual potentialities beneath. Only the surface of the ocean is whipped to waves by the 'winds of karma', its depths are unstirred. Let us gladly accept all that is denoted by 'Fortune' instead of gambling with her and losing all in trying to win all as her wheel turns. If we seek the depths (=deep experiences) we will have chained the wheel of chance and are free from her rotations. Triumphant living does not mean making no mistakes but making

A Saint can work in a brothel
A Sinner can be at church

only our own mistakes, mistakes conditioned by our *own* and not adapted principles. The spiritual quest has in our time been supplanted by the quest for Security and yet man remains fettered to the evanescent. Only an immature soul strives for security by attempting to modify the external conditions of life. It is like attempting to be secure in a gale at sea by trying to control the winds. The mind if shallow sees only the mundane which being transitory is unreal and so powerless; it is insecure ie: the very opposite of what it seeks. The eyes of the initiated see the supramundane. The mundane mind feels restricted by its external environment, be it ideas, persons, or surroundings. All ideologies pertaining to utilitarianism, technocracies, social utopias is so much happy talk; Bhoga-Bhūmi or 'enjoyment-ism' instead of Jñāna-Bhūmi or 'wisdom-training'. It is exactly when our contact with life is shallow and superficial that we find real or imaginary discords in our external environment. We would then fain cure all 'social ills' be it by bullet (=revolution) or ballot (=Politikerei) rather than begin with the real spade work which consists of improving ourselves. Superficial life consists in selecting (out of the totality of data reaching us from the external world) an inchoate group within which attention oscillates. Thus the more our inner life has dried up the more do difficulties in the external world loom insurmountable. When we are exhausted within we seek solace from without. What slows down our enthusiasm for the spiritual life is a lack of profound interest for the QUEST. A mere change in our fortunes would not for certain renew our interest. The problem remains : how to enter the very depths of our Being-in-itself.

We can and should work at improving our external circumstances. Yet we should make the end also the means in that we look upon the situations in which life places us not as so many obstacles but as so many fields of expression for our spiritual urges. Then changes in environment will follow (and not precede) the enfolding of profound interest. A mind devoid of profound interest will not even notice the advantages an improved environment brings him. He carries his bad habits into the new environment and poisons it to boot;

he carries ruins to ruins. On the other hand external obstacles are swept away under the impact of genuine enthusiasm resulting from profound interest. What is subjectively felt as 'profound interest' finds its expression in the objective world as 'genuine enthusiasm'. By profound interest we mean an interest so deep as to cease from being interest for, in or about a specific thing and becomes an interest-in-itself unrelated to any specific object. It is this state of interest-in-itself which brings about 'genuine enthusiasm'. Interest in a specific object excludes that open-mindedness essential to heightened sensitivity. Heightened sensitivity and enthusiasm go together. Without heightened sensitivity and enthusiasm even great pleasures (be they earthly or heavenly) would subjectively be experienced as dull. No welfare-state, no earthly Utopia, no heavenly paradise can pour blessings into a mind having no space to receive them—as is the case with a shallow mind :

"Oceans of Hochheimer, a Throat like that of Ophinchus... cannot make a Shoeblack happy."

If, on the other hand, we can expand our sensitive receptivity then our life will undergo moments of deep experience even in everyday drudgery. Even routine and trifles become significant when seen in this light.

Now, the 'Centres' of Zenoga (=all imaginary points in the 'four-sectional' mind) should *not* be confused with the 'Chakras' of Kuṇḍalinī Yoga. To begin with, wrong are all explanations which assert that these Chakras are situated inside the spinal aperture. Only the first Chakra (situated at the base of the spinal column) may properly be said to be located inside the spinal aperture. Already the second Chakra, slightly higher up the spine, is to be located outside (and behind) the (gross) body; and so on till a kind of half-moon (concave to the back of the gross body) joins with its tips the spinal base with a point hovering above and almost touching the summit of the head.

The Chakras when developed cause reciprocal points to arise in *front* of the body equidistant to their own deviation from meridian; the corresponding half-moon now projected in front of the body constitutes (including the horizontal axises joining the 'Chakras' behind the gross body) what is called the 'causal' body considered still more subtle than the half-moon line of Chakras behind which collectively forms the 'subtle' body. The centres in Zenoga have little to do with all this.

At this point we may anticipate an important term, or rather twins of a term :

The word vāsanās when used in the *plural*, and with a *small* 'v'
means :— predispositions
—including inclinations and disinclinations of all kinds psychic and otherwise.

The same word Vāsanā
when used in the *singular*, and with a *capital* 'V'
means :—the general mental tendency or rather 'constitution' (analogous to 'constitutional' law)
arising from the above-mentioned predispositions.

A mental resolution contrary to one's own Vāsanā will meet with pitfalls just as a statute 'against the constitution' is void. The Vāsanā consists of vāsanās yet is a something above and beyond the total of its added units—for the essential elements of the past (including pre-natal past) persists not so much in memory as in being. In the moment of death the single vāsanās regroup to crystalise according to a said pattern; this pattern will then serve as prototype for the Vāsanā of the next incarnation. The principles, according to which this regrouping takes place, I have explained in detail in my book : Die verborgene Weisheit.

Only by a qualitative transformation of the vāsanās do we create in ourselves a capacity for deeply-felt experiences so necessary to 'profound interest'. The vāsanās resemble the cells of the physical body; there is a constant process of removal and renewal. The ejected vāsanās like eliminated cells are replaced by new ones. Of what stuff are these new cells created ? In the main out of the nutrition (food and drink) we take. And of what stuff are the replacing vāsanās formed ? Out of, and resembling the mental quality of, the thoughts accompanying each and every act of taking nutrition. If we are full of hatred while eating we create an undue supply of vāsanās of the 'hate' variety; if full of anger, of the 'anger' variety and so on. Thus Zenoga gives paramount importance to how you think and feel while eating and drinking.

The psychic tempest has a therapeutic value. It casts off all dead things and so the burden of the past is swept away. This is what SHAKESPEARE really meant by using the word Tempest as the title of his most occult play. Without a tempest our mind would remain placid and so cannot be deeply stirred by profound interest. Even the German word 'beben' (as also in 'Erd-beben') had originally this meaning of 'sea-quake' (=Sturm, storm) derived from the Indo-European: Viprah, meaning one who is inwardly stirred=the sage.

Such a psychological tempest is no honeymoon. One is torn by the temptation to resist the storm (out of a fear of being swept away altogether) and a wish to surrender. These contradictory desires create much confusion. Indeed confusion is a concomitant of the gale and whatever decisions one makes at such a moment makes confusion worse confounded. In the psychic upheaval one must find a jury anchor—anything which will help us to stay out. If we offer no resistance, the tempest will get a chance to work itself out, the result being a transformative cleansing of the Vāsanā. A new mental attitude will open out for the storm-purged psyche. Needless to say, a 'new' Vāsanā (with its new all-round attitude to life) is always accompanied by torrents of enthusiasm because profound interest has now been awakened. Dare to be brave: invite tempests to put some pep into your life. Forget 'security'—it is the weltanschauung of a mouse. Even a crow will live for hundred years by eating the proferred grain. Be not like dumb driven cattle, be a warrior on life's battlefield. All life is a challenge. How do you expect to find 'security' when all life is a challenge? If all life is a challenge then, unless you are alert and vigilant, all you will get yourself is a *false* security; like the security of a savings bank account during a galloping inflation. If you are not vigilant then either you are not aware of life's challenges or even knowing them you are so stick-in-the-mud as to have become totally stagnant. Now how can there be 'profound interest' (for anything except kicks) in an existence totally stagnant?

"Fixed like a plant in its own peculiar spot
To draw nutrition, propagate and rot."

Burden of past is swept away.

To weather a tempest is an undertaking involving considerable courage. Yet that condition of inward solitariness when you are facing the full impact of a psychological storm brings with it psychic renewal of a high order. In that kind cruelty of the tempest, obstacles of our previous environment are eliminated as dead leaves and branches are shedded by a tree during a storm. The past is blotted out leaving no 'complexes' behind. Behold the post-tempest future fraught with untold spiritual possibilities.

Evolution has, for the continuity of its operations, the principle of gradualness. Indeed, according to KANT (who coined this term and not, as many suppose, DARWIN) it is called 'Evolution' for that very reason because any change divorced from gradualness is to be termed 'Revolution'—eg. : Industrial 'Revolution'. Yet spiritual life is an entirely new dimension of Being so it is not the principle of gradualness (nor for that matter 'revolution'), but that of *instant-ness*, which operates here. This instant-ness becomes possible in that Critical-Certain-Stage (C.C.S., for short). The C.C.S. provides the soil in which the spiritual plant may take growth. In the C.C.S. the mind is poised at the point of psychological *transition*; transit from Sec. 1 to the Higher Sections. At this point of transition spiritual transformation ceases to be evolutionary and becomes revolutionary; the mystic event of this sudden change being instant; hence our term: instant-ness.

The spiritual path cannot be treaded until it is discovered. Attempts to tread the spiritual path before having found it give rise to untold needless difficulties. The result then is weariness, dejection and frustration because that element of inner joy (called Prīti in Zenoga) is missing. The attempt to imitate a particular pattern of living taught in spiritual books is not a discovery of the Path but a mere attempt to mould and confine Life to fit into that pattern. This joyless imitation may be called uncreative discipline in contrast to the Prīti (=joy-through-creative discipline) of Zenoga. Without spontaneity and creativity, any hidebound 'system' of living (=living according to some 'system') is bound to be joyless because it is only in the mood of 'functional wellbeing' (=that feeling you get upon discovering something or even upon discovering your own progress on the way to Discovery—or, for that matter, that feeling of 'making progress' in or at anything) that a creative joy in the day to day unfoldment of our own life becomes apparent. If every man were a thinker there would be as many spiritual paths as there are individuals. Yet for each specific individual there is but one Path; he may rightly tread only *that* path which he has discovered for himself in this life and which at the same time is suited to his Vāsanā.

On such a path everything becomes natural and spontaneous for him; while on other paths he feels constrained to become what he feels he is not. The discovery of the path certifies its existence. Discovery implies new data or a new relationship between already-known facts. Where the discovery is a psychological moment (as in the 'discovery' of 'love', 'faith' or a spiritual path) it has a dynamic dimension to it. To discover such psychological entities means also discovering at the same time that the discovered moment is now no longer where it was—for all life is movement.

"That awful daring of a moment's surrender
which a lifetime of prudence cannot retract."

As our psychological constitution is changing ceaselessly from thought to thought, mood to mood, the Path also must be rediscovered every day in changing psychological settings. The once-found path tends to get concealed in a changing psychological environment and must be aufgedeckt anew. The person ignorant of Zenoga may think this constant re-discovering of the path as monotonous and tiring an exercise as the finding of the L.C.M. and G.C.M. of arithmetical fractions which plague his schoollife memories. Psycho-spiritual discoveries, however, exclude monotony—for this kind of discovery has always a thrill about it.

Even the repeated discovery of the spiritual path is an invigorating experience accompanied by thrills. Thrills better than any provided by kicks. The thrill lies in finding out (like a clever detective in TV-dreadfuls) where the Path could be hiding in every new psychological situation with which life constantly confronts us. Can playing the detective be dull? We say 'playing' because spiritual life is play not grind. Nietzsche explains spiritual life as a camel (= beast-of-burden, grind) becoming a child (=child at play). The thrill of re-discovering the path in ceaselessly changing psychological situations provides that element of zest (=prīti) which differentiates a life of spiritual adventures (LAO-TSE) from a life of ethical inflexibility (CONFUCIUS). Ethical drill signifies movement according to the set terms of an established static code. (The 'thou shallst' and 'thou shallst not' generalizations). Spiritual adventures signify movement according to the dynamic particularities of each specific situation. The principles' of ethics are based like the vices (greed, envy, hate, etc.) it denounces on particular psychological states irrespective of individual situations. (Thus, for example, ethics overlooks the cruelty arising from refusing to be cruel to a masochist). Do the 'virtues' and 'vices' of Ethics have an existence apart from an individual having them? A vice like 'greed', for instance, can mean in practice only someone having or showing that property. And that psychological state of 'greed' will differ not only from individual to individual but also fromsituation to situation. So that in the end it is but a psychological incident or event whose content is depicted as 'greed'—usually for want of a better name to facilitate generalizations. In Germany this is made worse by using adjectives to qualify vices when they appear in incidents of which one approves. Thus 'anger' comes to be labelled 'positive anger' = gerechter Zorn = Entrüstung. In the same way one could justify entertainment as 'positive asceticism'! The psychological content of a 'vice' like anger, greed or lust does not lend itself to generalizations for every incident in which they occur will have an individuality of its own. G.K. CHESTERTON delighted in showing in his short stories how easily virtues and vices lose all meaning once disconnected from the peculiarities of the incidents in which they occur. Each psychological incident has an individuality of its own and our own individuality changes according to the psychological settings of an incident. Here we have two variable factors. But the spiritual path in itself is a constant.

This constant ever again appears in a field dominated by the above-mentioned two variable factors :

i) our changing (perhaps 'evolving') personality
in
ii) a life full of changing incidents.

One of the sixteen laws of spiritual mathematics says that where of three given things two vary in terms of each other and of a third which remains constant, the one remaining constant will lie on the diagonal of the two variants. Thus the Path is always to be found no matter what the situation. The path never gets lost; we get lost when we do not find the path—for there is no 'getting lost' apart from a definite destination. Thus the path has to be 'un-covered' anew in each changing situation; this kind of discovery is a dynamically constant process giving day-to-day existence the thrills that explel boredom. The discovery of the path is a journey to that C.C.S. After the C.C.S. comes initiation. The treading of the spiritual Path after initiation is a journey not only to but also with God; for after initiation you walk the Path not alone but with the MASTER, the Master Himself (—MAHA-AVATARA). The discovery of the Path means, in the long run, the discovery of the Master's Divinity.

PLOTIN describes the Soul's journey to Divinity as a flight of the alone to the Alone. It is only when we are alone that we become one with the Path we tread. In order to reach the Light (of Divinity) which is Alone we must begin our search in a condition of aloneness. It is only when we search earnestly that our asking for wisdom acquires a depth distinguising such asking from inquisitive curiosity. Yet depth of any kind is difficult when the mind is distracted by drifts. Yet our psyche is also 'alone' in another sense of the word :

We can see only when the wavelengths of light are between :

0.00008 and 0.00004 centimeteres
(all else is invisible to the naked eye)

We can hear only at vibrations occurring between the frequencies of :

30 and 20,000 per second
(All else is inaudible to us).

When we compare such paltry figures with the range of electro-magnetic vibrations existing around us (=radiowaves

It's betn me & my God.

of wavelength 20 kilometres, down to cosmic radiation of 0.0000000004 millimetre) it is evident that we are very much 'alone' or 'blind and deaf' to a wide range of events; for we are sensitive only to a very limited field of vibrations.

By proper preparation through Zenoga our range of perception can be increased well beyond the average. Enlightenment comes only when we are alone. Yet man fears to be alone—and being alone is a state he wishes to escape from. So he is always on the look-out for someone or something. If modern man cannot find anything at hand to occupy his mind. he digs out some subject through sheer curiosity so that his mind need not be alone with itself: e.g: driving a car without any real destination so that the mind be occupied with the attention paid to driving; this he calls 'relaxation'. Aloneness, in opposition to this kind of pseudo 'relaxation', is a state in which the mind has nothing to hold on to. Our experiences in Life are superficial because we are so seldom alone. Our receptivity to experiences of the Spirit thus becomes poor in depth. No wonder if our spiritual radiation becomes even poorer. Spirituality, once it takes roots, is a plant of rapid growth.

> "This will I do because the woeful cry
> Of life and all flesh living cometh up
> Into my ears, and all my Soul is full of pity
> For the sickness of the world;
> Which I will heal, if healing may be found
> By uttermost renouncing and great strife."
>
> *Light of Asia*

The purpose of this book is to provide an opportunity of understanding the purpose of Life, to work and progress within Life, whilst living a regular 'normal existence.'

God—(that most elusive word, that most exploited word, that most misunderstood word), if God be, could He be such that He requires the most difficult and strange practices along with special conditions, in which He can be found by the very few? Then He is—not the God of our age!

As one matures, certain vital questions inevitably come to mind:—

1. What is the purpose of birth and Life?
2. Can the simple 'man-in-the street' ever know the answer or is it beyond his understanding, and is best left to the few?
3. Is free will given to man or is everything predestined, marked and drawn to the least detail for an eternity to come? Life would indeed lose some of its charms if this were so and there would then be no hope for honest men who sincerely wish to do something worthwhile with their lives.
4. There is some Power behind Creation by whatever name we know it. Is it possible to know and understand Its Laws or have we to accept them blindly as, being finite, we cannot fathom the Infinite?
5. Is there a golden middle road—one of neither extreme indulgence nor of absolute denial?
6. Must man renounce knowledge and progress to find the answer or must one renounce everything worldly and became a hermit?

From early childhood these and similar questions oppressed me; "One passionate note of interrogation, an unappeasable hunger for enlightenment, on the basic problems of life."

I experimented with many different ways, the pleasant and the unpleasant, the easy and the difficult, the strange and the commonplace. I tortured myself in many ways. I kept my mind open and I gave every theory a fair chance. I opened my heart to all religions that I may gather the good in them all. I searched in many books, but was often disappointed! I searched for schools and for gurus, but was again disappointed, (not that I did not find them!).

Then God guided me through one of His advanced sons. The name of his teaching was Zenoga. Under his guidance I slowly progressed. Under his guidance this book is written.

If what is written contains wisdom, then God be praised that my mind could finally grasp what my Teacher could explain. If the reader finds anything inconsistent, know that I have not been able to grasp what was explained, or must have added something inadequate of my own. If this book serves

I opened my heart to all religions to try to understand reality.

any purpose I shall feel happy that the struggles of over thirty years have found solace in a few.

This is yoga without glamour. What you do will be strictly between you and your God and no man shall know of it.

In this book you will find simple practical thoughts which have been tried and successfully put to the test. You too can, if you so desire, put them into practice, and succeed.

Above all, there does not exist in this life nor in all Creation, "something for nothing". You will have to pay a price. We have all heard the story of Ramakrishna, who simply by a touch of his hand made Vivekananda see God. None is prepared to tell us, how much Vivekananda had worked and progressed (before this event) to fit himself for that Divine touch from the Master.

This book is dedicated to that Great Soul who guided me—I so unworthy. If we can only be as he was, certainly God could be wonderful ! He was instrumental in inspiring in me a deep and unshakable love for the Divine. "The journey of a thousand miles begins with the first step." Take that first step today and may God be with you. We have come from somewhere and we are going somewhere. Surely the Great Architect of the Universe, could hardly have built a stairway that leads to nowhere. The guarantee of arrival is in practice.

Chapter I

MIND AND THINKING—AND HOW BOTH DRIFT ?

> "It was but yesterday I thought myself a fragment quivering without rhythm, in the sphere of Life. Now I know that I am the sphere and all Life in rhythmic fragments moves within me."

Let us begin our study with the question: What is man ?

In trying to understand this question we will understand the process or internal working of the grey matter which is called, in common parlance, 'thinking'. Experience shows that whilst engaged in thinking our mind carries a main subject, but off and on we go off the track into other disconnected subjects. Such a process is called drift or drifting (from the main subject).

There are two intensities of drifts; (a) controllable and (b) uncontrollable or unrecognised.

(a) This occurs when we drift from the main subject, but in the midst of a drift realise what has happened and bring ourselves back to the main subject.

(b) This occurs when we drift from the main subject, but are not aware that we have done so and drift further into some other unconnected subject till we end on a subject so different that we are not even able to recollect the original subject or the in-between drifts.

Both (a) and (b) can take place when an individual is thinking or rather is engaged in the process of thinking. Or this can even happen when a group of people are engaged in light conversation.

Let us now proceed to our study: "What is man, the human being ?" and let us watch our thinking process.

*Drift I.**

I refer to a dictionary to find the meaning of the word 'man'. A dictionary is so essential for spellings and meanings ? I think of my spellings and this in turn makes me think of my office stenographer whose spelling makes me doubt my own at times. But how neat she is in her dress and makeup, and how fine is her clear cut nose and her round cheeks and her glances they are full of meanings that no dictionary can give,—but I have drifted. To come back to the meaning of "man:" the dictionary defines this as, "a human being as distinct from the lower animals and from angels or divine beings, with intellectual qualities, peculiar to man."

Drift II.

My eyes glanced over the phrase, "half-a-man." I looked up, turned round and asked my friend who was near, "Say ! What is half-a-man ?" My friend said, "One who is unmarried" and for some inexplicable reason left the room very annoyed. It was clear he was angry. But I have drifted again !

Drift III.

Coming back to the dictionary and to the meaning of "man",—"as distinct from lower animals and from angels or divine beings." "Darling", I called to my wife and said, "Here, read this. If you are a human being, you are not an angel. I will call a spade a spade and no more will I call you 'my angel'."

"Not a bad decision, and I will not call you names of any lower animals", she retorted, "would it not be a better idea to call your office stenographer an angel ?" she asked and I could see she was hurt. But blessed Lord, I have drifted again !

Drift IV.

To come back to the dictionary and to the meaning of

*** The enumeration of the different hypothetical 'drifts' though fanciful and perhaps needlessly tedious, plays an important part in elucidating later chapters. The reader is counseled to have patience.**

"man." It says, "man, as distinct from lower animals". Man is, therefore, not expected to behave like an animal. Animals do not build fine houses and wear good clothes and have rich ornaments, nor deal in diamonds and currency, I thought. I visualised myself, in possession of a lovely marble villa at every hill station or health resort, richly decorated and furnished with servants attending in uniforms, silks and nylons everywhere and what more—in every villa a fair damsel with a diamond necklace round her shapely neck ? But what on earth am I doing ? I have drifted again.

Drift V.

To come back to the dictionary and to the meaning of "man". It says "lower animals." Are there higher animals ? Is man lower than a higher type of animal ? Could a woman be higher ? But often, when a woman looks at another woman, she does it with jealousy; does man betray no such envy ? But I have drifted again. I think, I will have to hold my mind firmly with both my hands and stop it from drifting any more. But I can only hold my head with my hands not even my brain, let alone the mind—and who has seen the mind of man ? But I must stop drifting and go back to my dictionary and to the meaning of "man."

Drift VI.

"Man is distinct from the angels." Perhaps he is greater than the angels ? Has he not created a few miracles ? The millions of stars in all the galaxies perhaps have no creature on them, equal to man on earth. Perhaps the universe is empty and all is for the glory of man. Perhaps, there is no equal of man who has conquered Nature and bent her to do his will. What can he not do tomorrow ? I saw myself flying faster than light to distant stars.

(Example of an unrecognised drift).

Drift VII.

Maybe I thought, as yet he does not understand what the substance of life is, nor perhaps can he understand what that elusive state of sleep is, nor does he know what tomorrow will bring, neither can he succeed in separating himself from his own shadow. But I have drifted once again.

Drift VIII.

But to come back to the dictionary and to the meaning of "man." It says, "as distinct from divine beings." Are these beings superior to man ? Has not man come through the hardest test Nature could subject him to—the survival of the fittest? I thought of the Ice Age and the Stone Age and then of the days of the Romans and the gladiators and how the spectators would shout 'Kill' 'Kill', and how pretty women dressed gaily, found joy and entertainment then, even as today when in the stadium one boxer rains in blows for a knock-out; our modern version of 'Kill', and even today pretty women dressed gaily shout and enjoy the spectacle. Of course man always believed that such sport was and is manly ? My poor brain, where am I ? The dictionary remains in my hand and my mind, God alone knows how it roams and where ?

Drift IX

To come back to our main subject. The dictionary says, "as distinct from angels and divine beings". But in Roman days and the days of the gladiators, I thought of a man who was crucified for His great faults—for his grave crimes against humanity—for teaching, guiding and healing mankind ? Jesus — the Christ. Could one call such a person a human being or a divine being ? In so far, how is man distinct from divine beings ? The Cross, once a symbol of torture for the wicked, became then and onward, the emblem of hope, tolerance, and charity.

Drift X.

But to come back to our main subject. The dictionary says, "with intellectual qualities peculiar to man". Why only intellectual qualities I thought, and not spiritual qualities ? And why are spiritual qualities not peculiar to men ? Are such qualities peculiar to divine beings ? Then surely man is not expected to be divine ? Then why should there be Karma or destiny that is so unforgiving to man and so exacting ?

If there be no cause and effect, then there could be no predestination either and that too in spite of man's endeavour as it appears today. Is man then a machine? Has man's birth therefore no purpose? But I have drifted again.

Drift XI.

Let us come back to the main subject. The dictionary also further says, "humanly possible" as "so far as man's knowledge and skill are concerned, apart from divine help". Now what does, "apart from divine help", mean? Where is this divine source? Is it within us or invisible, in the air or very high in the sky, or on the distant stars, or in the depths of the oceans, or on the top of the highest mountain, or in all these places and everywhere? Can anyone tell us how we can ask for this divine help? Is there a regular way or method of asking for this divine help, and is it ever given, or does it come to a select few by accident or by some arbitrary decision? Does it imply prayers? Are prayers answered? Can we pray as Jesus did?

Drift XII (again unrecognised).

This reminds me of what Omar Khayam says:
"That inverted bowl we call the sky,
Underneath which we creatures live and die,
Lift not your hands to it in prayer
For it revolves as impotently as you or I."

Do not people pray in every conceivable manner and yet remain miserable all their lives? Then what is this Divine help?

Is man subject to predestination? i.e., do the laws of cause and effect operate? Does man have free will within however small or large a measure or is he a kind of domestic animal serving some other beings as domesticated animals serve man? Or does everything happen according to the will of some Super-Being—so man has to submit quietly to that Divine Will? Is he born once only on this planet and then disappears for all time and eternity or does he take birth to return again and again?

(Unrecognised drift)

If he has no choice, if his life is already charted out and

he cannot deviate; if he has no free will or choice to act in a particular manner then his birth if once or many times on this planet or elsewhere, is meaningless, for he is then a plaything in the hands of some other Being. Even the existence of that "some other" Being is meaningless if this is His only full-time occupation ? If there be, God surely He, as Creator of this immensity, of this gigantic universe, of this vast array of law and order, cannot be credited with sentiments and qualities which would not be a credit even to man, His creation, and yet we see around us indignity, injustice, death, diseases, chaos, with man struggling, plodding and groping in the dark, seemingly helpless, and frustrated. What then is the purpose ? Is Man a Divine Being capable of becoming a part of God Himself or is he condemned to be only dust in spite of all his aspirations ?

But I drift again ? This is dear reader, thinking like an average person and "drifting" during thinking. Whenever we have a main subject, there are associated 'pictures' in our mind which slowly take hold of the mind, and, before we realise it, the last picture we end up with and the first picture we began with, seem to bear no relation or link.

Our minds, if not trained, will always act in this manner even during our most serious thinking. We shall feel exasperated for what we call lack of concentration on the main subject. Picture forming and the associating of pictures is the supreme quality of our mind.* What then is the remedy ?

Fortunately, this habit of drifting is *not* the quality of the *entire* mind but of a *part* only. Let us, therefore, first study the proper methods of training the mind so as to separate the functions of its different portions. Thus we come to the higher aspects of concentration, insight, identification, and higher stages.

An average human being thinks that : "it is easy to concentrate or meditate ?" Let us take this very thought for serious thinking as our main subject for about fifteen or thirty minutes *and note* the drifts of the mind. Then read the next chapter.

*Vide Hume's Theory of Associations.

CHAPTER II

DRIFTS OF THE MIND AND WHAT THEY CONVEY

> "The technology which built a human brain was obviously of a superior order to that developed by the brain."

There are three forms of consciousness :

1. *Simple consciousness* : which is possessed by the animal kingdom. By means of this faculty a dog or a horse is as conscious as man of the things around him. Even an animal is conscious of its limbs and body, and elementary sense perception.
2. Man does possess the same simple consciousness as that of the animal kingdom. In addition to this, he has what we call '*Self-consciousness*'. By virtue of this faculty he is not only conscious of the things around him, or of his own limbs and body, but he is also conscious of himself as a separate entity. Man, due to this faculty, is able to feel his own mental states as objects of consciousness. This was precisely what we were engaged in during the previous Chapter; unfortunately Man does not, in general engage in this practice and form of training, but (like the animals) lives solely in the realm of simple consciousness, and so has only a small degree of self-consciousness—in the sense we use this word here.
3. There is another still higher type of consciousness, We call it *Cosmic consciousness*. This is as far above self-consciousness as is the self-consciousness of man above the simple consciousness of animals. It is a very high form of consciousness not yet practised, understood or possessed, by the average man. The chief characteristic of this type is a consciousness of participating in the life and order of the universe. This cosmic consciousness cognizes not through the laborious process of reasoning and deduction but by awareness. It thus places a human being endowed with

such consciousness on a plane of existence superior to that of a normal human being—so much so, that it would make him almost a member of a new species.

What are the richer qualities and greater dimensions of such cosmic consciousness in an individual? Does he belong to a human race of the future?

The direct and visible reaction is a radical yet constructive change in attitude, towards, and also in, all aspects of life. The soul aspect, which today is the subject of idle gossip or complete disbelief, will become as much a reality in the future as physical existence is today. A sort of spiritual, and not merely 'religious' attitude, will dominate such an individual. All past traditions will be swept aside. The question of belief or disbelief in the metaphysical side of life will not exist for it will be seen, heard, felt and verified.

No more will a few be privileged to know and to lead, for each will be a teacher unto himself. No particular book of religion will lead, as the level of being or consciousness in the awakened man will be beyond the use of books and subsequently no more will Truth be the monopoly of the few.

The word sin will disappear and no one need appear to come forward to 'redeem' mankind; for by taking this vital step of cosmic consciousness mankind would save itself from all possible retrograde actions.

God, heaven, immortality will have quite different meanings. The new-found cosmic consciousness will govern correct and proper actions and reactions to impulses. 'Salvation' will also have no meaning. The future will hold no suspense or worry for what may be in store after the cessation of earthly life or in a life 'beyond the grave'.

It seems that such a day for mankind is far away, just as the present age was in comparison to our Ice or Stone Age consciousness. That day seems far away for two main reasons:

1. No one has shown in a practical manner the mechanics of self-consciousness, or in simple language how one can, by simple and gradual steps, arrive at the first step of cosmic-consciousness.
2. Even after this is shown, man finds it difficult to break away from the inertia long imposed on him by the predominant state of self-consciousness. It is like the enormous

The word Sin will disappear
There are errors - trial & error

pull of gravitation which exhausts us as we climb higher. It pulls us to the ground and prevents us from making a fresh start by practising simple steps along new lines. Man is therefore content, even prefers, to move within the old patterns of thought.

We now realise that the mechanics of self-consciousness are not easily understood. Not that they are difficult to understand but because of the long association of the mind with set patterns. Man finds it difficult to adjust himself to new patterns or is not bold enough to break away from old patterns and so every time falls back into the rut even when he takes on new methods and practices.

The methods to be followed (as we will show in this book) are simple and direct and will encourage the mind to give up the old patterns and take more to new ones.

In the first chapter we saw how the mind plays its tricks. Whenever a person is engrossed in profound thinking, the drifts occur to disturb him. So quickly does the mind run away from the main subject (selected for meditation or concentration) that we notice it much later (or sometimes not at all). The mind flies away and comes back a number of times. In most cases the mind never returns to the main subject if left to itself.

In Sanskrit there is an interesting though simple story illustrating this 'drift' of the mind and the great difficulty of preventing it; the main subject being quite forgotten or put aside.

One day the sage Narada and Krishna were passing by the river Ganges and were discussing man's place on earth. The sage said, "Lord, the only thing that I cannot understand is, how and why so easily does this poor creature, man, fall into the snares of illusion. If he could only keep his mind, on one subject and not let it drift, (—i.e., have one subject only in mind) there is no chance for him to go astray and take such ages to be enlightened." Krishna said, "Yes, Narada, if their minds were as steady as yours then perhaps they would be able to avoid the snares of illusion. But let poor man go his way for, as I see the Ganges below, I would like to have a cup of water from this cool and refreshing river. Can you oblige me?"

The story goes on to say that sage Narada came down to

the banks of the river with the purpose of fetching some water when he saw a young girl. She started discussion on the subjects of life, death, immortality and the Divine Being. The sage was anxious to know who this young girl was. He spent a long time discussing with her, the cup with the Ganges water in his hand. He completely lost sight of the fact that Krishna was waiting for him, and of his purpose in coming down to the river. The young girl then once again took the form of Krishna and said, "You see Narada, even after seeing and knowing the Divine Being, it is possible to forget. Even a mind steady as yours, drifts from the contemplation of the main subject—then how much more difficult it should be for mortals who, though they know not well their purpose as you do, drift away and completely forget the goal."

In the first chapter we noticed that the mind drifted away from the main subject: "What is man". Time and again it had to be brought back. It was a hypothetical case, for normally it does not happen. If the mind drifts away a second or a third time, it generally drifts away for good. In drifting there is always a certain pattern of drifts varying with the inner mental constitution of the individual concerned.

The great sage Patañjali very rightly said that if a man can bring his mind again and again to the main subject (whatever the subject may be) and keep it there even for a moment, that alone is entitled to be called the beginning of concentration.

The point of study is to watch ourselves. We may take any subject for serious thinking. The mind will naturally drift away, but fortunately not the whole of our mind. Only that portion of the mind which forms innumerable pictures, learns by pictures and even puts pictures into pictures (=day dreaming) does this mischievous drifting.

The working of this portion of the mind must be observed during the daily period set aside for our practice. We must maintain a diary and note the drifts. For example, let us study the drifts as enumerated in Chapter I by way of demonstration:

The first drift was prompted unconsciously by the sex-nature-predominant and we learn from this that at that given time the Sex centre within the mind was the most active.

(We shall come to this subject of centres later). A person is as weak in sex as the intensity of the drift that would carry him away. Please note the word "prompted". All drifts are prompted unconsciously in relation to our conscious state of mind, i.e. our conscious effort at serious thinking on the main subject by that particular portion of our mind.

We normally say that the mind drifts. What actually happens is that we ask that particular portion of the mind which forms pictures, to steady itself and focus itself on the main subject. We have a different portion of our mind which can focus itself on the main subject if asked to do so. Yet not knowing which and where *that* portion of our mind is, we ask our small portion of the conscious mind to be our "maid of-all purpose". The respective portions of the mind have a natural tendency to do their allotted work, which is their inherent quality created by God (or Nature) for the benefit of man.

However, that portion of the mind which continuously forms pictures, will go on incessantly forming pictures and those pictures will depend on which centre is predominant at any given moment. Even the centres are predominated by turns so fast, that the drifts depending on them go on changing continuously. Observation, however, and notes made therefrom will give a conclusive pointer to, or proof of, the centre most predominant over a given period of time. Such drifts give a clue to the tendency on our part to harbour certain types of thoughts in preference to others.

The second drift shows anger or a show of temper as a weakness in a person. Note the sequence of drifts. The greatest weakness even among the aged and the wise is sex and next comes anger. This may not be true for all, but is certainly true for most of mankind as a whole (irrespective of education or academic qualifications). As *this* science of the mind has been a neglected science, both the so-called educated and the uneducated will suffer equally from these drifts.

The third drift shows the sense of ego, a great and common failing, oft-times the root cause of all other failings; viz., telling of lies, living beyond one's income, etc.

The fourth drift depicts avarice or greed arising from possessiveness. Mortals know they are not immortal, they even freely advise one another that all possessions are to be left behind when death overtakes one; and yet few there be who are free from this weakness.

The fifth drift denotes envy or jealousy. Man attributes this weakness to woman though he is just as weak.

The sixth drift, shows the arrogance of man. He thinks no end of himself; even disant stars are his to conquer, and so thinks even the man in the street.

All persons suffer from arrogance in varying degrees, that is why all persons love praise. If we do not suffer from arrogance, we will react in the same way to praise as we would do if someone were to insult us. Though we think that we do not like praise it certainly makes us happy, whilst an insult, even if we can control ourselves, certainly makes us unhappy. One sage has said that arrogance is the twin brother to ignorance. Where there is an exhibition of arrogance, under the surface is ignorance. The next drift after arrogance is ignorance; i.e., the seventh drift. Should a person be so lucky as to know that he is ignorant, he has a chance of looking into his own self and correcting the fault. The seventh drift is from the previous sixth, directly, without the mind being brought back; what we call the unrecognised drift.

The eighth drift shows courage. Courage is a good quality though it tends to drive a man into the next stage which is cruelty. Courage by itself is not to be considered a positive quality, though certainly it is not a negative quality, but like transparent glass, courage will take the colour of other qualities outstanding in a person.

Should the mind of a person be not noble, courage will make him cruel; just as there are courageous wild animals, who, without other nobler feelings and thoughts, are reduced to cruelty.

The reader will therefore notice that the eighth drift is from courage to cruelty. In the ninth drift however, the noble mind of the sage rises to higher sentiments and gives hope, which is the very balm of life; for if there were to be no hope in man, there would be little room for kindness. Those who can hope, can also tolerate and those who can tolerate can be compassionate, as exhibiting kindness.

Therefore we note from Chapter I that courage in an

Anger is weakness.
Doubt lead to depression

untrained mind leads to cruelty and in a trained mind it leads to hope and compassion.

Then follows the pardonable habit or weakness in man, to drift generally. To drift in life with the tide, without compass and without rudder, to drift from "the purpose of life and birth", to drift when reading and writing or thinking, to drift from friendship and from love and from human relations, to drift from the status of a human being to the rank of an animal; all this is drift and to what?

Should we not watch our mind, our heart, our eyes, our tongue, our hands and our feet from drifting? Can we stop this drifting? Is there a method? Is any price too high to achieve this one success—the control of the tendency to drift; from God the Divine Being, from Soul the essence, from having a body to the thought of being somebody having a soul—this kind of drift is more dangerous than any drift in the Arctic or Antarctic during thick, impenetrable fog among the icebergs.

The next drift illustrates how doubts creep in. At the hour of our task they come in and assail us incessantly. Yet we forget that our very life rests on doubts and beliefs. We are asked to have 'faith' in God, though as to His various laws we may have little conviction. We are sure day must follow night. Yet we are asked to have 'faith' in the ultimate goodness of man and some even doubt whether man can ever be good?

Doubts lead to depression. A person in the grip of depression, having discovered what doubts made him (or her) drift from the main subject, is in a position to come out of that grip of depression.

The next drift leads to day-dreaming. It is a natural sequence of thought. A person in doubt drifts into thoughts of depression, and depression in turn leads to day-dreaming. In day-dreaming we replace all that we miss in actual life. Most people even find happiness in day-dreaming. However, no sooner does a person indulge in day-dreaming than he shuts out the possibilities of effort, struggle, success and reward He becomes more weak, more fretful, more depressed in turn, and indulges all the more in day-dreaming. It is the escape for weak minds who cannot and would not work or strive to get what they want.

Many such idle day-dreamers become drug addicts. This is, therefore, the next possible drift.

There are philosophers who preach that man is a machine, that he can do nothing of his own volition, that he has no free will or choice, that every moment of life is predestined and that there is no remedy.* They make a mockery of both God and man. According to them, the Creator is a mathematician, an autocratic, who according to His Divine will subjects man to all and any sort of humiliation. He (supposedly) torments and frustrates man, even in his work when such work is noble. He treats man in the way scientists of 'Behaviour-Psychology' treat rats. Therefore, the next drift is fraudulent Metaphysics, or Logical Positivism. Such philosophers play with words to invent false theories.

Do they know themselves? Have they achieved control over their appetites? Have they control over their senses? Do they have a purpose in their own lives or is not their purpose actually a motive? What sacrifices have they made for the fulfilment of their purpose?

The next drift from philosophy can be devotion and prayer or it can be towards disbelief or atheism. Thus do drifts follow each other.

Dear reader, the first step is to set aside (daily) fifteen or thirty minutes. Then take a single thought as your main subject. If you have not such a thought refer to the thought at the end of any chapter. Let the mind drift. After the allotted time note whatever details you could register, and classify the drifts according to chapters I and II. Summarise every fortnight. Do not miss this exercise. As this is to be done in the privacy of your home, it is better to be very honest with yourself. Never believe in that misleading term "making your mind blank". Fortunately and mercifully no one can do it because Nature has prevented such a possibility.

According to the drifts of some persistent nature over a period of say three months (=i.e., six fortnightly summaries) note your weaknesses in order of intensity i.e., most persistent followed by less persistent. These drifts ultimately lead to

*Watson and the followers of Behaviourism; see A. Koestlers : Ghost in the Machine.

In day dreaming we replace all that we miss in real life

innumerable emotional or psycho-physiological fixations or what is known as 'behaviour patterns' of a person.

How to correct these weaknesses and drifts and make the mind more steady, we shall study in subsequent chapters.

Take this thought for serious thinking for about fifteen minutes and note the drifts of your mind "why am I, what I am".

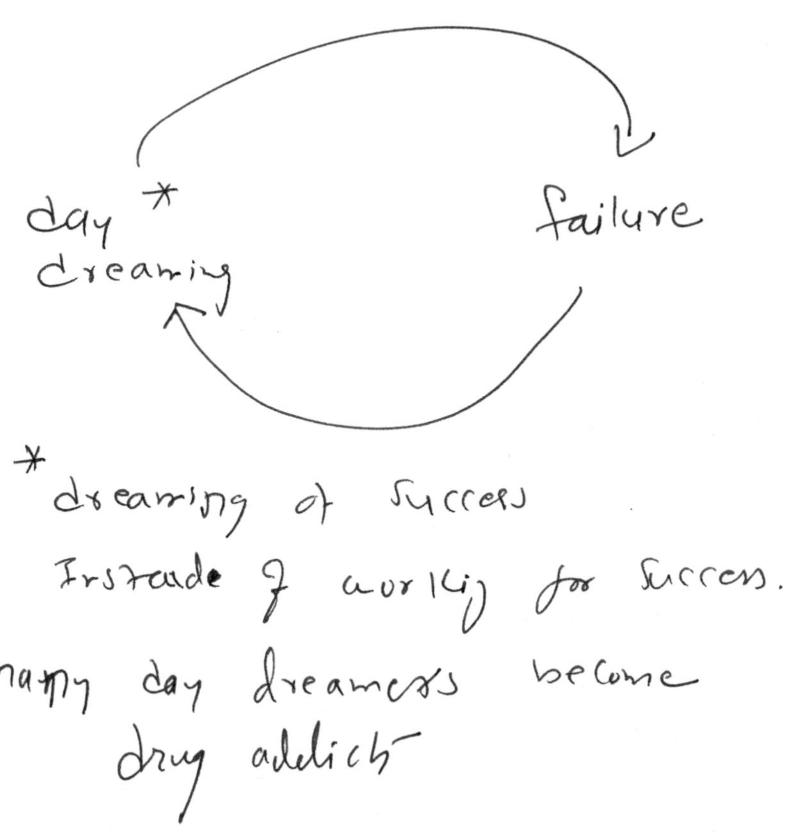

day dreaming *
failure
* dreaming of success
Instead of working for success.
many day dreamers become
drug addicts

Chapter III

WHAT IS THIS MIND OF MAN ?

There is no struggle of Soul and body save in the minds of those, whose Souls are asleep or whose bodies are out of tune. The brain of a thinking man does not exceed in size the brain of a non-thinking man in anything like the proportion in which the mind of a thinker exceeds the mind of a savage.

It is not reading, it is not study, it is not reasoning, it is not deliberation, it is not self-recruiting. It furnishes immediate perception of things divine, eye to eye with the saints, spirit to spirit with God, peace to peace with heaven. Later we shall study this possibility when we discuss the portions II, III and IV of the mind and the cellular-molecular, molecular and electronic bodies or 'vehicles' and their vast added dimensions of consciousness.

But for the present, what have we learnt from this ? What is brain ? Are mind and brain synonymous ? Are they different ? If so, how ?

In the first two chapters we have seen that the mind drifts away from the main subject again and again. This drifting gives us a clue to the inner states of mind. Whenever a brain is observed or subjected to tests by sensitive instruments, it will be noted that the brain or grey matter shows agitations, certain subtle movements, certain giving off of rays, certain striking of notes, certain creation of intensity or for want of a better word or explanation, a certain "something". This certain "something" is the mind of man or the effect of the impact of impulses reaching the brain through the senses.

These impacts or reactions to impacts are invisible, yet have a definite existence and can be recorded and noted by sensitive instruments. In common parlance such effect is called a thought.

Therefore the mind of man is invisible, unlike the brain which is visible. Such individual reaction to impulse or impact on the grey matter, is called "a thought" and hence, thought is also invisible. Thoughts grouped together make up the mind of man.

The 'grey matter' called brain has four sections or main portions. These four sections have certain special characteristics peculiar to each. Hence the reaction to impact in each section is different according to the characteristics of the different portions of the brain.

Every single mind, due to its inherent characteristics of that "certain something", creates an affinity, or repulsion, or indifference, towards other minds (i.e. : of other persons).

1. *Affinity* : leads to friendship, love, courtship, sex, possession, courage, hope, devotion, attention.

2. *Repulsion*: leads to anger, egoism, greed, envy, arrogance, cruelty, doubts, disbelief, and in sex even rape.

3. *Indifference* : leads to ignorance, drifts, depression, day-dreaming.

For example :

1. *Affinity* : between one mind and another leads to a master mind, groups, camps, United Nations, religions, philosophical, scientific or social groups.

2. *Repulsion* : between one mind and another leads to misunderstanding, resulting in crime and every conceivable nature of misunderstanding. This, in turn, leads to every conceivable nature of crime such as war, violence, destruction etc. because of frustrated reactions registered in the grey matter.

3. *Indifference* : The relation of indifference between one mind and another; a mind which can feel neither repulsion nor affinity. It lives alone in very restricted surroundings and, if not given repeated opportunities of feeling either affinity or repulsion towards other minds, tends to become morbid and to develop various mental and psychological diseases.

Frequently, due to its habit of taking the line of least resistance, the indifferent mind becomes repellant to every other mind and we see then the early traces of insanity. We can call all such people "mentally unhappy".

3. The mind of man is like a cloth, the strands of which are the thoughts with which the cloth is woven. Emotions give colour to this cloth. Repetition or habit gives the cloth strength or durability. The quality of the internal states or stored-in thoughts give it coarseness or fineness. The grey matter or brain then shapes this cloth into clothes which manifests itself as character. Likes and dislikes give fashion to the clothes, i.e., give shades of expression to the character and life of the individual.

Constant daily practice as explained in Chapter II, and taking proper steps to remedy or correct, (which we shall study later) must refine our emotions and with it the quality of our thoughts. Our likes and dislikes will change, which means a revaluation of the things of the world, which in turn will enable us to have a higher 'quality' of character or level of thought than the old.

We have noted that mind is invisible. Were it to become visible, we could observe and study it. Because it is invisible we cannot observe and understand. If we cannot observe and understand our own mind, it is much more difficult to observe and understand another mind and this leads to misunderstanding.

There is however a way to overcome this obstacle. The ancient sages were able to both observe and understand.

All reactions of the grey matter to impulses or impacts received from what we call collectively "the mind", consists of a reaction which occurs. How is an impact registered? Our senses in the physical body do this. These senses are mediums which note the impacts as coded impulses received; they also in turn receive decoded thoughts (or messages or commands) sent out by the brain as a result of the coded impulses being received. This change over, from coded impulses received to decoded thoughts sent back is done with the help of the brain and certain mechanisms of the body-system which we shall study later on.

Coding and decoding i.e., noting and translating of the impulses received is the work of the mind in conjunction with the 'greymatter' brain.

Each human being has a number of thought patterns. The number is really large and grows daily. These patterns

Practice = watching drifts

repeat themselves as a person lives his daily life. They accumulate from infancy, through parents, teachers, schools, colleges, friends, home and other environment, and general experiences.

The important point is that nobody makes an effort to carry out certain daily mental disciplines which would analyse these patterns, and no independent thinking is done apart from the play of regularly stored up patterns. Any sort of corrective method is seldom considered. The drifts of the mind are not even examined, and indeed, often go unnoticed.

On the other hand, most persons live by playing back some of these stored-in patterns as if from a tape-recorder, depending on the stimulation, inhibition or irritation received from the outside world through the senses. Such a person drifts through life and makes no attempt to improve his situation. We would go so far as to say, —HE DOES NOT EVEN PROTEST. He is probably not even aware of it.

Some predominating drift makes a person do one thing in preference to others and he may do that to perfection. But whatever a man does, he should at the same time ask the question, "What is the purpose of life and birth and am I approaching nearer to it however slowly?" If the answer is not honest and forthright then whatever he is engaged in is a drift—however nice, grand or noble it may appear to him.

Take this thought for serious thinking and note the drifts. "All that I have read so far, is elementary. I know more."

If we can not even understand our own mind it is almost impossible to understand another person's mind.

NON-ATTACHMENT

Non possessiveness

CHAPTER IV

DO WE THINK AND HOW ?

What operations take place in the grey matter when we think ? Coded impulses are received by the brain from the five senses, and at appointed spots in the grey matter are decoded. This decoding is what one calls thinking and whilst emerging out of the appointed spots in the grey matter it is called 'pure mind-energy'. This outgoing decoded impulse can be either held in suspense i.e. 'filed' (= given no outward expression), or could be expressed by words or actions. The 'filed' outgoing impulse is suppressed thought, the expression of an outgoing impulse in words or deeds is called action. Action is normally understood in Yoga as a function of Karma; actually, it is the emerging 'outgoing' impulse (from the appointed centres in the brain) which, in its pristine state of pure or 'unexpressed' mind-energy, is called Karma.† The specific expression in words or acts is further modified by the dictates of culture, character, education, circumstances, environment, individual health, etc.

In breathing and eating an injudicious use of our free will would soon cause trouble and thus call attention to it. In thinking, however, it is felt to be one's own absolute domain ordained to be free from any kind of excess or misuse. We are, therefore, tempted to feel that we are safe with whatever misuse of free will we indulge in and assume there will be no trouble.

This is a wide domain where one feels "I am the master of all I survey, my right there is none to dispute". In this domain some paint pictures, some compose songs or music, some do day-dreaming, some cross bridges before coming to them, some make progress, some go over the past and some visualise the future. Everyone is confident that this is absolute private ground and is all harmless; for we have as yet given nothing to expression in words or acts. One perhaps even feels that no Karma has been created !

†As understood in the sense of a creative energy.

The four states resulting after coded impulses have been received by the brain and decoded are :

1. Pure mind-energy state,
2. Held in abeyance state, i.e. thoughts suppressed,
3. Pure mind-energy not expressed in acts but in words or 'mental pictures' i.e. : day-dreaming,
4. Pure mind-energy expressed in acts.

Actions will be judged according to their intentions. That which is lawful is clear and that which is unlawful likewise, but there are certain doubtful things between the two from which it is equally well to abstain.

We say, however, that there is no difference between the four states explained above though there may be difference in the eyes of the law. As free as the texture of the thought is basically, so is our free will in the pure mind-energy state.

Patanjali in his Yoga Sutra, Book I, very clearly explains what is so difficult even in our days. He writes :

Stanzas *Book I*

5. The mind's states are five and are subject to pleasure or pain; they are painful or not-painful.
6. These modifications (activities) are correct knowledge, incorrect knowledge, fancy, passivity (sleep) and memory.
12. The control of these modifications of the internal organ of the mind, is to be brought about *through tireless endeavour* and through non-attachment.
13. Tireless endeavour is the constant effort to restrain the modifications of the mind. (Use of free will in trifles.)
14. When the object to be gained is sufficiently valued, and the efforts towards its attainment are persistently followed without intermission, then the steadiness of the mind (restraint of the Chitta) is secured.
30. The obstacle to soul cognition are bodily disability, mental inertia, wrong questioning, carelessness, laziness, lack of dispassion, erroneous perception, inability to achieve concentration.
33. The peace of the Chitta (or the mind) can be brought about through the practice of sympathy, tenderness, steadiness of purpose and dispassion in regard to pleasure or pain: (Corrective methods).

Purify your mind

34. The peace of the Chitta is also brought about by the regulation of the prana or life breath. (Three-step rhythmic breathing).
37. The Chitta is stabilized and rendered free from illusion as the lower nature is purified and no longer indulged. (Change of the mind's 'basic ratio' or the development of the 'disinfection chamber' as will be shown later.)
48. His perception is now unfailingly exact. (Sections 2, 3 and 4 of mind developed.)
49. This particular perception is unique and reveals that which the rational mind (using testimony, inference and dedication) cannot reveal. (The operation of the Sections 3 and 4 of mind; Sec. 1 of the mind has its limitations.)

What we refer to as Section 1 of the 'grey matter' or brain, is mind Sec. 1 or what is in Yoga called Kama-manas = "mind tinged with feeling". It is mistakenly also called the "lower concrete mind".

Chapter V

MUST WE SLEEP AND HOW MUCH

> "Half of what I write is meaningless; but I say it, so that the other half may reach you."

Before we begin let us suppose that the reader is the busiest man on earth. It is precisely for him that these few lines are written. If such a person sleeps daily for eight hours we request him to sleep seven hours and we assure him that it is going to do him no harm. If he is sleeping already less than eight hours, i.e. if he is not a believer in such fads that eight hours sleep is essential and that the quality of sleep cannot compensate for quantity, then we request him to further reduce his sleep by one hour. The best hours of sleep are from midnight to four in the morning. Nearly as good are the hours from eleven at night to five in the morning—and that is also the maximum one needs.

Sleep is like one's income. If the family drain or other indulgences exist, a large income looks small and a person is soon in debt; whilst on the other hand a judicial use of a lesser income would create savings for the family.

If a person's drain on his physical, mental, emotional and sex energies be great due to certain excesses or indulgences then not eight but even eighteen hours sleep will not suffice.

Due to certain negative and positive polarity currents flowing through and around us, sleep can be of six distinct different types:

1. Very intense, invigorating, and highly beneficiai.

2. Intense and beneficial.
3. Indifferent, or that which adds not an ounce of energy.
4. A little wasteful of energy instead of being able to give energy.
5. Damaging, (will damage the nerve tissues).
6. Highly damaging, conducive to sickness and diseases.

The hours of the day corresponding to the above six types :

1. Midnight to 4 a.m.
2. 11 p.m. to midnight and 4 a.m. to 5 a.m.
3. 9 p.m. to 11 p.m. and 5 a.m. to 7 a.m.
4. 7 a.m. to 12 noon
5. 12 noon to 4 p.m.
6. 4 p.m. to 9 p.m.

The vibrational colour zones which the currents build within the body are also of six types as under:

1. Pale blue,
2. pink,
3. green,
4. yellow (dark),
5. orange (deep),
6. red (deep).

The only mental satisfaction we get from more sleep is the thought that we have slept. It is a kind of self-hypnosis that gives us the feeling that it is well and good that we had eight hours of sleep. By all means rest. Resting and sleeping are two entirely different things.

Rest may give you rest, but not so sleep unless it be during certain specified hours.

"Meditation is not for those who eat too much; nor for him who eats not at all: nor for him who is over much addicted to sleep, nor for him who is always awake. But for him who regulates his food and recreation, who is balanced in action in sleep or in waking, it shall dispel all unhappiness."

If we observe the lives of illustrious persons we will usually find that such persons have slept (or do sleep) for hardly four hours in 24 and have done so even with advanced age and have maintained a sharper intellect and better health.

There is another benefit arising from observing lesser hours of sleep. We get more valuable time to do some constructive work without disturbing our daily normal life. It then happens that these hours and our constructive programme (in the hours we have saved) mould our pattern of thoughts for the rest of the day also. This results eventually in a diversification of two different types of persons: one who indulges in sleep and finds that he drifts the whole day and the other who enjoys the right quality and quantity of sleep and in the hours

See the futility of unhappiness

saved progresses, so that finally he is able to make the right use of the gift of free will.

Should we decide to reduce sleep it should not be at a greater rate than ten minutes in a fortnight. When one hour has thus been cut down, continue without a further cut for one month. Again proceed at the rate of ten minutes a fortnight and when another hour is cut down, continue without a further cut for one month. The cutting down of ten minutes should be before 11 p.m. and after 5 a.m. till the exact 11 p.m. to 5 a.m. period is reached.

With this valuable waking time saved and the damaging hours of sleep avoided we now can more profitably employ ourselves to certain practices, methods and corrective thinking. These hours saved are a seed which will ultimately grow into the whole tree of life. These practices should not be regarded simply as exercises but should be regarded as a disciplined life in miniature.

Take this thought for serious thinking, "Reading, thinking, living—what is the common link—which hour of the day or night can forge this link? How best can I make use of this hour?"

Sleep

Very beneficial 12 - 4

beneficial 11-12 4-5

Chapter VI†

THE EXPANDING CONSCIOUSNESS

> "The obvious is that which is never seen until someone expresses it simply."

Life and consciousness seem to be synonymous. It is obvious that without life, there can be no consciousness and on the other hand it is also true that without the most elementary concept of consciousness, there can be no life. What then exactly is life and what is consciousness !

In our age of interplanetary travel are we nearer to knowing life than the proverbial ape, our one time ancestor ? What exactly is life ?

This vital factor Life makes us live, just as it allows the animals, birds, fishes and plants to live. But accompanying life is what we call consciousness or awareness, which is imperceptible in the mineral kingdom, very limited in plants, less limited in the animal kingdom, still less limited in an average human being. This makes man a rational intelligent being as compared to other entities. But man thinks that in all creation, there is not a kingdom or kingdoms with consciousness as much or more advanced than is his in comparison (or as his consciousness appears in comparison) to the other lower kingdoms.

Yet consciousness alone does not make man a Divine Being. There is another subtle, vital principle in man which, when it is able to function within man, makes of him a Divine Being—we can say that man *is* the vital principle and has consciousness, life and a physical body, just as a man may 'have' a house, furniture and a car.

Supposing we were to live in a world of perfect darkness. Now suppose, that we come into possession of light equal to

†Most of the practical exercises are given in Appendix II at end of the book; it is wrong to practise anything before reading the whole book at least twice.

one candle power. Even so, we should be able to differentiate between light and darkness. If this one candle power of light be not there and only darkness existed, then we could never distinguish between light and darkness.

In the same way, we sleep at night; our consciousness (by comparison to other standards) is one candle power during our waking hours ! However, if we were always asleep, we could never understand what consciousness is. Are we actually conscious for sometime, however short the duration, or are we completely asleep and always so ?

We do not understand even today what sleep is. We have another state in which we are not aware or conscious of our body even though awake. In deep sleep we are not conscious or aware of our relation with other people, our knowledge, our possessions, our worries, our health or ill-health, even our own body; in short, we are in oblivion. Nothing exists, neither we, nor God, nor the world. Yet when we get up we say, "I slept wonderfully. How time flies. To think I had eight hours of sleep ! Seems as if I went to sleep only a moment ago."

If we were in oblivion how could we say, "I slept wonderfully ?" What is that state of consciousness ? Who testifies to it ? and who is this 'I' that slept and who is that 'I' that testifies, or is, or was, conscious of the fact ?

During deep sleep,the body had its own type of consciousness; for it continued breathing regularly. The circulation of blood, the beating of the heart, the digestion of food and even turning on our side in sound sleep, all continued. What is this state of consciousness within ?

When we are not aware of our body as in deep sleep, it is life that makes the body exist. That state when you are not dependent on your five senses is the state of the vital principle. It lives by its own inherent capacity independent of any material or physical laws or the consciousness of circulation, breathing, etc. It is the inherent consciousness in matter of all forms and grades due to the prevalence of the substance Life in all creation. All creation therefore breathes; from those taking in very short breath to those taking a very long breath—and everything moves, rotates, circulates in all the various realms of creation.

It is not due to want of consciousness 'beyond our Earth', but want of observation and the means to observe beyond our Earth, that we presume there is no life or consciousness in interstellar space.

It is this rate of flow of life, it is this rate of flow of consciousness, it is the state of the vital principle in its original state as in deep sleep; or as identifying itself with the physical body in what is known as the waking state together with the inherent different levels of consciousness that makes men different from each other. Circumstances, environment nor heredity could be the sole cause.

Take this thought for serious thinking. "What is sleep and who keeps awake to carry on the vital functions during sleep?"

man is not created as a finished product.

Chapter VII

BREATHING AND ITS RELATIONSHIP TO CONSCIOUSNESS AND LIFE

All forms of consciousness and life, whether lower or higher, live by a particular and different way of breathing and thus of coding and decoding the incoming impulses as well as the outgoing reactions called thoughts. This holds true for all creation. In all creation there exists Life and Consciousness in different states.

Breathing is essential to all normal functions of living. Life and breath are not quite synonymous, though they seem to come together at birth and depart together at death. What relation then has breath to life ? What is the purpose of breath ?

We are made to understand that the respiratory system has a particular function to perform, viz., purifying the blood in the lungs. The heart beats and works regularly, sending blood to the lungs, and with each breath the millions of air cells in the lungs are supplied on the one hand by air and on the other hand by blood which is brought by the veins to the heart and from the heart to the lungs. There is another important organ of the respiratory system, though much less known and appreciated, which keeps constant movement. This organ is the diaphragm and it is the movement of the diaphragm that makes the ribs rise and fall and create a vacuum that sucks air in the lungs or work like a bellows to throw it out.

The cleansing of the blood is not the only purpose of breathing. Nature is a past master at economy. Nature quietly makes man take in with every breath the very essence of Life. Many times vaster than the envelope of atmosphere is the all pervading Life essence. Within this ocean of Life that pervades all creation like water in a sponge and around it, all creation subsists. Nature makes man take in a 'something' more than just oxygen with every breath.

1. In breathing we introduce outside elements into our system. They are impulses reaching our nerve centres within, causing the 'grey matter' to give out its reactions. Or, in

other words, we receive coded incoming impulses and the brain centres give out decoded thoughts.

2. Similarly, when we eat and drink we introduce outside elements into our system. They are also impulses reaching our nerve centres within from which the 'grey matter' gives out reactions. Or, in other words, we receive coded incoming impulses and the brain centres send out decoded thoughts.
3. Finally, in the same manner we receive from outside elements coded impulses through our sense of touch, sight, hearing, smell, and also magnetic, electrical and cosmic impulses. All these coded impulses reach our nerve centres within and the grey matter gives out reactions. Or, in other words, the brain centres within send out decoded thoughts on receiving such coded impulses.

We have an appetite for food as well as emotional, mental and sex appetites. The impulses are received as explained above in (3) and come in to feed our emotional, mental and sex appetites. Just as in the case of food, we find that even here we must exercise some care. We shall find later on that much more care is required in the selection of these incoming impulses which form 'food' for the human appetites of emotion, intellect and sex.

At the same time, just as we take food so that the body is healthy we should take the incoming food of impulses and not inhibit the emotional or sex appetites by certain "denial" practices. There is a way to select such impulses. We can note their incoming, their effects and reactions and the satisfaction or over-indulgence of these appetites in respect to the emotional, mental and sex appetites. This involves a study and a method and the scientific approach to this study is termed by ancient sages as Zen or Yoga; which, combined = ZENOGA.[1]

Do these impulses introduce themselves to satisfy or irritate our appetites? Do they enter according to our directives? This could account for the difference between man and man. This control, let it be very plainly known, is not possible by the use of 'will'. Use of will-power for exercising control is the surest way of losing all control. Control is possible due to

1. It is included in my original method called: VITAL-YOGA.

conscious or unconscious use of corrective methods and disciplines. Corrective methods and disciplines when they become habits, enable one to experience, what is called effortless effort or effortless control. Will-power or use of one's will, never gave anyone any control over the least of human weaknesses.

From infancy we collect a great many 'patterns' together with certain habits of food, drink, sleep, breathing and the incoming coded impulses of emotion, intellect and sex. There is a wrong way and a correct way of doing each or all. It is easy to do them incorrectly by over-doing; for strange though it may seem (when each one of these is done incorrectly) we get a certain sort of wicked pleasure or physical (perverse) satisfaction. This sensation of pleasure or satisfaction makes us repeat the performance and as noted earlier the repeat performance is also done incorrectly. Repeating this many times, we form a wrong habit.

Why is it that each of these when performed incorrectly gives us pleasure? To do correctly or only to an optimal extent, the I. centre is activated and very little excitement of the E. or S. centres is involved, less than the decoded impulses would require when doing it wrongly. However, ninety-nine per cent of people work the E. or S. centres only, or to a large extent with very little excitement or participation of the I. centre. All human life, all human enjoyment, all human pleasures are more attached to the emotional and sex reactions within than to the intellectual. The few that activate the I. centre go to the other extreme of completely inhibiting the emotional and sex reactions.

Therefore change of habit should be painful as explained above because the intellect has to come into operation more and emotions and sex less. The pleasures of the flesh are woven around the sex and the emotional reactions only. That is why it has been said: "But O mighty One! who understands correctly the relation of the qualities to action, is not attached to the act, for he perceives that it is merely the action and reaction of the qualities among themselves."[1]

Further: "It is necessary to consider what is right action

1. "guṇā guṇeṣu vartante"—Gītā III, 28

and what is wrong action and what is inaction, for mysterious is the Law of Action."[1]

Knowing that a particular habit is wrong is not enough. The resistance we experience from within us when changing a habit is not overcome by will power ! Temporary triumph by imposition of will finally makes us indulge in that habit all the more ! Such repeated failures of the use of will power makes our will weaker still. This leads us to the thought of giving up trying to improve ourselves or correct our habits. This is natural in the absence of a correct method of approach.

Man is created not as a finished product but is created with certain rich potentials and has been given access to knowledge and awareness that may prove fruitful in evolving further and in reaching the state to which he is ultimately destined. This means that man is given an unique type of independence, the vital presence of which he denies.

To man Nature gave a special place. For the fulfilment of this great trust, man was given a will, so that his acts should reflect God's universal Will, law and mind. Freely choosing whether he should experience the sublime joy of being in harmony with the Infinite and with the great drama of the world around him;...man fell through vanity when his will was warped and he chose the path of discord. Sorrow and pain, selfishness and degradation, ignorance and hatred, despair and unbelief then poisoned his life.

Man is either honest in his belief, that is, of his denial of having free will because he is not aware of the real situation; or he is not honest in his denial of free-will because he is anxious to start a new theory or cult.

If man is aware of his great heritage and can work to achieve it he would certainly be far better than he is today, and if today he is, what he is, it is understandable that he is unaware of his great heritage or that he is careless of it. He must overcome his initial inertia in order to live a new life.

Of course it would mean a little hard work in the beginning. It would mean, following certain disciplines; and yet man is prepared to spend a minimum of fifteen years at the rate of six hours a day merely for elementary and high school

1. gahanā karmaṇo gatiḥ"—Gītā IV 17

Pleasure which turn painful in long term

education. What is more objectionable is that during these years only a few thousand tape-recorder type thought patterns are learnt, which later in life are played back, as if from an automatic record-player. The total time, in the average life of a person, spent in real independent thinking may be at best a few minutes in his whole life and even this is doubtful ! If man insists on living this kind of life, well, none can help him—even God and Nature are helpless, for then, even they cannot impose their will on him.

We human beings have bartered away our free will for a few meaningless pleasures, which in the long run we find painful and damaging. We have been created to enjoy supreme bliss but we are searching for pleasure. Pleasure is more obvious and easily obtainable because of the coarseness or because of the line of least resistance or because of the free use of E. and S. centres. Man does not care to look below the surface of pleasures.

Let us take this thought for serious thinking. "What is the difference between pleasure, happiness and bliss ? What acts lead to each and during all these years what have I been heading for ?"

Knowledge is NOT enough
Knowing that Smoking causes Cancer is not enough to quit Smoking.
Temporary victory by force is defeated soon & then makes us over indulge

CHAPTER VIII

SPIRITUAL PLANES

"All knowledge that is *divorced from justice* must be called cunning rather than wisdom."

In the life of all persons comes eventually that moment when he finds himself standing on the threshold. What is this threshold and of what kingdom is this the threshold? In the life of such a person comes a moment when without being told or even without passing through trials and tribulations the zest of life seems to leave him. No longer do the usual pleasures of the flesh or mind give satisfaction; on the contrary, a distinct disgust is experienced. This is indeed a blessed moment and at the same time a terrible one.

A few persons, due to certain reasons, come to this stage unconsciously without any deliberate thinking about it, whilst some earn this blessed moment. But not knowing the laws which bring about this experience they miss the opportunity and even misunderstand this moment. We call this moment: "that critical certain stage".

In the last chapter, we noted that 'outside factors', food, or impulses (in different forms) introduced within ourselves are through :

(a) breathing (b) food and drink (c) coded impulses received through our senses.
The test of a person is how these elementary factors are introduced within his system. These seemingly simple factors create two more simple factors, viz. (d) sleep and/or inertia (e) sex appetite.

Let us therefore examine how we treat these five factors (a) breathing (b) food and drink (c) incoming coded impulses received from our senses (d) sleep and/or inertia (e) sex.

The gravitational pull of life, the inherent pull of matter the hypnotic spell of the self-consciousness state in which we find ourselves today and the fear to be different from the norm of others, keep us as if held in a vice in the drama of this world where we seem to perform and also to behold the performance of others.

Life and consciousness are relative terms. All light, all understanding, all truth, good and evil and all religions are relative; but relative in what manner? We say relative to the position of a person to "that critical certain stage" or the threshold of that blessed moment in life.

It is never possible by reading or intellectual gymnastics, dry philosophy or mundane theology, or misleading yoga practices to understand life, consciousness, or vital values much less anything higher. This is all understandable only when one crosses over the threshold to reach "that critical certain stage".

The question is, how should one find out whether one has or has not reached "that critical certain stage" and by what means or methods or disciplines can one reach "that critical certain stage?"

We on our part will endeavour to guide, but the reader should honestly examine and judge himself and then unfailingly and painstakingly follow day to day the methods and disciplines outlined.

It is a prevalent notion that such guidance is only given by a teacher to the disciple. It is to be presumed that a teacher, after ascertaining the peculiar tendencies of the disciple, gives a particular line of treatment. Yet a general course in a book form would immediately meet with resistance.

This is very true and should be so. However, this book is not written for those few who have laboured and crossed the threshold and have become accepted disciples. It is also true that one often sincerely believes himself to be a disciple of some teacher or guru or master. This is usually self-imposed or imaginary and such teachers and such disciples are countless. When a person has crossed the threshold (=Einweihung) we hear the oft repeated, "When the disciple is ready, the master will appear"; and unfailingly it is so.

The main question is, how should a person make himself ready? We, therefore, wish to guide those who would first like to reach that fruitful, Critical-Certain-Stage and then be ready for a real master or teacher. There are many sincere people who in their very eager search unfortunately lose their

You are not ready yet
So the techniques will not work

way, their heart and even their heads for so-called schools, ashrams, teachers, methods new and old and theories old and new—but who would not take into account this very important factor, viz., that of *first* reaching "that critical certain stage". Not knowing this fact, or ignoring the same, they apply certain higher methods and disciplines rather prematurely! How can they then expect results without first reaching "that critical certain stage?" All such methods outlined as dhāraṇa (concentration), dhyana (meditation) and Samadhi (identification) are for persons who have already reached "that critical certain stage". Let there be no mistake about this unimpeachable fact. Experience, not theory, reveals this miracle-moving law.

The four most misunderstood, exploited and even abused words are : God, Religion, Love and Yoga. The great yoga systems, as the other ancient systems, have deteriorated and are now looked upon with suspicion. This is because they have been followed and practised by people below "that critical certain stage" and by many foreign scholars who after getting a few fragments, clothe the same in appealing language and postulate fancy theories.

Sometimes, due to the operation of a certain law, a person crosses the threshold to that Critical-Certain-Stage, for a split second. When this happens without conscious effort, it is not possible for him to control it or to remain long enough in that state. However, by conscious effort and methodical approach, it is possible to live the rest of one's life in that blessed state.

The effect of the intensity of such an acceleration of the flow of consciousness on the physical body is too strenuous. Thus (before this stage) it is better, nay rather it is necessary, to consciously pass through certain methods and disciplines. We thereby raise the intensity of the body replacing generations of weak cells, by cells able to withstand the blessed event.

The body and brain being ill prepared to meet and withstand the intensity, will have to depart from such a state, within fractions of a second. Mercifully; for without preparation, the body and mind would be damaged irrepairably by prolonged flow of such high intensity.

Such a person, so to say, passes through a new state rn 're-birth'. He is born into a new way of life and rises high oo the moral and spiritual plane and is never again thesame old

Self created drama

self? This stage is not a supernatural stage. It is just a normal human growth promised to man by God which gives us a taste of things to come! Only if man were not to use his free will unwisely, the blessed day for the whole race would soon be at hand!

Can we define "that critical certain stage?" Can we find or know the practical ways and means or have a yardstick to measure and find out in a simple and direct way 'where' a person is at a given time in this life? Can we give simple and straightforward instructions? The methods and instructions should be such that nothing is left to faith, fate or chance nor should they be impracticable.

Men should deserve to be classed as conscious beings; such as could deliberately work out their causes and weave patterns to that effect. Whenever a person reaches such a high stage, the internal self-diagnoses reveal even microscopic faults and defects of the left-over previous patterns and as such a desire to remove the same; such a person's aim being, Perfection. To that end, therefore, it is imperative for such persons to bend their whole will and work for that one purpose—Perfection. To reach that end, such persons work out causes, deliberately setting out to fulfil through efforts which carry moral lessons for the average person and once having fixed causes consciously, they work out unflinchingly the effects. The higher the order of being, the more poignant is the way in which the causes are set to create most hair raising effects. The last traces of the ego are destroyed completely. The self-created drama therefore includes, insult, humiliation and a subdued mind which refuses to act even in self-defence; besides setting less advanced people an example.

Chapter IX

AVOIDABLE MISTAKES

"Poor Soul, the centre of my *sinful* earth,
Fooled by those rebel-powers that thee array,
Why dost thou pine within, and suffer birth,
Painting thy outward walls so costly gay?
Why so large a cost, having so short a lease,
Dost thou upon thy fading mansions spend?"

Shakespeare

Substitute ignorance for 'sinful' and replace 'rebel-powers' with the I., E., and S. centres within Sec. 1 of the brain which are 'in rebellion' (as explained further in this book) and we would understand the above quotation better in the light of Zenoga.

We note that the three distinct ways in which coded impulses enter our body are: (1) Food and drink (2) breathing (3) sensations of sound, touch, sight and smell. We shall first note their operation and effect and then pass on to the corrective methods.

The senses are not the Self, the organs, the limbs, the grey matter, the impulses, the nerve systems, the mind; nor all these put together make the Self.

Yet we say *my* hand, *my* foot, *my* heart, *my* nerves, *my* brain, *my* mind, *my* hearing, *my* sight. What is that *thing* which claims all these and yet which all these put together cannot claim "it". Let us give a more descriptive word for "it" and call *it* the "Chairman". This chairman has under him a senior managing director and a junior managing director. These two have under them five directors. Between them they are *supposed* to manage this wonderful mechanism; the human body. (Read next chapter later for further clarification.)

The five directors are :

1. *The I. Centre* : is the spot which consciously commands, reasons and guides.

2. *The E. Centre* : is the spot which spontaneously arouses all crude or noble feelings.
3. *The S. Centre* : is the spot which commands all sub- or unconscious reflexes; (= reactions) arising from a concealed memory of man's pre-evolutionary past; activistic perversities and/or reflexes conditioned therefrom.
4. *The M. Centre* : is the spot which combines the above-mentioned thoughts, feelings and reflexes to form a specific decision. It is like a mathematician.
5. *The In. Centre* : is the spot which takes care of the unconscious biological functions within our body and is responsible for the internal repair and maintenance work; the working of the heart, lungs, circulation, digestion, secretion, excretion, etc. All these processes are mercifully kept 'outside the jurisdiction of the other centres, which are subject to erratic behaviour (reactions) in an average person. All activities of this centre are looked after by one sub-section i.e. : one half of the centre. The other sub-section or the other half we shall examine later.

Of these five, the I. Centre is the most senior.

The coded impulses which enter the human body through (1) nutrition, (2) breathing, (3) sensations (of sound, touch, sight and smell) reach these five spots depending on the impulses; they will reach the particular spots where they are decoded, i.e. translated and the centres issue the command accordingly and the outgoing command is the 'pure mind-energy' state.[1]

In Yoga the first three centres are described as gunas : Sattva, Rajas and Tamas.

Sattva	Rajas	Tamas
= I. Centre	= E. Centre	= S. Centre

1. In an average person, all centres have leakages. When we have a subject on which we think, we find that we drift from the main subject and come back to it. All the time that the mind is drifting from the main subject, it is expending energy. This spending of energy is a waste of the I. centre's energy and is hence a 'leakage'.

1. Cp. Buddha in the Dhammacakkappavattana Sutta.

2. The leakage in the E. centre is of a different type. It is not normal thinking but 'playing with debit accounts' as it is called. We have been hurt or are afraid of some event; in short, our worries are the leakages of this centre.
3. The leakages of the S. centre consist of nocturnal ejections and other ejections connected with the physiological functions of sex life.
4. Many people have a habit of shaking their head or hand or leg or drumming their fingers. Any unnecessary motion is a drain or 'leakage' of the M. centre.

Such drain of energy from the four centres is like water which is wantonly allowed to run from a tap. There are leakages which are noticeable and those which are less noticeable.

Exercise :

Every morning and evening seat yourself in an armchair for two minutes and make your joints loose from head to foot. Continue the three-step rhythmic breathing.* Do not move even an inch of your body, not even the eyelids. Remember that *all attempts to relax are to no avail if not accompanied by the three-step rhythmic breathing* ! In a healthy body and mind, there are no leakages. The leakages of the four centres and the drain they impose within the areas of their jurisdiction, have to be met with and repaired *by the instinctive centre over and above its normal work.* The result is that this centre suffers from the added load and is not able at times effectively to carry out its functions. Then the internal organs and nerves begin to complain. Complaint in the early stages is in the form of pain in the body and later we have more serious complaints.

In whatever you do, let the purpose of that act and thought be traced (actually should have been traced before commencing); and if satisfied that it is not correct, insert or introduce the corrective method. Can a man live all his waking hours purposefully? He can—and he cannot. It all depends on how serious he is. This way of living purposefully daily and hourly, is called Jagrati (=*vigilance* or *awareness*). Jagrati means being awake and till then one is supposed to be living half-asleep or rather half-dreaming.

*Will be explained in detail later on.

We cannot acquire Jagrati (or total awareness) by mere use of will-power or by the force of so-called concentration or still less by enthusiasm. Unless every moment our mind questions the purpose of its activity and on finding any reply not satisfactory, changes its activity to a satisfying purpose, there can be no progress towards that Critical-Certain-Stage.

But the reply we give should be an honest one. Should we have a tendency to justify whatever we do or say however well-meaning, then we should be all the more cautious.

Man is not born perfect but is a self-evolving being. He cannot expect to evolve automatically, because then he would not be a self-evolving being, but some kind of a vague evolution would be thrust on him whether he wishes or not. But we think that such a gift of evolution is not to be thrust upon anyone, even on the gods or by the gods on man.

Therefore to be self-evolving man must remain conscious of the fact that he has constantly to evolve. This consciousness of evolution is the purpose of life and birth. This consciousness or purpose is usually absent or comes in only for a fleeting moment to disappear again.

This purpose must be *held aloft* before our eyes and by constant practice of certain methods shown later, it will become possible for us never to lose sight of it. This purpose must run like a thread in all our words, deeds and thoughts. Am I working consciously for this purpose? Am I furthering or hindering the Purpose? Am I indifferent to the Purpose?

Whatever we are able to do or have done in the field of science, medicine, industry, electronics and even the atom, is cumulative knowledge only. Suppose two hundred years ago, our great, great, great grand-father knew a hundred words of language and a hundred facts of science and each generation based on that knowledge added a hundred more of each, then today we may know much more, but that is not evolution. This is only cumulative knowledge.

Can we express today better thoughts than those which the Christ, the Buddha, or the Rigveda expressed? We can express different thoughts on subjects they never knew about, because very slowly but imperceptibly we drifted from one thought or one subject to another; but can we today express *a better thought or a nobler* thought? If we cannot, then our evolution is a misconception. True evolution is the changing of the basic ratio of the first four centres from 2:4:8:2 to 5:2:2:1 as we shall study later.

The five centres are the five important 'egos' in us. Each director has a retinue and these, when the director is away, are additional 'egos'. Any one particular "I" is dominating at different times of the day. It would not only be interesting but educative if we kept a diary to note each day in what centre and under which "I" we find ourselves. Out of this we could plot a graph to show a diagnosis to be studied.

Do we spread our ego or sense of 'I am' over all the centres equally, or do we exclude one entirely to indulge exclusively in others? How long do we thus indulge? If we check up our leakages together with this we will very soon be on our way to that Critical-Certain-Stage. These different 'egos' account for our moods. Combination and permutation of these egos colour our moods.

Each centre has its own intensity. Each centre can be compared to a planet having its own speed of rotation on its own axis and its own speed of revolution round its 'sun'. This creates a certain intensity which is responsible for its contents, growth, and evolution. The centres with their sub-centres, each have their own specific intensity. This in turn gives a varying intensity to our different moods.

Take this thought for serious thinking. "Which of my centres suffers from a leak? Leakage would mean waste. How much intellectual, emotional, sex and physical energies can I prevent from going to waste?"

Chapter X

THE CENTRES AND THEIR MECHANISM

A person may be at his desk in the office reading a letter sitting in a chair. His legs may be swinging and the fingers of one hand may be drumming. From the corner of his eye he may be observing someone and on that someone will depend certain thoughts. That someone could be a person stamping letters or a clerk fumbling with his papers or a secretary arranging her skirt. The person observing may have had a heavy lunch or may be looking forward to a good lunch and finally the contents of the letter could be evoking certain other thoughts. Try to imagine the different functions of his mind and the different thought patterns attendant thereon. We are tempted to ask, "How can such a person be capable of clear thinking ?"

The difference between an average person who plays with the four centres of Section 1 of his brain and the evolved person having developed up to Section 4 is this :

Though he hears, sees, touches, smells, eats, moves, sleeps and breathes, the evolved person knows that it is not he who acts. Though he talks and though he gives and receives, though he opens his eyes and shuts them, he still knows that his senses are merely disporting themselves among the objects of perception.

One is enjoined to live a normal life but one has to understand the working of Section 1 and bring about harmony of the centres and then co-join Sections 2, 3 and 4 and in due time inherit what Nature has declared as the right of man to become a god.

If you suddenly watch yourself twenty or more times a day you will surprisingly find that every time your thinking is in a mess. By such constant checking, you will be able to improve. Sincere, regular practice will certainly help.

When the diagnoses of these checks is to be done (once a week) classify as under:

1. Percentage of exclusive indulgence in one centre.

2. Percentage of one centre dominating other centre or centres.
3. Percentage of interference by or influence of S. centre.
4. Percentage of 'debit accounts' (=wasted energy).
5. Were you doing a particular task exclusively?
6. Is it too jumbled up for honest analysis?

The incoming coded impulse is received through a particular sense and reaches its respective centre for decoding and it results in a thought. This process has speed and vibration. This creates intensity. We can compare the normal or average intensity of each thought of each centre and then also note the minimum and maximum positive and negative intensity possible in each centre for each thought.

Impulses reach our brain through the five senses, automatically and even without our conscious knowledge. They reach Section 1 of the brain. Herein again (in Section 1) are four points or spots or centres. We call them 'directors' for the simple reason that these points or spots or centres are a very conscious and intelligent collection of cells capable of reacting and thereby translating the incoming coded impulses. For example we see sour lime and our mouth waters as it is commonly expressed. A man sees a beautiful woman dressed lightly and he passes through certain mental and emotional convulsions. A woman sees a fine dress or a diamond necklace and her mental mechanics are activated.

Now whenever an impulse enters and reaches the brain, it brings in a tiny fragment of energy. This impulse is in coded form and when decoded in the brain it (like an inflammable gas) flares up and thereby the tiny fragment of energy becomes either a sizable amount of energy or just burns up and leaves nothing behind. When it is decoded by improper methods it burns up and when by proper methods it becomes a sizable amount of energy which can then be stored or further dissipated. When stored, it increases the inner tone of a person and when it is dissipated it exhausts a person physically, emotionally, sexually or intellectually through the various leakages as explained above.

The sun is the source of energy. The sun pours its energy liberally on this earth and which is in turn converted to heat, plants, minerals and in short, all life. Those in turn we take in, through (1) food and drink. (2) breathing, (3) sensations of sound, sight, touch and smell.

The sun also likewise receives energy from the central point around which it revolves and so on ad infinitum. Therefore, cosmic energy reaches this earth from innumerable sources some harmful and some useful to humanity. Those which are harmful are stopped automatically by Nature whilst passing through the atmosphere[1] which serves as our disinfection chamber. The atmosphere is so arranged that exactly the right amount of the right kinds of radiation are allowed through, while radiation which would prove inimical to life-forms is filtered out. This planet was prepared over long aeons by a Creative Source for the coming of Life. From everywhere, therefore, pour impulses or tiny fragments of energy in coded form i.e. the impulses are invisible. Thus, decoding releases the energy of the incoming impulses. By proper methods of decoding these tiny fragments of energy are created into sizable amounts of energy. This energy is absorbed by the cells and this in turn gives rise to the emission of a force which could be subdivided into physical, intellectual, emotional, sexual, molecular and electronic energy. The impulses keep pouring into us as into every creation or created thing at the rate of 120 per second.

Each decoding repeats this operation and, therefore, accumulates in the human body and mind a certain amount of force. This force could be negative or positive, constructive or destructive, plus or minus. We call this force 'Plus-Resultant-Intensity' when accumulated, minus when not. Seldom is the decoding energy release absolute zero. Mostly it is a small unit with a plus or minus intensity due to proper or improper methods of decoding.

The points where this energy accumulates as I., E., S. or M. energy are called the I., E., S., and M. centres respectively. All these points are in Section 1 of the brain. Section 2 of the brain accumulates cellular-molecular energy. Section 3 accumulates molecular, and Section 4 electronic energy.

1. =The so-called solar-winds of cosmic dust filters

The other centres are: the 5th centre or In. centre,[1] the 6th centre we call Paramental and acts as a 'junior managing director' and the 7th centre we call the Transcending centre or, as it were, the senior 'managing director'.

No control is possible over 5th, 6th and 7th centres as long as proper methods are not followed and harmony brought about between 1st, 2nd, 3rd and 4th centres. When that is achieved, the 5th develops. Later 6th and 7th are also developed with the attendant expansion of consciousness and the acquisition of higher powers.

Why or how do we arrive at the intensity rate of the different energies and their points of accumulation in Section 1 ?

The M. centre's intensity-rate is nearly as much as that of the I. centre and its average is also the same. On this earth, average humanity spends 'physical' energy and 'intellectual' energy much less than 'emotional' or 'sex' energy because the potential spending power of emotion is as high as intellectual and physical output taken together and all the three, viz. intellectual, physical and emotional put together equals the potential 'spending' of sex energy. This is the unhappy state of affairs today on this planet. Let us take as an example a figure of 1000 units for the I. and M. centres. The E. centre then has 2000 units and S. 4000 which yields our present-day ratio of 2:4:8:2 for I., E., S., and M. respectively.

This rate can become double itself at best then we call it 'plus' or (at its worst) it can sink to its lowest level in which case we call it 'minus'. Evolution will slowly change this ratio and when the whole race will 'arrive' the ratio will be 5:2:2:1 for the I., E., S., and M. centres respectively. In the meantime certain individuals can 'arrive' by acquiring this proper ratio through Zenoga.

For convenience we take 1,000, 2,000, 4,000, 1,000 as the average unit force for the centres I., E., S. and M. respectively and double this could be the maximum either plus or minus. This is the result of energy released by decoding incoming coded impulses in Section 1 of the brain at the points I., E., S., and M.; *if decoded properly* we get a 'plus'. Seldom

1. In being the abbreviation for Instinct as well as Intuition; this centre has two distinct sub-sections; the first '(a)' dealing with instinctive processes, the latter '(b)' with the intuitional.

does much energy accrue from decoding because the methods applied are wrong. Nevertheless the possibility of energy accruing at the four points are in the ratio of 2:4:8:2 for the I., E., S., and M. centres according to our *present* state of evolution. If four impulses reach the four points in Section 1 of the brain, the decoded energy release in each centre (should the decoding be equally correct or incorrect in all four cases) as well as the rate of intensity of energy-release after decoding will be in the ratio of 2:4:8:2 for the I., E., S., and M. centres respectively. How this force is gathered by proper methods will be shown. When a certain quantity of forces is accumulated, certain results are possible. Until a sizable force, either plus or minus, is accumulated, we find nothing special in a person. Yet if the accumulation reaches (as explained further in the book) one Z.-Unit[1] then this force travels through a special nerve (nadi) called Sushumna (or the nerve in the centre of the spinal cord) and reaches (by turn) Sections 2, 3 and 4 of the brain. Such a force is called Parameshwari and unless gathered into an integral Z.-Unit lies 'coiled' or sleeping.

These centres are like senses, like tongue for taste, like nose for smell, like ears for hearing, like skin for feeling; and so one sensitive point in Section 1 of the grey matter will decode, coded impulses of sex, the other will decode impulses of emotion, the third will decode impulses of intellect and the fourth will decode the impulses of movements.

Section 2 has also such a centre which decodes chemically the impulses received. Section 3 too has such a centre which decodes solar and interplanetary coded impulses. Section 4 has such a centre which decodes even cosmic and galaxial coded impulses when received. However, if these sections are not fully developed, these impulses are not registered, just as defective ears or vocal cords do not register and translate certain impulses.

At each decoding the 'resultant-intensity' moves vertically (i.e. higher or lower) in the same centre or centres but horizontally from centre to centre, if it is the same grade i.e. both plus intensities or both minus ones. In each centre when the intensity has to move from more to less (=lower) or less

1. **Zenoga-Unit=Z.-Unit**

to more (=higher) intensity of the same grade (i.e. either only plus or only minus) then it will simply slide up and down like mercury in a thermometer.

For example let us examine the I. centre. Suppose for average thinking the intensity is one Z.-Unit, therefore if the intensity falls to zero, it would be clouded and when it rises to two, it would be original and intense like that of a genius. If it drops to minus one or minus two, it would be negative and criminal respectively. 'Positive' means here constructive and negative is destructive or obstructing. However, in this centre the intensity can rise to 2000 plus vibrations at a maximum.[1] On the other hand it can sink to minus. We have taken in the following example plus or positive the maximum reaching 2000; and going down at the most to —2000 (negative or minus). Positive and negative aspects are described as plus and minus respectively. In comparison and based on this same proportion we arrive at the intensity in other centres in a human being, e.g. in the E. centre where the intensity is double, that of the I. going as high as 4000 plus and going down to —4000. In the S. centre the intensity is four times that of the I., i.e. going as high as 8000 plus and going down to —8000.

But if an intensity quotient has to jump from minus to plus or plus to minus, in that case it has necessarily to come to zero each time, e.g. if the resultant intensity has to go from +1000 to +1500 or to +500, it will slide up and down and also similarly if it is from —1000 to —500. If it has to go from —1000 to -500 then in that case it will rise to zero from —1000 and then rise to +500 or higher as needs be. However, if it has to go from +1000 I. to +1000 E. it will move horizontally; also if —1000 I. to —1000 E. If it is —1000 I. and has to go to —2000 E., it will move horizontally from —1000 I. to —1000 E. and then—fall vertically to —2000 E.

Sudden change to high minus or to high plus and vice versa is a great shock to the body. Loud noise or surprise, suddenly moves us (within) from wherever we are to take us high up or down, i.e. to a minus in the E. and or M. centres. Seldom does it happen that all the centres suddenly fall to zero

1. One Z-Unit=15 billion vibrations or rotations.

simultaneously but whenever it happens it is the end.[1] If we could see the movement up and down, coiled and horizontal, we would find the movements serpentine. The ancients seeing this internal movements of the intensity in each centre, or from centre to centre with their molecular and electronic visions, saw it all as a play of qualities; of Sattva, Rajas and Tamas.

The M. centre has also an intensity and the maximum it can reach is +2000. It can drop to zero but cannot be minus.

One of the first four cells of the body is retarded and later this retarded cell divides and re-divides the same as other cells, *but all of its descendents become 'sex' cells* and go into the organisation of the sexual organism. Thus we might say that one-fourth of the tremendous potential creative power stored within the fertilised ovum is later released as vital energy of the S. centre.

Therefore, we find that in an average human being the highest intensity is in the S. centre, followed by the E. centre. All life is coloured by emotion whether thinking, moving or sex. It is half in intensity to the S. centre though at one time in the very distant past it was as high as the S. centre and the I. centre was very near zero in its intensity on the plus scale. This is the work of evolution so far. Now let us summarise the intensity fluctuations on a very broad basis. Every time we talk of intensity it is the intensity of the decoded thought in its pure mind-energy state and unless minus accompanies it, it should be read as plus:

The intensity of any given centre could be as follows:

1. The I. centre could be between zero to —2000 in its own centre without dominating or being dominated by other centres.
2. The I. centre could be between zero to +2000 in its own centre without being dominated or dominating other centres.
3. The E. centre could be between zero to —4000 in its own centre without dominating or being dominated by other centres.
4. The E. centre could be between zero to +4000 in its own centre without being dominated or dominating other centres.

1. i.e. death on the physiological plane.

5. The S. centre could be between zero to 8000 in its own centre without being dominated or dominating other centres.
6. The S. centre could be between zero to —8000 in its own centre without being dominated or dominating other centres.
7. The M. centre could be between zero and +2000 in its own centre without being dominated or dominating other centres.

Such pure working of a single centre normally does not exist, in fact, can never exist. Interaction of two or more centres always takes place. The centre which is at a higher intensity dominates other centres. Therefore, at that moment, other centres are dominated by that centre. The result of each such decoding which results in thought in the pure mind-energy state will have the resultant intensity i.e. the sum or resultant total of all the centres involved, some being (i) plus (ii) some being minus, or (iii) all being plus (iv) all being minus (except moving).

Suppose the I. centre receives a coded impulse and sends a command to the other centres. If the intensity of that centre or centres were to be higher than that of the I. centre the resultant intensity will be dominated by the other centre or centres with the result that the command given by the I. centre will not be carried out, and the command issued by the other centre will instead be carried out, which may be quite the opposite of the command issued by the I. centre. This is called domination of one centre by another.

Normally the I. centre sends many such commands to the E. and S. centres but the command is reversed by these centres. Such repeated failures keep the I. centre permanently dominated by these centres.

It is also a fact that the E. and S. centres are very friendly with each other and normally join hands with the result that the I. centre finds itself at a definite disadvantage and often makes no further attempt to dominate these centres.

The M. centre is not affiliated to either the I. or the E. and S. group but obeys the centre having stronger resultant intensity.

To summarise; any centre receiving a coded impulse, can on decoding send a command which might be obeyed or reversed or carried out, depending on the harmonious or inharmonious working of all the centres. We can take a few examples in explanation. However it should be noted that man has so far been dominated by the E. and S. centres only. As long as that happens the free will of man is bound to be misused and hence cause results which are unpleasant.

When all centres work in harmony they co-operate to work jointly so that no one or more centres dominates the rest. The command then given is correct and the use of free will seldom misused. Whenever an individual consciously learns the correct methods which permanently retain this harmony, there is co-operation of the centres.

Further, if one remains too long in a particular centre, and should the resultant intensity therefore exceed a certain particular pitch, a marked effect on the physical body (sickness or diseases) would become apparent. Should the E. and S. centres together have too high a resultant minus intensity for a prolonged period, we get the brutal or 'animal' type of person. Should the S. centre be predominant and the intensity be minus, we have the morbid and the pervert prone to sex crimes. Should the E. centre be predominant and the intensity be a small minus, we have the complaining idealistic people with fads. Were neither the E. nor the S. centres to dominate and yet the I. centre be below the average, we have the dull-witted type. The I. centre if not dominated by other centres is usually normal (i.e. plus intensity but if the E. centre disturbs it with a very high minus we get a nervous breakdown). If the I. centre is normal (=not dominated) yet the S. centre has a plus intensity we get deaf and mute children. When the I. centre's intensity is normal and yet the E. centre has a little minus intensity we suffer from minor bodily complaints. If the I. centre's intensity is normal yet the S. centre has a high minus we get various kinds of skin diseases. If the S. centre has a high minus intensity in its own centre and the other centres are normal and non-interfering, we have diseases like T.B., Cancer and Leprosy. This high minus S. intensity is intensity of the suppressed sex urge. Should the I. centre have a high plus intensity which balances the S. and

E. centres, the resultant intensity is a great plus. It depicts a well balanced mind and a well balanced life and such a person effortlessly maintains mental poise.

Even though the total may be the same, the difference between the intensities of different centres ensuing in the final resultant intensity is in effect, quality, or behaviour dominated or coloured by the centre with the highest intensity regardless of the total score of resultant intensity. For example, the I. centre has +2000 and S. —6000. The interplay of centres results in the resultant intensity being —4000. Now if we have an I. centre with a strength of +2000, issuing a command dominated by the S. centre with —6000, the I. centre is forced to change its score to —2000 (instead of *plus* 2000) and the resultant score is thus —8000 (—6000 plus —2000). The I. centre has here issued a command which the S. centre has reversed.

After each decoding the emerging thought is in a pure mind-energy state and thus has a resultant intensity. Such particular operations are like depositing or withdrawing from the bank as the case may be. Such continuous operations from early childhood create a kind of 'bank account' which could be a plus or an overdraft leading to spiritual insolvency. When the 'bank balance' is a huge minus and the resultant intensity of each operation of coded impulse to decoded thought further continues to be predominantly minus then it so happens that the I. centre becomes permanently dominated by the E. and S. centres.

Such a person becomes negative in his personality, having continuously 'negative' (decoded) thoughts which form negative habits; and soon all this is translated into 'negative' or harmful action. A little later criminal tendencies show up and the person becomes a seasoned criminal.

An average person believes in that vague term *will*, and attempts to use will to control such inner processes. Not knowing the right method he faces defeat and dejection. He loses heart and then even faith in God and in the goodness of man. He then considers himself the aggrieved party and reacts accordingly. It is as if he were to use a broom to sweep a room of utter darkness and thereby expect it to be lighted; such efforts not only will be fruitless even if continued to eternity but also useless, because it is never done and is never possible. To increase your mental dimensions (the working of these centres) by will or resolution is just as stupid, for even after an eternity you will not be able to succeed. That is why man is what he is even after ages of "civilisation".

If we examine the inner life of most people, we shall find that in each and every case the inner struggle was great and the defeat and humiliation within was also great. Then such a person says, "What is the use?" This is a dangerous mental state. It suggests the surrender or complete domination of the I. centre. After such a surrender the I. centre co-operates with the E. and S. centres without resistance. This causes the difference in the total score of the resultant intensity.

Mercifully it is ordained by God or Nature that all those who have surrendered their I. centre to the E. and S. centres get several chances during what are termed 'astrological periods' when, momentarily, (due to the position of Mars and Sun in relation to that person on earth) the I. centre casts off the domination of the E. and S. centres. Such periods, though of small duration, come several times in each person's life. It is a kind of interest Nature's bank pays on all deposit accounts of the person. Such periods coincide with certain positions of Mars and Sun but it is Nature's work which mercifully makes the I. centre in all persons revert to normal. The periods being, however, of very short duration, the absence of proper methods prevents a person from making full use of such opportunities and he falls back to the degraded state. Sensing the chance, but being unable to comprehend it, such a person thinks himself frustrated just when he was beginning to improve. Many make fresh resolutions, only to fail again!

If during such a period the I. centre could find ways and means (=*proper methods*) to remain *un*dominated, the person would make rapid progress in every way. Such opportunities are given to everyone for the simple reason that Nature wants man to evolve further so that she can stop spoon-feeding him.

The methods in this book will show how a person can make proper use of such opportunities given by Nature. Fortunately, during the I. centre's "cycles of return" a person is momentarily free and his mind is clear but not knowing the proper methods he registers such moments as moments of atonement only.

We have earlier seen the intensity of each centre. That is, the speed and vibration of each incoming coded impulse to decoded thought. To recapitulate:

	Average	*Max.*	*Min.*
M. centre's intensity	+750	+2000	zero
I. centre's intensity	+1000	+2000	—2000
E. centre's intensity	+2000	+4000	—4000
S. centre's intensity	+4000	+8000	—8000

From this we come to some very important conclusions:

I. The exhaustion, elation or inspiration we can experience, as well as the proper or improper use of physical energy through the M. centre, resulting in physical movements of all kinds, is the least tiring.

II. Much more is the exhaustion, elation or inspiration we can experience by the proper or improper use of mental energy through the I. centre. As the average is higher and as the possibility of a negative expression is also higher, it is much more tiring than the M. centre or purely physical energy.

III. Twice as much is the exhaustion or elation one can experience through the proper or improper use of emotional energy via the E. centre, resulting in expression or suppression of emotions.

IV. Finally, four times the I. and twice as much as the E. centre is the exhaustion or elation we can experience by the proper or improper use of the sex energy through the S. centre resulting in expressions or suppressions of biological urges.

The method of working the centres is as follows: whenever a coded impulse is received by the I. centre (and before giving out the command or decoded thought) it must contact the E. centre and induce it to call forth suitable feelings and then with the E. centre's average intensity contact the S. centre if necessary in the operation or just issue a JOINT COMMAND in which case the M. centre will without the least questioning carry out the command or decision. The body then makes all necessary movements to carry it out. The I. centre *must realise and never forget* that a complex administration is not a one-man show. The moment the I. centre contacts the S. centre (after having contacted and mutually agreeing with the centre as to the command to be issued), the S. centre gives its formal acceptance *because the E. centre is the great ally of the S. centre.* It is therefore imperative that the I. centre realise that all commands, before being issued, should be jointly passed or accepted by the others. Once the I. centre creates this habit, the E. and S. centres will always enquire of the centre how to act and not be hostile or eager to dominate the I. centre. The trouble is that the I. centre being the seniormost 'director' thinks it not necessary that others be consulted before issuing a command. This attitude is strongly resented by the other centres and their 'directors' so they join forces to form a group which opposes all decisions of the I. centre as a matter of principle.

Let us examine, what happens normally and, with a little care, what could happen within our brain.

The I. centre can when its intensity is at 1000 or 1500 (plus units) issue a command *directly* (i.e. without consulting other centres). Simultaneously, as this command reaches the M. centre (as it *must* at every issue of command) the E. and S. centres issue a joint (—2000 + —4000 = —6000) counter-command. The resultant —6000 less 1500 = —4500 is predominant and the M. centre merely carries out this reversed command. The resultant intensity of this single operation is not —4500 but rather (as +1500 of the I. centre become —1500 through reversal of command) —6000 + —1500 = —7500 !

Had the I. centre, before issuing the command, consulted the E. centre then it might have joined in, i.e., accepted; i.e. 1500 rotations or units +2000 of the E. centre =3500. Would the pair of them now contact the S. centre (before the issue of command) and should the S. centre accept the proposal, then 3500+4000=7500 rotations would be the resultant intensity of that single operation. It would be a satisfying command without the least internal friction and as such would result in happiness.

This inner operation of the play of centres for the issue of a 'command' (=a thought or a decision of the mind) takes only the fraction of a pulse-beat in point of time. Should this operation however take *longer* or should the particular decoded thought be held longer (=duration) then the resultant intensity is to be multiplied by the number of beats for which this particular thought is held e.g. the operation we just noticed had a +7500 score but the plus 7500 if held longer (in time) would result in an even higher score. This holding on to one specific decoded thought (to the exclusion of all else) by all three centres together is normally (though wrongly) understood as 'concentration'. All the world over, people break their heads in vain to achieve this. Such wilful thought-binding is not concentration in the real or Yoga sense of the word. Real concentration is not possible by the centres of Section 1 of the brain. This cannot be done because it is not natural. The centres must in a split second react individually to the coded impulses received. There can never be a pure or unalloyed intensity of one centre, i.e. a command issued by one centre only. Therefore, each decoded thought or each resultant intensity is a product of the intensities of different centres of which some may be plus, some minus or zero, or all plus, and so on.

Each internal operation actually takes $\frac{1}{12}$ of a pulse beat and this is the period fixed for the score to be calculated. No operation proper or improper can take more than $\frac{1}{12}$ of a pulse beat. The 'inside bank balance' is operated for each decoded thought at the rate of one operational score added or deducted at $\frac{1}{12}$ of a pulse beat.

The balance may turn out to be either what we call wisdom or foolishness; better still — (vidya or avidya) i.e. knowledge of the law or the ignorance of the law. Proper methods for each operation and function within is called focusing the mind. But which mind? It is nothing but being aware consciously in rare cases, and unconsciously in most cases, of the need for internal harmony whilst decoding and issuing a 'command' i.e. a thought of any kind.

The internal 'balance-sheet' is drawn, presented and passed by these 'directors'. Let the four directors (=centres) be told how and in what manner they are responsible for their 'company's financial standing'. But who will tell them? In some cases the directors do not even attend this meeting and the job is carried out by their subordinate staff. Yet the business is good and sound and with a little care could be highly profitable. They, the centres, should resolve to apply the proper methods.

The trouble is that the higher centres, those of Sections 2, 3 and 4 of the brain, seldom or never attend such 'board meetings' of the centres of Section 1. By the law of averages the plus and minus go on adding and substracting and at the close of a normal person's life the net resultant intensity is very much the same as at birth and, therefore, has hardly any chance to *evolve* further. Or the progress, if at all, is infinitesimal and long drawn out. An average person usually thinks haphazardly and at the rate of twelve thoughts to each pulse beat. Thus during waking hours he entertains $12 \times 72 \times 60 =$ 51,840 thoughts per hour. By correct methods this rate can be suitably decreased, then we have plus resultant intensity. However, by corrective methods and diligent application as shown in this book the thought-rate could be reduced more substantially. The experience of the ancients gives the following table:

(a) Domain of Mind Section 1[1]

Resultant Intensity	*Time taken per decoding operation*	*No. of thoughts per pulse beat*	*Remarks*
1. ∓ 10	$\frac{1}{12}$ of a pulse	12	Lesser than this
2. ∓ 20	$\frac{1}{1}$,,	7	may occasional-
3. ∓ 30	$\frac{1}{8}$,,	6	ly be as shown
4. ∓ 50	$\frac{1}{6}$,,	5	but unconsciously.
5. ∓ 75	$\frac{1}{4}$,,	4	Normal shallow
6. ∓ 100	$\frac{1}{3}$,,	3	thinking & routine
7. ∓ 200	$\frac{1}{2}$,,	2	and mechanical
8. ∓ 300	One pulse beat	1	thinking give very
			low scores.

1. Please note that the sign ∓ means = + or -, that is to say=plus or minus the indicated number.

		(b) Domain of Section 2 (transfer from Section 1 to 2)		
9.	Neutral			By corrective methods one can have deeper thinking as shown later.
10.	∓ 750	2 plus beats	1	
11.	∓ 1800	1½ ,, ,,	1	
12.	∓ 4500	3	1	
13.	∓ 6000	3½	1	
		(c) Domain of Section 3		
14.	∓ 9000	4	1	Higher, more refined thinking or intense negative thinking. One rhythmic breath.
15.	∓12000	4½	1	
16.	∓15000	5	1	
17.	∓18000	6	1	
		(d) Domain of Section 4		
18.	Where no minus or negative intensity ever takes place.			

When the three-step rhythmic breathing has been perfected, the breath rate falls from 18 or 20 a minute to 12 per minute and as such the pulse rate also drops. It is known to drop from 72 to as low as 51 and is on average anywhere between them. The slower the pulse rate, the slower as well is our breathing and the longer is every complete breath. This in turn causes an automatic drop in the rate of coded impulses being decoded by the brain.

To expect to reach the domains b, c, d in the above table is to be an applicant and an accepted applicant among the masters. It is not possible, unless with dedicated years of practice every thought achieves a huge plus resultant intensity. The average person operates in domain (a) and is at No. 1. Sometimes, unconsciously he fluctuates as far as No. 6 (in the table) or on rare occasion up to No. 8. Even this appears to him as an inspired moment or as a moment of grace.

What is the difference between the Nos. 1—8 and 9—17 in the table? There is one vital difference. It is like filling up a page by writing something which is all incorrect or all correct. Secondly Nos. 1—8 are reached unconsciously and No. 9—17 are reached consciously. Consciousness or awareness in each such operation is a mighty step forward. To explain further : in Nos. 1—8 the I. centre has to a small degree the co-operation of the other centres.

In Nos. 9—17 the E. and S. centres willingly accept the I. centre as their seniormost director and work in co-operation with him and under his guidance. We do not consider the M. centre for the time being. From No.8 onwards the 'higher' mind works. The mental 'bank-account' goes on making entries in the ledger. When the 'funds' reach certain levels (either plus or minus) the account is classed as 'superior' and when it reaches still higher levels, it is classed as 'superlative'.

When an ordinary 'account' shows a balance of (plus or minus) 1,50,00,000 rotation units (of vibrations in resultant intensity) it is transferred into a superior account and such a balance equals one super-unit. When the account gathers 10,000 such super-units the balance is then transferred to the superlative account and equals one Zenoga-Unit. Such an account shows a (plus or minus) balance of 150,00,00,00,000 ordinary units of resultant intensity. When two Zenoga-Units (=2 Z.-Units) are gathered the person reaches the Critical-Certain-Stage. (A normal person's account is a small minus account.) Then comes the No Man's-Land stage beyond the Critical-Certain-Stage. Herein again two such Z.-Units are to be gathered and added to the score, the additions here being expected to be only of the plus kind. Then one reaches the other side of the No Man's-Land.

When one is on the other side of No Man's-Land then only is one able to use free will *correctly* and to reach the desired goal. *Only from this stage* onwards are concentration (dharna) meditation (dhyana) and Samadhi (identification) possible in perfection. One becomes free from the 'gravitational pull' of life, i.e. one is able to exercise free will in all aspects. This is the stage of the use of pure free will and gives the needed thrust to escape the stage of bondage. The resultant intensity of the individual is always registered in mental ledgers under the headings I., E., S. and M. intensities or rotation units of vibrations in such intensities respectively. The score can be plus or minus and can be predominant in one centre only to the exclusion of others.

In an average person the operation of the centres is normally in the ratio of 2:4:8:2 for the I., E., S. and M. centres.

By proper methods this proportion can be altered and brought to the required proportion of Nature's laws. The correct proportion is 5:2:2:1 for the I., E., S. and M. centres. Nature's laws allow a person to accumulate up to four Zenoga-Units in any proportion, but further progress is barred if the correct proportions are not introduced. Such disharmony is considered by Nature as a fault. Beyond this limit it is essential to get rhythm and proper proportion of the Z.-Units.

When the vibrations are high enough to be transferred to the 'superior' class it becomes possible for a person to concentrate (dharana) in the right sense of the word. When the same is transferred to 'superlative' it is possible for a person to meditate perfectly. Above that stage is the stage of identification (Samadhi) in the full sense of the word though at first it is 'Samadhi-with-seed' or near-perfect-Samadhi.

By the collection of resultant intensity we amass a certain force within our system which raises our vibrations and creates another level-of-being which makes us spiritually superior to the average person. There are two types of force, one slightly superior to the other, and those are the forces accumulated in our system by the accumulation of high (plus or minus) resultant intensity.

Above the four already mentioned centres are the sixth and the seventh centres respectively; the fifth centre or the In. centre has a dual capacity:

(a) all internal functions of the nerves and the other centres are spread over it.

(b) it provides the ability to reach the root-cause of a problem and enables deep thinking on any subject. It can concentrate on a single thought for as long as ten to fifteen minutes to the exclusion of all else.

By its means the straying intellect becomes steadied in the contemplation of one object only; whereas the minds of the irresolute, stray into innumerable bypaths. By 'irresolute' is meant those who try to control thought or 'contemplate' through Section 1 of the mind, that is to say: through the four centres I., E., S. and M. only. Straying into bypaths signifies the various drifts or fresh pictures very rapidly formed by Section I. of the mind.

The sixth or Paramental centre shows the road to freedom from bondage only after the first four Zenoga-Units have been accumulated. The sixth or Paramental centre is able to function on the molecular plane and the seventh or Transcending centre is able to function on the electronic plane. When the required Z.-Units have been accumulated, the sixth centre requests the seventh centre to take over and for the first time they work hand in hand. In other words, the sincere disciple who has come so far is now ready and the Master appears on the scene to take him by the hand. From this stage on the aspirant needs no one else and nothing else—except his inner guide. But we have to study and understand much more before the Paramental centre (junior managing director) hands over his charge to the Transcending (senior managing director) as shown above.

Take this thought for serious thinking. "How much do I increase daily my resultant intensity score? How quickly have I to move forward daily to arrive in reasonable time? What efforts to that end am I making daily? Am I awake to the purpose of Life and Birth?"

Chapter XI

USE OF FREE WILL IN TRIFLES

There is a state so happy, so glorious, that all the rest of life is worthless compared to it; a pearl of great price, to buy which a wise man willingly sells all that he has. This is a state which can be achieved. In Yoga there are certain steps leading to this state. The last three are d h ā r a ṇ ā (concentration), d h y ā n a (meditation) and s a m ā d h i (identification). But before these advanced steps may be taken, other steps must be mastered. This is very clearly laid down by Yoga. The earlier steps are by no means less important. These are : y a m a, n i y a m a, ā s a n a, p r ā ṇ ā y ā m a. These are practices in corrective methods and a kind of 'disinfection chamber', and include rhythmic breathing. Between these four and the last three is the most important step, — P r a t y ā- h ā r a or that Critical-Certain-Stage.

Normally the steps y a m a and n i y a m a are described by writers as rules of conduct for normal behaviour. Our intention is to explain these at great length. How a normal person can in his daily life take conscious action regarding these steps. Along with these we shall also see how p r ā ṇ ā y ā m a can be done successfully. We presume these have never been rendered in books clearly enough to explain the great thoughts hidden behind those obvious looking eight steps.

Let us first see how we use our so-called free will in the trifles of daily life. Why should there be a difference in the various actions of our daily life? Because, we presume we are conscious of the results attendent thereon. The fact that comes out is our 'consciousness' in relation to the act. This consciousness can be due to 'punishment' administered on man by God or Nature. This is the most primitive but essential step in awareness or consciousness in our daily life made up of many trifles. The next step in this 'consciousness' is our own desire to act in a particular manner even if there be no resultant punishment. When that stage of consciousness or awareness dawns on us and we act out of choice and natural inclination (and not when we are guided or frightened into behaving by the operation of man-made laws or God's and Nature's laws) then only do we earn the right to use free will !

Let us examine in brief a few trifles, and our desire to use our free will, or our desire to follow the line of least resistance, will be put to the proof:

A day (including night) is made up of twenty-four hours. How do we spend this day of twenty-four hours ? How much really constructive work do we do without either being paid for it or without any motives of praise or recognition ?

Suppose we owned a large factory and worked in three shifts round the clock. We have to give a weekly off or a staggered weekly off to all the employees. There would be in addition some public holidays and some paid holidays. We have to give the annual leave and the other leave mandatory under law. Such a factory running to full capacity for three shifts a day at the end of the year declares profits and, for the employees, bonuses whenever permissible. Now our wonderful factory of the stomach works for three shifts, where millions of millions of workers (cells) work in three shifts, round the clock, for three hundred and sixty-five days of the year under conditions worse than in the days of the ancient Romans and their galley slaves-and we do not even revolt at this thought. What should be the working hours for those cells in the stomach ? In what manner should they be given rest and holidays and pay and bonuses? Do we care to think ? We even laugh at this thought as an ancient Roman captain of the galleys would have laughed if such thoughts had been suggested, by a trade-unionist of our present day, for his galley slaves. Are we at least fair, if not merciful to these workers (our cells) within the stomach ?

Further, whenever we are eating, do we care whether we are standing or sitting, whether we are silent or talking, whether we eat with pickles or wash down the food with drinks, whether we are arguing, angry, sad, moody or thinking about some pressing problems ? Do we care whether we are eating fast or slowly and so on.

The other very important function is that of breathing; let us examine this now. All of us breathe. We begin our life with the first breath and with the last breath it is all over on this planet for us. A normal person breathes eighteen to twenty breaths per minute, i.e., in twenty-four hours, a normal person breathes between 25,920 to 28,800 times. What should be the duration of each breath ? What are the cubic contents of each person's lungs ? Is it the same or in the same proportion in all cases ? Are lungs like the limbs in proportion to the size of the body or like the eyes or nose, which may be out of proportion in size ? What is the ideal number of breaths for each individual or is it the same irrespectively? Should we breathe through the nose only or often through the mouth also ? Is it bad to breathe through the mouth ? Should we smoke if smoking violates the basic principle of breathing through the nose ? Do we fill up the lungs properly to give oxygen to each of the million of million cells in the lungs ?

These are commonplace daily functions of eating an breathing and you may wonder why so much attention is being paid to these functions, but in these trifles, we build up unconsciously a mental make-up or we create a certain mental pattern, based on which unconsciously we weave other mental patterns jor more serious consequences. Thus slowly we build up that unseen but much respected web, we call 'character'.

We have compared the stomach and the lungs to factories and our body cells to workers. If we take this analogy a little further and bring in the very important factor of tolerances, i.e., the allowable variance in the manufacturing processes in the factory, we realise that there are very strict tolerances in all processes in factories, and beyond a certain tolerance (which is very minute) we cannot go ! In some cases there is no tolerance at all ! In the same manner, we should also lay down certain reasonable tolerances for the important functions of eating, breathing, sleeping, thinking and sex. However, with the passage of time our mental tolerances go beyond a limit, which is not safe. That is why, we observe that with age, our frailties and weaknesses grow, and what was possible to control in youth, becomes increasingly difficult in middle age and becomes impossible in old age, until with repeated failures we willingly give up even trying?

Take this thought for serious thinking. "What is y a m a and n i y a m a; should free will be used in trifles and in our daily routine functions ?; do our mental tolerances reach the danger point ? What is the remedy ?"

CHAPTER XII

CORRECT METHODS IN DAILY LIVING

(Food and nutrition habits)

The three ways in which outside impulses enter our body in coded manner and reach our brain, there to be decoded are:—

1. Food and drink

2. Breathing

3. Sensations of sound, touch, taste, sight and smell.

Between these there are the five human physical senses being made use of. All our thinking arises out of this play of incoming coded impulses and outgoing decoded thought. Sleep and sex are by-products of this action and reaction, so that when the reaction reaches a certain 'flood' resultant intensity the action is sexual intercourse and when it reaches the 'ebb tide' (the exact reverse) the result is sleep. Our study, therefore, in the first stage should be around these three factors, viz.:

1. Food and drink

2. Breathing

3. Sensations of sound, touch, sight and smell etc.

(1) *Food and Drink*:

To begin with, let there be no fads about eating and drinking. That vegetarian food could be better than non-vegetarian and vice versa; for it is not the food we eat but *how* and in what particular manner we eat that makes the difference. "Kill not your hearts with excess of eating and drinking", say the Masters. Food should be simple and never rich; one course is better than many. Do not begin like a hungry lion but with gratitude that we have been given a chance to live this human life as a stepping stone to a much higher life.

As in sleep, we should curtail the size of our meal and its frequencies, and by very slow stages form new habits of eating. Do nothing in a hurry.

"Therefore I say unto you, be not solicitous for your life, what you shall eat, nor for your body, what you shall put on. Is not life more than meat and the body more than the raiment?"

For persons over the age of twenty-one the main growth of the body is over. Food then meets the need to replace worn-out tissues of the body. Therefore we do not wish to recommend this way of life for those who have not yet completed twenty-one years. Should they wish to follow, they are welcome to do so as no harm will result. Our reason in not recommending is that the seriousness of life should not be brought in too early in life, unless of course it surges from within a person.

If we avoid waste of physical, emotional, mental and sex energies, we shall be able to create a great economy so that with controlled food habits and reduced food intakes and less of sleep, we will feel better and fresher and healthier.

After preventing waste we also take remedial steps.

The first step is to reduce all food intake to zero before 10 or 11 a.m. This should be done gradually over a period of fifteen to twenty weeks. Then only one meal between 10 a.m. and 2 p.m. (depending on convenience and other circumstances) should be the major meal for a time. Nothing should be done simply because of feeling that we are missing something. Take longer to curtail food, if this feeling is registered. Make no use of will-power; (should you think you have) and do not mention to anyone that you are on diet. You are certainly not dieting but only correcting. If we have given up the 'pleasant' way of life, i.e.: eating, drinking and sleeping as much as and whenever we like, let us now with intense enthusiasm find great happiness in outgrowing all old-established wrong habits of food, sleep and sex.

Let us not have water or any other drink during meals and thereby give our internal system the opportunity to do its work.

We may have formed a habit of taking something with tea in the afternoon or evening, let us, therefore, over a period of fifteen to twenty weeks slowly eliminate all food intake till the night meal. Slowly, but resolutely, reduce the food intake at the night meal over a further period of fifteen to twenty weeks then drop this night meal altogether.

Now let the body be accustomed to one meal only anywhere between 10 a.m. to 2 p.m. and certainly never after 4 p.m. (local time) should any food enter the body. It does not matter how long one takes to come to 'one meal a day' (and nothing before or after) without the feeling of weakness or 'sacrifice'. There should be no added fruits, milk, juices besides our one normal meal. We should take more time if necessary till we are finally convinced that our one meal constitutes a well-balanced diet.

A well-balanced diet, with an ill-balanced way of life is more harmful to physical, mental and emotional life than an ill-balanced diet with a well-balanced way of life. This is not to deny what science has to recommend; for science is perfectly right in recommending a well-balanced diet and an eight-hour, well-balanced sleep. With our present ill-balanced way of life (added to an unbalanced diet and unbalanced hours of sleep) the average person would die young.

All this talk of balanced diet and sleep and life are good, but as all good is relative, they are good in relation to the person. In all cases change should be very gradual, yet sincere and resolute.

Some may prefer the dinner to lunch because of social obligations. Let us quote here, "Even in our deepest sleep, within the great hushed factory of the body, the swarming scavengers, repairman, chemical workers are busy clearing up the debris left over by the day's activities, replenishing the exhausted stores of hormones, repairing the wear and tear on the structures and organs and building-up supplies of bio-electrical energy within the ganglia and the plexuses for the next day's activities." There are important functions going on inside the body when we rest at night. The workers within should not be exhausted further by eating at night and thus adding to the other important functions, the extra functions of digestion and excretion. We should, therefore, endeavour not to put into the stomach anything after 4 p.m. local time. If we feel that we have to oblige someone by accepting an invitation to dinner, party, or wedding, we should join in without making a fuss. But we must compensate on that day by forgoing the usual lunch and on the next day following by eating nothing at all. The day after that: the usual mid-day meal. Suppose we have dinner on Saturday night, then on Saturday we miss our mid-day meal and the whole of Sunday eat nothing. On Monday, as usual, we take our mid-day meal. It is not harmful to eat after thirty-six hours once we are used to twenty-four hours, but normally it is not proper to have anything after 4 p.m. (local time) and the less we indulge in dinners the better.

Nature has not yet created anything better than water to drink. Man has not manufactured anything better than water either. An occasional cup of tea or coffee is understandable. Never put into the system any kind of alcoholic drink, either diluted or neat in any quantity. It is the most damaging substance a human body can be subjected to.

Take this thought for serious thinking, "am I some insignificant mortal or am I the very essence of God ? What does it matter what I am, it is how I live that matters. To live, I have to eat, drink and sleep and therefore how I eat and drink and sleep is important; to live I have to breathe, therefore how I breathe matters, to live, I have to think, therefore how I think, matters."

Breathing in the three-step Rhythm

(2) *Breathing*:

An art of living which will enable one to utilise each activity of the mind as an aid on the Path, is indispensable. Of the three factors, the second factor is breathing (the first being nourishment along with sleep). We have already given a fleeting thought to some aspects of breathing. However let us go into details and study the very important three-steprhythmic breathing. It is known as 'three-step' because the *first* step is technique, the second step is Volume and the third step is rhythm. When all the three-steps are mastered it is known as the all-purpose, three-step rhythmic breathing.

Neither the three-step nor any other rhythmic breathing is the same as p r ā ṇ ā y ā m a. No person can do p r ā ṇ ā-y ā m a who has not reached that Critical-Certain-Stage. We shall explain p r ā ṇ ā y ā m a in detail later. The three-step rhythmic breathing will subject our body to a new rhythm. This breathing is to be made natural by constant practice.

To learn it properly and to practise the f i r s t step, lie down flat on your back. Put a fairly thick and heavy book on your navel. Keep your hands under your head. Now breathe (not very deeply but only normally) and raise the book, but n o t the chest. Do it gently, as normally as your normal breathing had been before you tried this out. The raising and lowering of book should however be p e r c e p t i b l e. Do n o t hold the breath between breathing in and breathing out. This is the first step to be done lying in bed but preferably on the floor.

The actual spot which rises and falls can be located as follows: Put your palm on the stomach (remove the book), the little finger's tip touching the navel. The spot four fingers above the navel, i.e. the spot where your index finger is and midway of the index finger is the spot that rises and falls with each breath. Endeavour to take care that no portion below the navel rises and falls with the breath and likewise there should be no movement of the chest *when practising the first step.*

This first step should be practised for ten minutes a day gradually increasing this time by five minutes every fortnight till you can do it for half an hour. Do it sitting, do it standing and do it walking and without the book now. Slowly do it the whole day and let it cease to be an exercise for now it should be your natural way of breathing. You should now be able to do it u n c o n s c i o u s l y and yet correctly. Be very persistent. Do not be in a hurry.

The s e c o n d step requires one to stand near a wall but not touching it. With your back to the wall breathe as in the first step. As you breathe in, raise your hands above your head so that the back of the palms touch the wall. As you lower your hands breathe out. Do not hold the breath at any stage. In the second step we breathe as we did in the first step and the stomach rises with the breath we take in (as in the first step) but when the hands reach the shoulder level, also raise the chest a little by filling in the chest as well. This is helped by raising the hands from the shoulder level till they touch the wall.

In the second step we fill in the lower chest as well as the higher chest after the lower chest is raised. Once you understand this method, there is no need to stand near the wall as we did in earlier practice. Now practise the second step sitting, standing and walking, and it should be possible unconsciously. Do not begin the second step till you have perfected the first step and have practised it for at least six months.

The first step with the book was to give you the feeling of breath in the l o w e r chest and this standing near the wall as a second step now gives you a feeling of the breath in the chest h i g h e r up. The two steps combined, mean that we breathe and expand the lower ribs and the top ribs also, both simultaneously. Do not hold the breath at any stage. Do not make efforts to breathe deeply. Do not do this as an exercise but as a way of normal breathing and make an effort to breathe in this manner the whole day. Do not expand the ribs either of the lower or the higher chest as in deep breathing; this is merely correct breathing and not deep breathing. Take time to master these first and second steps combined.

The best study is to observe a child about a year or two old, and watch it when asleep, flat on its back. This is the natural way every child breathes from birth. As the child grows it changes this correct way to the incorrect way of the world. Nature wants us to breathe as explained in this chapter. The child is tiny and the growth rate at that age is tremendous and so the breathing is faster and has its own set rhythm. Persons over twenty-one years of age have completed their physical growth and though the size of the body is bigger than the size of the body of the baby the physical growth is as such, nil. The rhythm of breathing will, therefore, vary. It is, therefore, the t h i r d step where we shall differ from the child's breathing rhythm *though not in technique*.

After twelve months of the three-step rhythmic breathing our whole body will appreciably change. The changes will be within us yet unfailingly felt by us. It must change, for we have now imposed a new rhythm on the whole system and subjected every ounce of blood and every cell in the blood to this new rhythm. Continuously the cells are replaced. The new ones will be born with the new rhythm. Simultaneously we are also changing our food habits as explained earlier and so also our habits and hours of sleep. All these, though slow and gradual, will be like the dawn after the dark hours, which will surely though slowly burst into the morning glory. There will be a complete renovation of the body from head to foot.

How shall we know whether we are taking the three steps correctly ? If we are doing so (and if there is no movement below the navel) we will get a deep, long, outgoing breath every fifteenth or twelfth breath in the early stages and later when perfected it shall be at the ninth breath.

To get a very clear idea of the movements from the navel, lower chest and higher chest we should go to the seashore and observe the sea at high tide. Watch carefully and you will notice that either every ninth or twelfth wave is longer, i.e., will sweep up the shore towards you. This is the lower chest near the navel.

Watch the mid-sea waves and it will be first and second steps combined, the lower and higher chest heaving and lowering simultaneously. See the sea at a distance and you see much less heaving and lowering and merely some white foam or a little wavelet, travelling and merging with the mid-sea. This is analogous to the topmost portion of our chest and the narrow portions of our lungs as distinct from the broad and immense area of the mid and lower lungs.

Observe, practise, repeat and check up. Be enthusiastic but be modest and sober and above all wait *very patiently* for results.

Whilst carrying on with the three-step rhythmic breathing corrective methods are to be introduced in the very process of breathing, i.e. whilst we are introducing the impulses within the body.

Select any quiet half hour at home, or in the bus or train or in the office, in the break-hour (whatever is convenient) and repeat mentally any one of the following thoughts depending on your choice:

1. "One so freed from bondage of senses transcends all material relation."

2. "If thou objectest, how should I grasp all this?" "Pray do not grasp it."

3. "It is not attainable by the most constant attendance at lectures."

4. "Trees continue to vegitate, so do most men live."

5. "The Self unfolds its full essence to him alone who applies his self to Self."

6. "Having obtained this priceless birth he who does not understand the good of Self destroys himself."

7. "He who sets himself not at liberty by cutting the tight bond—his mind—*with his mind*, can never be freed by anyone else."

8. "Death is the law of being. The wise describe it as 'Life'."

9. "If the wise man of the world who carefully picks holes in the characters of others, would but expend the same skill on himself, what could prevent him from breaking through the bonds of ignorance."

10. "If thou feelest anger at him who does thee the smallest evil, why dost thou not feel anger at passion itself which entirely spoils the chief aim of existence—Liberation."

11. "Let all be happy; let all enjoy perfect health; let all find the good of their heart; let no one come to grief."

If by now we have cut down our hours of sleep, if we have altered our food habits, and if we have perfected the three-step rhythmic breathing, we have gone a long way indeed, though much still remains to be done. The one great additional advantage which will accrue will be the saving of valuable time by cutting down the hours of sleep and much that still remains to be done can be profitably done during these hours.

Take this thought for serious thinking. "How do all the kingdoms in Nature breathe? What are the different rhythms of breath in the different kingdoms?"

Chapter XIII

PROGRESS ON THE PATH

In Chapter XII we have stressed the need for one meal a day and how gradually we could come to that stage. We have not, however, discussed how much to eat and how to eat and what factors affect food and how. Food and drink as we have seen are one of the three ways in which the human body takes in coded impulses.

It is an absolutely inflexible rule (whether we like it or not) but one must observe silence whilst eating. Besides this, the other rule we have to observe is that one good morsel for each hour of the day, (i. e. twenty-four morsels in that one meal), ought to be sufficient and is the ideal food-intake. These twenty-four morsels include desserts and everything else. This much for the actual food-intake.

Now, we all know that blood circulates and replaces the worn-out dead cells and tissues. Worn out and dead tissues are a result of expenditure of energy of that part of the body. Continuously hundreds and thousands of cells die all over the body and hundreds and thousands are replaced all over the body.

In the human body, the race of cells like the human race is split up into nations, groups, camps, into big and small nations. It has in remote places 'backward' tribes as we have in Central Africa and Australia and such other places. Even among the civilised class, there are groups of cells that form the criminal group, as also the disabled like the blind, the mute, the deaf, i.e. (with permanent disabilities), the leprous, the cancerous, the mutilated, the physically sick, the mentally sick, the emotionally sick, and so on.

As in our sorry world, those cells which are normal (=slightly better than the common masses) are too busy with their own trifles and their own routine lives to care a hoot for any higher code or purpose. This is the sorry state of affairs, this is an exact picture of the inside contents of a human being. If you have a flair for social work and have time and energy, be prepared to render your insides utmost attention; for it will not only be a social service rendered but a duty fulfilled! If by correcting your inside, you cure one human being, i.e. yourself, you have rendered indirectly social service to the world, to God and Nature and you will be suitably rewarded. We would repeat that your first duty demands that you put straight this great world of cells within you. This is a sacred duty. Only those who have been able to render this service within have been able to render service to mankind.

We have seen the inside state of our cell life. There are some methods for correcting this state, but the best methods we know of are operative only whilst we are eating. Therefore, instead of talking during meals we shall adopt the corrective method during meals. This is the best method, because like an injection it immediately reaches every point within.

Whenever we eat, if our thoughts are frivolous, passionate, angry, depressed, blind to reason, deaf to sensible advice, egoistic, cancerous, parasitic or mutilated, the repair material will replace the dead cells with cells of similar nature as the quality of our thoughts while eating. It is therefore not enough that you do not have these types of thoughts. As the Gītā says :

"Those in whom passion is dominant, like foods that are bitter, sour, salty, over-hot, pungent, dry and burning. These produce unhappiness, repugnance and disease."

Let us now diagnose our drifts and seek out our failings. Lose or waste no time in regrets. Miss not a single meal from now on without practising the corrective methods so that the repair material is charged with the proper vibrational tone. Deliberate and precise thinking along the lines charted out for you is essential for reconstruction within. You will be surprised what Nature can do to help you correct your inner world in twelve months' time provided you are regular and sincere in following all the methods given.

Please note very carefully that this is not a faith cure, if you think so, you will fail. Here we understand; and deliberately do what we want to do. This is to be tried out practically and the results tested. Do not think of the aches, fever or cold you may have and do not try to work on that to get a particular cure. Such cures will also follow but only as by-products for such ailments are the results of a deeper ailment—viz. the diseased cell life within and so let not such thoughts interfere. Keep your eyes on the goal and the rest will follow.

"Blessed are the soldiers who find their opportunity. This opportunity has opened for thee the Gates of Heaven. Refuse to fight in this righteous cause and thou wilt be a traitor, lost to fame, incurring only sin. On this path endeavour is never a waste, nor can it ever be repressed. Even a very little of its practice, protects one from great danger."

The method to be followed is this: By following the methods of tracing our drifts as shown in former chapters. we analyse and pinpoint our weaknesses.
Take one weakness at a time and apply the corrective method *for at least a month* and then go on to the next one. Later, in explaining corrective methods, you will learn to pick up the correction according to you analysis. *This application is to be done whilst actually eating.* The result is almost miraculous.

We assure you that no amount of reading, philosophising, regrets, repentance will cure your weaknesses. Even renunciation (or sannyasa) and torture of the flesh is only misdirected effort; for unless we make use of proper chemical and technical methods (as further explained in detail) nothing happens; nothing can help. Your first duty is to correct this inside world of cells. Later we shall add the correct emotional exercises and remove the wrong administration of emotions. All this is essential to reach first, that critical certain stage.

We cannot live and die with our inside world uncared for. If we do not like our inside world now, it is a pity that we did not realise it earlier.

Live your life so well, let your life be so exemplary, that God himself should come down to you and ask, 'What can I do for you?' Let us live well without any guilt complex, and let us make use of our free will in daily routine so well that God or Nature may feel justified in giving us permission to use our free will in *all* matters big or small.

Take this thought for serious thinking. "Shall I take the glamorous road to Yoga and all other philosophies by first practising, dhāraṇā (concentration), dhyāna (meditation) and samādhi (identification) in the way the others blindly do without understanding the deeper laws or shall I first take this simple and commonplace looking advice about one meal a day, three-step rhythmic breathing, and the corrective methods ?"

Chapter XIV

WILL-FORCE

One may not reach the dawn save by the path of the night.

'Sin', according to us, is due to minus resultant intensity. A 'sinner', therefore, has high minus resultant intensity. By following methodically all the techniques outlined in this book one can change this minus resultant intensity into *plus* resultant intensity and even gather 'plus Zenoga-Units' as explained. Once the correct technique is adopted, all minus resultant intensity, i.e. all 'sin' is washed away or burnt out.

If man is responsible for the horror that we see around us, then he is a free agent and thus answerable for his action. He cannot then be not responsible and say that a power is sporting through him over which he has no control, and which makes a mockery of man. If there be such a God, such a heartless God with deeds which do not make sense, but which He wants his creature, man, to believe as Divine Will, this is not worth a thought !

How and where man's identity becomes meaningful, that point which we seek, that is the point we call the Critical-Certain-Stage. We do not mean to say that man has no free will until that stage is reached, nor that until that stage Nature's laws do not apply to our every decoded thought. We only mean that when one reaches that Critical-Certain-Stage one is able to make a conscious and correct use of free will and so man is able *consciously* to create his destiny. Then we go beyond this fourth kingdom of human beings and know and bring about true evolution.

We have noted earlier that man can function in four out of five centres; in all except the In* centre. The decision to function in and operate the four centres in a particular pattern is a choice never denied to man and which he, though unwisely,

* i.e.: centre 5, in Sec. 2, Sup-section (b). In=Intuition.

does exercise. If we select bondage—we will keep our bondage! If we see many in bondage it does not necessarily mean either:

1. that liberty was denied or is denied

2. that all have accepted this bondage

3. that now those in bondage cannot be free.

Whilst on this subject, we would like to make a statement, though we realise it will hurt many. "We are all criminal by birth, by instinct, by education, by pedigree and by the law of creation."

The difference between us all is this, we are all biological and chemical beings and our biological actions and chemical reactions and our chemical actions and our bilogical reactions are equal and opposite. This action and reaction is the same in all of us, but we all do not behave in the same way, because of several factors attendant thereon. But do not for a moment believe that our actions are dependent on education or environment. They all depend on the equilibrium or non-equilibrium of the centres within and the degree of control possible. In the absence of any treatment of our own inner self, how are we going to condemn anyone? Whatever we do after the event is of no use, like water to a man dead of thirst. No remedy is good after a man has acted and is declared a criminal. The question is, what remedy have we which will prevent him from becoming one?

There are more things today a normal man wants and enjoys than was possible for the very rich to enjoy in the past. Therefore, he is goaded or tempted to go wrong much more today than ever before in the past..

Normally, the S. and the E. centres always work in co-operation.* The S. centre is incapable of working satisfactorily without the needed emotional stimulus; and the E. centre is not able to get optimal results without the S. centre's 'vitality-giving' co-operation. The I. centre is the seniormost director of them all. In what manner is this 'director' senior? Just

* In women, particularly, the S. and E. centers are all the more interdependent.

as in planets, the centres have their individual speed of rotation, their specific speed of revolution and their particular 'mass', this together creating a certain maximum of 'intensity' for each centre. What 'mass' is to the planet the 'will' is to a centre. The following table will clarify:

WILL-FORCE*

I. centre	400±	The In. centre has its will-force at ± 200
E. centre	150±	
S. centre	150±	
M. centre	100±	

From this we note that the will-force of the I. centre is very high as compared to that of the other centres. Yet the + or —400 of the I. centre is jointly contradicted by the E., S. and M. centres thus reducing the whole to zero, whereas in fact it could be ± 800 if the centres work in harmony. The In. centre has its will-force at 200 and so the harmonious will-force could be a 1000 units whenever the decision is unanimous.

Usually when we speak of the 'will', we think of a force acting only by tortuous efforts, characterised by out-thrust jaws, beetling brows and clenched fists. The opposite is however true. The will is an integral function of consciousness and operates as effortlessly as does the hand of an engineer on the throttle which sets a locomotive in motion. An act of will (=consciousness in control of the mental centres) directs the entire output of our energy towards the accomplishment of a preconceived objective. What is usually mistaken for will is simply desire and *desire is usually the product of the conflict of the centres*.

Take this thought for serious thinking; "Is there rhythm within my inner world? What is the state of the cells within my body and how do the different *cells and* wills act inside of me? What method should I follow? Will this book show me the way ?"

*Should not be confused with capacity for vibrations or rotations; as then S. has 8000, E. 4000 and I. only 2000.

CHAPTER XV

THE INTERNAL NON-EQUILIBRIUM OF CENTRES

> "Hence oh Mazda? Through my own internal light, with purest unbiased mind, I compare alternatively these thy two Mainayus, who are both promoters of Righteousness and both of great strength, notwithstanding that they are in contest. I have ascertained the co-services of them both, the spirits of both of whom work together in association."
>
> —ZARATHUSTRA

Did Zarathustra visualise the struggle between the I. centre on the one hand and the combined E., S., and M. centres on the other; each able to build up a formidable four Zenoga-Units score of resultant intensity, plus in one case and minus in the other?

Let us imagine the working of these four centres in two examples; first in an incorrect and then in a correct manner.

(*a*) *Incorrect way*:

A person decides to get up at 4 a.m. the next day and to start enthusiastically a new (pious) life. Before going to bed the I. centre makes the decision and sends a command to the M. centre accordingly. To make sure, the alarm-clock is set for 4 a.m. as well.

Next day at 4 a.m. the alarm goes off. As the E. and S. centres were not consulted they decide to oppose. The S. centre takes the field. The person may be a married person. As he is getting up he bends over to kiss his wife. From this moment the S. centre gathers more and more momentum. It is 4.30 a.m. and both husband and wife are entangled in passionate embrace. It is 5 a.m. They both are tired and satisfied and in this momentary bliss embrace each other and decide to get up a little later. It is 7 a.m. as usual and the man staggers out of his bed with much regret and with a lot of mental conflict and the subject is the night's episode. How did it happen? He asks himself: "Why should the devil cross my path ? Why is God not willing to help me fulfil my best intentions ? I will try again."

The toilet and tea is gone through but the same thoughts come and go. If the person is sensitive, he inflicts various punishments on himself in various ways. The guilt consciousness or a guilt complex colours the whole day.

When this happens a number of times and failures repeat themselves in a different manner each time, it seems "will has deserted" the person in question. He looks into the mirror and starts a soliloquy.

Why does the mind betray the person who wants to improve? Why do such set-backs come when the desire is so noble? It is because there are many wrong ways of telling your mind to do a thing and there is but one right way of going about it. What most people do is that if they chance to read or hear something which makes them feel they should go in for a changed life, they decide to do it at once. This is the decision of the I. centre. The I. centre, because it is impressed, makes the decision, forgetting that it should consult and convince the other 'directors' on the subject and ask for their co-operation. The immediate reaction is that no sooner the I. centre decides on its own the other three also decide—they decide to oppose the command *whether right or wrong*, and either the S. or the E. centre takes the lead; and the M. centre gives added co-operation. This is the curse of all resolutions. *No devil stands in the way to oppose your every move. No God mocks at your vain attempts.* All creation is law and order. Obey the Law. A person becomes weaker and weaker every time a resolution is made and broken because the minus score goes on adding to itself.

It is an irony of fate that all good persons who make attempts to improve, yet doing it wrong fail, and slowly go the wrong way.

When repeatedly the I. centre's command is reversed by the other centres, the I. centre loses confidence and becomes diffident. This is reflected in a person's attitude to life and work. Thus his behaviour becomes slowly disappointing to others. When we see such a person, we judge from what we see and forget the immense struggles the person has had and is still unsuccessfully going through within. His only fault is his desire for improvement but regretfully he uses incorrect methods. Such a person falls below his own standards whilst trying to rise above them so that it seems to him better not even to try to improve. Whatever happens to the I. centre's intensity also happens to the I. centre's will. Thus the damage is two-fold. Such repeated failures weaken the I. centre, make it less confident, and later forms our bad, negative, diffident or pessimistic habits.

(b) *Correct way*:

Now let us suppose that the same person wishes to get up at 4 a.m. the next day for a picnic which has been planned in advance. He again sets the 'alarm' for 4 a.m.

The previous night very many thoughts pass through his mind regarding the next day's picnic and his contribution to the share of the fun. The thought of the picnic has thus been sent over to the emotions and the E. centre has already responded.

In the morning at the sound of the alarm, or even a few minutes earlier, the command reaches the M. centre and the M. centre receives a joint command. The person jumps out of his bed and just for today he is fresher at 4 a.m. than he normally is at 7 a.m. which is his normal time to get up. The reader will notice that in all commands the I. centre, were it to consciously or unconsciously consult the other 'directors', gets the required result.

There are four main appetites. We live to satisfy these appetites. When someone appears to us as a cause of obstruction to the satisfaction of these appetites we are annoyed and are in a rage and are put on guard, i.e. raise the E. and S. intensity and at best we become unfriendly; and when someone appears to be the cause of giving us the satisfaction of these appetites we are happy and become friendly. This is how good friends, husband and wife, parent and children fall apart, or come close together.

Whenever there is some friction or misunderstanding, it is essential that the persons concerned first trace out these four appetites. Normally when a person overindulges in one or more of these appetites, then troubles begin.

On the other hand, there are diplomatic persons who know how to satisfy the particular appetite of another person for ulterior motives? These four appetites are (1) Food, (2) Sleep, (3) Sex, (4) Ego and Greed.

If we understand ourself, it is much better than trying to understand someone else, and definitely helps one to understand others. By talking we make a noise, we do not understand. If our motive is to understand this will itself cause—the removal of the guard, in the other person, which is not possible otherwise. We have to follow the right biological and chemical processes of lowering the intensity and follow up with corrective methods as shown later in this book. Otherwise there is only one explosive way left for us—to meet a high minus intensity by an equally high minus intensity—this process is followed daily by many all over the world and everyday the newspapers all over the world are full of stories of the sad and violent results of such actions.

Take this thought for serious thinking; "Am I wrong when I think I am right and am I right when I think and consider I am in the wrong ?"

Chapter XVI

HOW CAN WE RESTORE THE INTERNAL EQUILIBRIUM OF THE CENTRES ?

"I believe in you my soul———
The other I am must not abuse itself to you,
And you must not be abased to the other."
—Walt Whitman

We are trying to explain in the same thought in regard to centres. We should never allow one centre to dominate others or be dominated in turn.

We have seen earlier that there are five spots or centres in the physical brain.[1] Four of which receive the outside coded impulses by way of (1) Food and drink, (2) breathing, (3) the sensations of sound, touch, sight, taste and smell. The fifth[2] centre which receives impulses from chemicals takes care of the internal functions of maintaining the body and its various processes and nerve fibres. There is also a sixth centre and a seventh centre. Upto the first four centres the activity is on the cellular plane. In the fifth, the activity is on the cellular-molecular plane. In the sixth centre the activity is on the molecular plane. In the seventh centre the activity is on the electronic plane. Now, what are these activities called molecular and electronic ? We mean that the 'molecular' consciousness and the 'electronic' consciousness are possible to man through these two wonderful centres of consciousness just as the first four centres give him self-consciousness.

All the first five centres obey and acknowledge the sixth one called 'junior managing director'. However, this 6th centre does not like the things of *this* world while the first four centres are only interested in the daily, petty, routine and material things of the world. The sixth centre not attending the 'Board of Directors meeting' does great damage because in his absence no equilibrium is possible and in the absence of corrective methods no equilibrium is ever brought about.

What is meant by molecular and electronic plane consciousness ? Suppose there is a hill. An average person with

1. See extra "Note" at the end of book.
2. That is the Reticular-Activating-Sytem or RAS for short.

cellular plane consciousness will see a section of the outside of the hill.

A man with molecular plane consciousness (i.e., with the sixth centre developed) can see the whole of the outside of the hill surface (from top to bottom of the hill) on all sides.

A man with an electronic plane consciousness (i.e. with the seventh centre developed) can see not only the entire outside surface of the hill from top to bottom, but can also see the whole of the inside of the hill. This is the tremendous difference between the fifth, sixth and the seventh centres.[1]

For further clarification we would say that if there be a book which is open and in a language we understand, the person with cellular plane consciousness can read the page which lies open.

A person with molecular plane consciousness can read any page without opening the book if it is in a language known to him.

A person with electronic plane consciousness can read the book even if it is closed and in any language printed or written.[2]

The last two centres are also within us and can be made to function.[3]

Each of the first five centres or 'directors' has an assistant, a secretary, and other administrative staff. These subordinates to the directors know of the friction between the I. centre director and the E. and S. centre directors; and the domination of these directors over the I. centre. These subordinates, therefore, take advantage of this friction and it so happens that the command issued by the I. centre director is reversed by these subordinates.

It creates the worst sort of mismanagement within. This is the sorry state of affairs in an average man and it is even more pronounced in the so-called criminal class. Seeing this state of affairs, it so happens that even subordinates of the I. centre misbehave. This is all due to lack of the knowledge of management, whether it be a small or a large administration of the vast inner world. If we could restore the prestige of the I. centre director and show him how to manage his staff then anyone doing so would render a great service to mankind.

The I. director, to avoid friction, should be friendly with

1. Cp-A Koestler, *The Roots of Coincidence*, London 1972
2. Cp. S. Black, *Mind and Body*, London 1969
3. Cp. R. Heywood, *The Sixth Sense*, London 1959

the other directors. He must contribute to, and think for them, and make them help him to carry out his plans.

We have seen earlier the moments when the I. centre is free and undominated.* Mercifully it is ordained that any person who takes advantage of such blessed moments is presented with many such opportunities and when knowing the correct method he can form new habits. Mercifully it is also ordained that when hundreds of thousands of human beings need this change, there appears in human form amongst them an advanced Soul we call a Saint or a Prophet or an AVATARA depending upon the state of awareness of the masses; in very exceptional cases even a MAHAVATARA.

Even after such a golden opportunity, the directors of E. and S. centres do not give up their domination easily. Slowly, the I. director becomes more free and the E. and S. centres become less and less aggressive. The M. centre becomes less disobedient. The I. centre's own subordinates and other subordinates again behave well; without strife and mutiny.

Care must be taken to note that just as putting off the fan switch, does not immediately stop the fan, so this constructive change for the better does not prevent that person from falling and erring many times yet. The person concerned has sincerely accepted the change. But others seeing that person err again shake their heads and say, "He is incorrigible. He pretends, but actually he can never improve." These are unkind thoughts due to lack of true knowledge. When the person takes the road to regeneration and knows the correct methods and proceeds along the right way in his food, sleep, sex and breathing practices, he finally (with analysis and diagnosis and corrective methods) reaches that Critical-Certain-Stage. We have seen that there are certain agitations in the grey matter, certain subtle movements, certain giving off of rays, certain striking of notes. This certain 'something' is the mind of man in action due to the effect of impacts on the 'grey matter' of the brain.[1]

This certain something, i.e., the creation of intensity now begins to change such a person. This change in intensity means that its affinity and repulsion patterns will also change

* Vide Chapter X.

1. Vide H. H. Price, "Psychical Research and Human Personality" in *Hibbert Journal* Vol. XLVII, pp. 105-113.

and this same person even if a so-called criminal will now be repelled by certain persons, places and acts he was formerly drawn to, and will be drawn to some other persons, places and acts he was repelled from before ?

The ancient sages found by long observation that *a certain rhythm always existed between a certain type of breathing and the mind of man.* This breathing they found was the three-step rhythmic breathing shown earlier. This breath they called the all-purpose breath, (sometimes known as "complete yoga breath").

If we were to impose this new rhythm on ourself for twenty-four hours a day we would soon be able to reach that Critical-Certain-Stage.

Earlier we have seen the wrong working of the I. centre and the resultant intensity thus created. The proper way is this: of the five directors, the I. centre's director is seniormost. However, the orders the I. centre's director would like to issue should be only after due consultation and due understanding and consent of the other directors; for I. by itself cannot do as he likes even if what it intends to do be right. So the I. centre must first analyse whether the thing to be done involves another centre or a combination of centres.
It must accordingly consult them, i.e. arouse plus E. and plus S. vibrations if needed and then issue a joint command to the M. centre. In the early stages only ninety percent of such commands given will be carried out. This we call, the re-educating of the mind. With practice and patience *all* commands will be obeyed. In the absence of a proper method of giving or issuing command through the I. centre the reader will find that it is not possible for him to improve rapidly and will be disappointed every time an attempt is made.

Have not most of our readers observed that no sooner one decides to reform, things seem to go wrong all the more ? It is only because of the wrong and hasty way of giving command by the I. centre which infuriates and antagonises the directors of the E. and S. centres. People complain that whenever they sit for prayers or meditation or concentration then precisely at that time only unwanted thoughts come in and intrude. This is nothing but the revolt of the E. and S. centres against the hasty orders and decisions of the I. centre.

If at such a time one were to arouse the other centres or

rather consult them and then decide to do what one wants to do, we would find that their co-operation is possible. Enthusiasm is wrongly mistaken for the right attitude, but enthusiasm is limited and mostly belongs to the I. centre only and so evaporates soon.

So also die all New Year's resolutions. On New Year's Day or on birthdays, it is easier to arouse enthusiasm of the E. centre and add it to that of the I. centre. The reader will forgive some repetition but such explanations are best repeated, they are of great importance.

Take this thought for serious thinking : "Have I tried to observe the agitations that go on below the surface of my brain like those in an electric computer ?" After thousand of years man will not be able to use his brain (where the finest computations go on and on) to full capacity.

The centres must work in harmony. This is helped by the nerves carrying the messages. We doubt, if even now, we know all the processes of conscious relation of the glands and body. There may be vibrations so subtle that the senses do not detect them as yet. This is all under the jurisdiction of the In. centre [i.e. : the fifth centre with its 2 sub-sections (a) and (b)]

The four centres along with the interplay of their qualities simultaneously, yet at different levels, transform all coded impulses into decoded thoughts. To do this *continuously* and without a pause is the inherent property of that portion of our brain we call Section 1 of our brain or mind No. 1. These four centres have their coding seats in the body and their decoding seats in the 'grey matter brain' we call Sec. 1 or mind No. 1. It is the inherent quality of this Section and to do anything else would mean not following its own law.

This non-stop picture forming, an inherent quality of this portion of the brain (Sec. 1 of mind), presupposes that it is unnatural *not* to form pictures every moment during the whole of our life. If it does not do so, there is some deformity in this brain Sec. 1. It is, therefore, its inherent quality never to give attention to even the finest, noblest picture for more than a fraction of a second. Therefore concentration, meditation or even continued serious thinking is seldom possible with this brain (Sec. 1). It is the privilege of this part of the brain

(Sec. 1) to form several pictures a second and that non-stop for as long as a person lives. This is done through those four centres, viz., I., E., S. and M.

The In. centre (5. centre) has its higher duties to perform and is put in charge of brain Sec. 2 (A and B) or mind No. 2. The four centres form the conscious life of man. Not knowing this, many people force Sec. 1 of the brain (even thereby tormenting the body) to make *this* portion of the brain do the impossible.

Our programme aims at certain disciplines of both body and mind, which help us to build up natural resources from within. It must be noted that when we talk of 'brain' the whole mass of grey matter is not involved but only a portion we call brain No. 1 or Sec. 1.

The intensity of vibrations rises many steps at a time or shoots up straight or moves sometimes hardly a fraction of a step. It moves simultaneously in all columns as impulses reach all the four centres simultaneously and so each centre is busy decoding the coded impulses received. These are a few of the qualities belonging to each centre. The plus and minus intensities are shown parallel or intertwined. Intensity not only rises and falls vertically in each centre but from each centre it goes to other different centres. If we could be given Divine sight or 'electronic vision' we could see the play of the intensities, or the play of qualities of the centre, as boiling liquids of different colours rising and mixing and separating and remixing. This play of qualities or the movement of intensities leaves a person so exhausted that in spite of all physical rest a person feels extremely tired and even tonics do not help.

Each coded impulse and decoded thought creates a pattern. Thousands of such patterns circulate every day in and between the centres. There are certain repetitions of patterns. *Those that repeat a sufficient number of times, impose their resultant intensities on the blood cells. The blood cells in turn, therefore, develop certain deformities within their inner structure. These deformities lead to various types of maladies and diseases.*

From this we realise that by corrective methods while eating, and three-step rhythmic breathing, we more easily correct the deformities than by any other method known and here we can even work in conjunction with other known methods.

Sec. 2 of the brain remains in a half-formed stage in the case of all humanity except for a few individuals. Unless brain 1 works rhythmically in all centres and proper rhythmic intensity is not imposed, the brain 2 (or Sec. 2) does not begin to develop fully. The half-formed brain 2 (or sub-section 2 *a* of the brain) carries on the activities of the In. centre. When the other half (sub-section *b*) of brain Sec. 2 is developed, we get the benefit of the functions of that part of the brain *and the most important of them is its ability to hold on to one thought at a time without any disturbance as long as is required*, i.e., the ability of that part of the brain to concentrate and meditate is denied to us as long as that portion of the brain is not developed and which cannot even develop unless a very high plus or minus resultant intensity is imposed on the blood cells. In ignorance, therefore, we force brain No. 1 (or Sec. 1) to do the work which only the other half (sub-section *b*) of brain No. 2 is capable.

It is the same story with penitence, resolutions, will-power, concentration, japa, prayers and the like. Brain Sec. 1 will go on forming pictures not at all connected with the subject of our serious thinking for it *has* to form many pictures per second out of all the impulses received. Even if you feel like doing some serious thinking it is obstructive. "Go to the right office and inquire", says brain Sec. 1 to us, "I cannot serve you exclusively and keep out the hundreds of thousands of the impulses that reach our office."

Only in deep sleep does brain 1 (or Sec. 1 of the brain) reduce by 95% its the picture-forming rate. In the soundest sleep, 5% picture-forming continues. It may or may not be remembered on waking up but we call such activity, "dreams". Sometimes this is transmitted unconsciously to brain 2 (Sec. 2 of the brain) and in that case we get unconsciously the concentration or meditation done on that subject. The answer or proper reply in such cases is what we call "prophetic dreams" or Führungs träume (Vide SAHER, Die verborgene Weisheit, p. 100).

This closing of brain Sec. 1 and passing on to brain Sec. 2 a particular thought can sometimes be done subconsciously. When one can do so *consciously* it is called YOGA. This gives a person the added dimensions of brain No. 2 (or Sec. 2) which is capable of functioning on the cellular-molecular planes.

Wonderful knowledge is gained, not ever possible to brain Sec. 1 by its methods of cumulative knowledge.

It is therefore ordained that brain No. 2 (i.e. Sec. 2) after fully concentrating or meditating on a particular thought passes down to the I. centre of Sec. 1 its findings and the I. centre then understands what would forever have been impossible by the unaided efforts of brain Sec. 1.

When a man attains to Pure Reason, he renounces in this world the results of good and evil alike. "Cling thou to Right Action." Spirituality is the art of living. It is very true that spirituality is the art of living and that art if followed methodically brings about Right Action. Brain 2 (or Sec. 2 *B* of the brain) is Pure Reason. Mind or Sec. 4 of the brain is Pure Intelligence, an uncorrupted 'Supraconsciousness' or the Ātman.

Further we can quote, "the sages guided by pure Intelligence renounce the fruit of action. When thy reason has crossed the entanglement of illusions, then thou shalt become indifferent both to the philosophies that thou hast heard and to those thou mayest yet hear."

When brain or mind 2 (sec. 2 *B* of the brain) functions, and when the Critical-Certain-Stage is crossed over, we need no books and no philosophies for our own wonderful mind gives us all the knowledge that is essential. (*Mind* 2 *is termed Buddhi or m a n a s and mind* 1 *is the mind stuff or the C h i t t a*).

Similarly we have Secs. 3 and 4 of the brain. But as long as brain Sec. 2 is not formed completely and functions satisfactorily, the brain Sections 3 and 4 cannot function.

We all know that a fourth of our entire cell population is formed of sex cells. This colossal, out-of-proportion population is therefore unwisely wasted by a normal person either mentally or physically. Actually, Nature's and God's prudent laws expect of man that HE WOULD BY A JUDICIAL USE OF THESE VERY VITAL SEX CELLS DEVELOP THEM FURTHER AND BY RYTHMIC BREATHING AND CORRECTIVE METHODS PROMOTE AND TRANSFER THEM TO BECOME THE HIGHER BRAIN SECS. 2 B, 3 and 4. When this happens, MIND (through Sec. 2 *b*) will begin to function and concentration as well as meditation becomes possible. Then, by proper process, Sec. 1 *through its I. centre* would be able to pass on to brain Sec. 2 B certain problems which brain 2 will concentrate or meditate on and give the right reply. Because this intercommunication between brain 1. and 2. (or Sec. 1 and 2 of mind) *is only possible through the I. centre, the I. centre is the seniormost director amongst the five centres and the other centres know this.*

When brain Sec. 3 is formed and is able to function it will open the great memory of Nature and her vast store of knowledge will be available. When translated through the I. centre it will inform the conscious brain of man about all and everything in interstellar space.

When further progress is made and mind No. 4 (or Sec.4) is formed, it will open the invisible worlds and the invisible operation of laws in the galaxies; it will be possible for man to have this unimaginably lofty wisdom which will come pouring through brain Sec. 4 and through the I. centre reach the conscious brain of man. This same insignificant looking creature man, when in possession of his brain or mind Nos. 2, 3 and 4 is an exact image of his Creator.

With the formation of Sections 3 and 4 are also formed the molecular and electronic bodies of man; these are an astral and spiritual replica of his physical body. Just as present day man, to suit his movements, makes use of a car, or ship, or plane or submarine, in the same manner God and Nature have provided man with cellular and molecular and electronic vehicles of the mind to enable him to function freely as desired in the three bodies.

The Universal Mind, the Absolute and such other terms have absolutely no meaning without man's conscious progress informing the Sections 2, 3 and 4 of his mind and thus also forming complete cellular-molecular, molecular and electronic bodies. Some call these cellular-molecular, molecular and electronic bodies astral, mental, and causal bodies.[1]

It is obvious that the intensities of the various centres are different. Man in his present stage of evolution has the intensities in the ratio of 2:4:8:2 for the I., E., S. and M. centres. Evolution is the changing of this ratio to the ratio God and Nature require of man which is 5:2:2:1. Man must then

1. Thus we read of the 'dharma' body of the Buddha and so forth.

transubstantiate his sex cells to form Sections 2, 3 and 4 of the brain; which then deserves to be called *mind* in its proper sense.

Some persons live exclusively in a particular centre. Most people live in different centres exclusively at different times and all people live simultaneously in many. Man, as his ratio today for the centres is 2:4:8:2, finds that whenever he dwells in the I. centre exclusively, the twenty-four hours seem thirty, that living in the M. centre he feels twenty-hours as twenty, that dwelling exclusively in the E. centre he feels twenty-four hours as twelve hours and that exclusively dwelling in the S. centre he feels the twenty-four hours as six hours. Whenever a person is engaged in patterns belonging to faster or higher resultant intensity centres, he finds time flying fast. When the balanced stage is reached due to the rhythm of life, twenty-four hours seem twenty-four hours as the ratio is 5:2:2:1 in all the centres.

Let us recount the incident of the person in an office, reading a letter, seeing from the corner of his eye the secretary arranging her skirt, and he has had a heavy lunch and the letter conveys some good news of brighter business. The impulses from the female secretary reach the S. Centre, the heavy lunch slows the M. centre by sending impulses to that effect, the letter and the news send impulses of profits and planning accordingly to the I. centre and the E. centre receives impulses from all the three, viz. the letter, lunch and secretary! Like boiling water, the intensities rise and fall in all the centres, each time the impulses of business, sex and laziness overpower or are dominant by turns, and the intensities fly from one centre to another. Imagine such chaotic messages flying through the telegraph. The effect of this chaotic state is physical, emotional, mental and sexual exhaustion.

Take this thought for serious thinking: "Why must I study this book most earnestly irrespective of whether I enjoy reading it or not ?"

Chapter XVII

WHAT IS THE PURPOSE OF LIFE AND BIRTH?

Understanding means knowing the purpose or the why of things as contrasted with mere belief which may be based on purely intellectual sub-conscious data and may have nothing to do with realities.

This book is devoted to practices, disciplines and methods which if followed with sincerity and regularity will bring any human being to the verge of the Critical-Certain-Stage.

Teachers are rare and a true Master never takes on a disciple; he befriends you and then just tells you in some simple way how to find the road, the strength and the clarification within. The more one reads and the more one hears and the more one discusses, the more one is confused.

We shall now give you the unfailing magic formula and it will bring you to that Critical-Certain-Stage.

Write down this formula where you are sure to read it daily lest you forget it some time or other.

It is the formula, the supreme "Mantra". God Himself repeats it without ever stopping as it is that which makes God what He is. And makes man look so small because he does not faithfully repeat it, meditate on it or think over it.

All those who have arrived, all those who have been guiding lights to man, have sincerely repeated the same and meditated over it. It is the unfailing sure guide.

Venerate this formula and with devotion keep it in your heart and mind. It is this:

"What is the purpose of Life and Birth?"[1]

Whenever you say something, or hear or read something, practise or think something, do or intend to do something, whenever you are puzzled or baffled or hesitate or yearn or wish to know what is good or bad, right or wrong, whenever someone argues or advises, leads or philosophises, ask :—

1. OM, Paraṁ satyaṁ dhīmahi.

"What is the purpose? Does this, whatever I am doing, take me nearer to that purpose, or take me away, does it create a wall or remove a wall, does it leave me where I was and as I was or will there be some progress?"

We recall those fine words.

"If you must defame someone, do not say it, write it, write it on the sand, near the water's edge." We say to you dear reader, do not say this formula only, write it, but not anywhere, write it in your heart, in your mind, on your tongue and on your brow. So that whenever you want to speak anything it will always be spoken first, and whenever you would think anything it would be the first thought and whenever you yearn for anything it would be sought first and should anyone approach you with new theories or should you approach anyone, the other person will read it on your brow and will quickly depart leaving you alone with your purpose.

Nothing matters in this life and in this world. All that matters is a life well lived. *A life so well lived in every step, in every breath*, that there itself is the purpose of Life and Birth translated. Such a life—*not a life of mere goodness* but a life of real goodness with the purpose of Life and Birth translated into every moment of the flow of life, is what Iqbal* visualised, when he said, "Oh Man, live your life so well, let your life be so exemplary that God Himself should come to you and ask, 'What can I do for you'?"

Up to this stage, let us not ask, discuss or think about religion, Karma, Life after death, Reincarnation, God, Creation, how long will this earth last? The subjects are very high and noble and good. However, for these two simple reasons we shall not indulge in such questioning:—

1. Even if the real truth about these subjects were told and explained, there is every chance of misunderstanding rather than understanding them.
2. Even if we did understand them, then this alone would not allow us to progress an inch or earn salva-

* Most famous Urdu poet of Pakistan: even the word 'Pakistan' was coined by him.

tion or be free or be at liberty to make use of free-will correctly.

We shall remain as much bound slaves as we have ever been. Even hearing from God Himself (if it were possible) and seeing God Himself (if it were possible) will not mend matters. It is first absolutely essential to reach that Critical-Certain-State. Let us keep on asking:

"What is the purpose of Life and Birth ?"

You may say, however, that there should be no reason for cutting down sleep or food. Is it not enough if we practise the three-step rhythmic breathing, analysis and the corrective methods? The question is natural and good. However it is like this: Imagine a thermometer marked zero, fifty, hundred, one hundred and fifty and two hundred, the normal being hundred. Suppose this is the safety point and that a temperature above this point would be dangerous. Then there must be a safety valve to avoid an explosion.

1. By experience you will also agree that more than one meal or even a heavy single meal, takes the reading to higher than a hundred depending on how much the indulgence is. Night meal in preference to lunch also does the same.

2. By experience you will also agree that more than six hours of sleep will take the reading to above a hundred depending upon how much the indulgence is. Sleep in the afternoon or any other inappropriate part of the day also does the same.

3. By experience you will also agree that indulging in (1) and (2) both, takes the reading to two hundred. What do we mean when we say that the reading goes to two hundred? Between 150—200 is the region of high minus intensity. It may lead you to laziness, procrastination, to sex indulgence and to debit accounts etc. Between 100—150 is minus

resultant intensity which leads to yawning, daydreaming, absentmindedness and to a willingness to sex indulgence, etc.

4. By experience you will agree that keeping to 11 p.m. to 5 a.m. as hours for sleep and one meal (average) in the noon every day will avoid the natural tendency of the mind and body to waywardness. The regular three-step rhythmic breathing for twenty-four hours and the corrective methods will help you to quickly change all minus intensity to plus. Hence your thoughts, when they are in the pure mind-energy state, will be free from all unnatural control and you will experience more and more the effortless way of life. Why would you like to make your task more difficult by sleeping more and at wrong hours, or eating at wrong hours ?

To control the flow of electricity we provide a fuse, which by bursting stops the flow of electricity temporarily till it is restored and so prevents greater damage. By over-eating or eating at wrong hours or over-sleeping or sleeping at wrong hours, by wrong breathing and by wrong use of the centres we overload the flow of life and Nature has provided fuses to stop the overflow of life for a few moments, to prevent greater damage. These fuses are set automatically when the imaginary 'thermometer' in our example reaches a hundred. The fuse system of Nature is a little complicated. The sex act, bursts of temper and by such other violent methods or ways we blow off the excess heat or pressure. Then the body reaches the normal hundred and the fuse is set again and this happens indefinitely. Therefore it is apparent that the load must be adjusted and there is no better way than one mid-day meal (average), 11 p.m. to 5.a.m. sleep, three-step rhythmic breathing, analysis and the corrective methods.

We have asked, desired and demanded a birth in the human form and this disciplined way is, therefore, necessary. Or else why should we not be wild animals and enjoy being wild beasts in 'freedom', for even the domesticated dog or horse has to live under some kind of discipline. Even an animal has to pay for immoderations with its life.

By all means read, by all means pray, by all means do all that you want to do, only observe the disciplines shown earlier *and seek true evolution.* There is no business on earth or in all creation so profitable, so devoid of all chances of failure as the business of self-improvement and the business of self-evolution, so long as you use the correct methods. Begin if you have hesitated so far, and God be with you.

Take this thought for serious thinking; "Nothing short of daily spiritual immersions in the spiritual waters of divine Reality will dissolve discordant films and open the way to pure knowing."

VOLUME II

THE UNPUBLISHED SECRETS OF ZEN AND YOGA

Chapter I

PRATYĀHĀRA

We have considered four important steps viz. yama, niyama, āsana, prāṇāyāma and have seen that all four steps together form the art of prāṇāyāma or the art of control of prāṇa* or impulses. These impulses are received from (1) food and drink (2) breathing (3) the sensations of sound, smell, touch, taste and sight. We have also noted the corrective methods for each. Sincere adherence to the methods and techniques shown would bring a person to the verge of the Critical-Certain-Stage.

The fifth step is Pratyāhāra. The first four steps bring one to the bank of a river. Then there is the river and then there is the other bank. On the other bank is the master waiting for the sincere disciple to come. The disciple has after a long journey come to the bank of the river. The 'river' we call 'No Man's-Land' or the fifth step of Pratyāhāra.

We have seen the interplay of the qualities of the centres and their repeated expressions of millions of patterns. The introduction of corrective methods bring about finally a state of inward agitation expressed usually as the "struggles of the aspirant". These inward struggles denote use of unmethodical methods. When the methods are methodical we term them as "the re-education of the mind" and then there are no such wild struggles.

Suppose we ask a friend to stand at the door and prevent certain persons from coming in. The friend is sincerely helping us in keeping these people out, yet is himself held in bondage in attendance at the door and he cannot peacefully come and be with us ! Such a friend is your mind within, the other people are the types of impulses you want to keep out, and so your mind remains busy in trying to keep these impulses from coming in i.e. instead of the bondage of indulgence of certain thoughts, you engage yourself in the bondage of preventing these impulses from coming in !

*Vital energy.

Every sincere aspirant has found to his or her dismay that no sooner is an attempt made for a better life then, as if from some unknown quarter of the mind, a host of thoughts rush in to suffocate this noble urge and the aspirant is himself astounded that such a host of vicious thoughts even existed within his own mind. Some piously believe that the Lord is putting him or her to the "test", never suspecting and utterly not understanding the strength of the E. and S. centres and the patterns stored within; this is the I. centre's unmethodical approach to the whole problem !

Taking refuge in repeating a mantra or holy name or visualising a holy face on which we have absolute faith, may not always help us in carrying out our daily life, for our mind can seldom properly dwell upon both subjects simultaneously. No sooner is the mind left to handle worldly life, than it plays its own tricks, and with a vengeance.

So, by putting into operation Part I of this book, one is also able to put into operation yama, niyama, āsana, and prāṇāyāma. Actually speaking, all the four steps *together* constitute prāṇāyāma or the art of controlling all incoming impulses. Sincere practice will bring one to the verge of that Critical-Certain-Stage which forms one bank of the river. Just as a river has two banks, so the flowing river of life has also two banks. One side of the bank is the life of the aspirant below and up to that Critical-Certain-Stage, and on the other bank, is the higher, more free, spiritual and Zenoga stage, or the goal, or the purpose of life and birth. Crossing the river is essential in order to go over to its other side. Whilst on the river we can choose the spot on the other side where we plan to land. For the higher, spiritual stage we must cross over and actually and factually land on the other bank. This river of life is normally a very turbulent river. Crossing from one bank to another one would need a good boat and a skilful boatsman. We do not normally carry a boat on our head in expectation of having to cross a river. But on coming to the river, we search for a boatsman with a boat. We neither search for nor find a boatsman before coming to the river !

The boatsman is your guide and the boat is his way of taking you to the other bank. Your arriving at the bank of the river is your preparation to be ready i.e. arriving up to the verge of that Critical-Certain-Stage. In other words you are then becoming ready for the Master to appear.

Normally we pay a boatsman for taking us across. What we pay in our case is our sincere adherence to his methods, regularly day in and day out. This crossing over is called the 'No Man's-Land' for though the land on either side of the river may belong to different owners, the river belongs to all. Just as the river is a different terrain from that on either side so is here the No Man's-Land. Quite a different type of effort, experience, and study are required *after*, as compared to efforts, study and experience required *before* or up to that Critical-Certain-Stage. What then is pratyāhāra ? It is normally called "preparation to concentration". The process of collecting the powers of the mind and restraining them from going out to external objects.

The aspirant finds that his every attempt is opposed by his wayward mind. There are some who bring in the question of the devil tempting the person who is on his way to progress.

A rocket, to be free from the gravitational pull of the Earth, has to develop a certain speed or power and for a rocket to escape the gravitational pull of the Sun, the intensity or speed required would be many times more. Is this gravitational pull a devil ? Is this gravitational pull of the Earth or the Sun a smaller and bigger devil ? Is the inherent gravitational pull of the flow of life a devil ? Is such gravitational pull in an ordinary aspirant and in a Christ or a Buddha a smaller and bigger devil ? Even supposing it is a devil, how is it that until this time i.e. until the day we decide to 'pull off' we did not realise that it was a devil for it would amount to saying that America did not exist till Columbus or Amerigo de Vispuze discovered it !

The inherent pull of the flow of life is the force that counters our efforts to be free from it and very naturally so. We have for a long time been very friendly and in line with the same flow of life, and now that we have decided to break off, naturally, parting company hurts and there is even a natural tendency to hold on.

The advanced souls are past the 'No Man's-Land' and are high up on the other side. They have already offset, so to say, the gravitational pull of Earth but, let us say, are satellites of the Sun. They again realise their new bondage and now seek release from that. The pull is however far too intense, but these wonderful ones are equal to the task. In figurative language this pull from outside is a mighty devil with great powers and the weapons with which he can oppose or 'tempt' are awful from our point of view.

The 'No Man's-Land' or pratyāhāra is the stage where an aspirant has to add two plus Zenoga-Units to the two already accumulated. Pratyāhāra is, therefore, a stage sufficiently long for the sincere aspirant to continue with the methods shown in Part I so that rhythmic three-step breathing is perfected. The decoded thought-rate keeps on diminishing till it reaches one hundred pulse beats for decoding one coded impulse. The ground is now prepared for the next and very important stage of Dhāraṇā (Concentration), Dhyāna (Meditation) and Samādhi (Identification) i.e. the proper use of brain and mind portion No. 2 which is still to be developed. This is done of course under the guidance of a teacher which the aspirant will automatically find when coming up to the verge of that Critical-Certain-Stage; this Stage is the equivalent of the higher grades of initiation (=Einweihung) given by a competent Master—or, still better, by a Mahā-Avatāra.

At this stage, i.e. stage of pratyāhāra occurs a two-fold change !

(1) The still higher stage of concentration is reached. The stage when for a duration of one thousand pulse beats, one single coded impulse is decoded, studied and 'held' exclusively. This means that the energy normally wasted in decoding 12×1000=12,000 thoughts is preserved and the intensity of that one decoding resultant is multiplied by 12,000. This makes it possible to hold intense plus resultant intensity for 1000 plus beats. This charges the whole body and the most important reaction resulting from such intense charging is the separating of the cellular-molecular and the molecular bodies i.e. the physical or purely cellular body with its functions from the molecular-cellular (=astral) body.

(2) The intensity is high enough to break away from the inherent pull of the flow of life. To reach this stage and be able to separate these bodies and to be able to function in them separately is, therefore, important and the only task at this stage of pratyāhāra. For this very important stage, a master appears to guide the sincere aspirant if he has regularly practised all that has been shown in Part I.

Take this thought for serious thinking, "What is the Supreme Truth? When does Supreme Truth appear on Earth in the disguise of a human being? What is such a Being called? How should we venerate Him? Could HE be the author of this book?"

Chapter II

SELF-CONQUEST

Now that the aspirant finds himself on the cellular-molecular and molecular planes, functioning, or able to function in his cellular-molecular and molecular bodies, some advice is to be given, for he will be sorely tempted to use his new found occult powers and his new dimensions of consciousness for ill-chosen purposes.

In part I we developed our mind (portions) 1 and 2 and even started developing mind (portion) 3. The cells, due to constant new practices and due to a new rhythm, change consciously. The intensity of the whole being is slowly evolved so that when the whole being rises to a particular pitch, the life giving essence i.e. prāṇa (it is also called prāṇa because life itself comes streaming in, by impulses) is able to come in from every pore of the body, for prāṇa is a force that can penetrate a body or any created substance. Prāṇa is on the subtle borderland between matter and non-matter. It is very, very hard to observe. It is able to penetrate every and any substance and for this reason life and consciousness could (in however limited form) exist in deep oceans and much below the surface of our earth or in outer space. The Moon provides Prāṇa for the entire cosmos.*

Yama and Niyama not only mean rules of conduct or precepts. They imply the training of the centres. A daily training according to this book and a perpetual awakening is essential to bring about harmony within.

In whatever we have stated till now there ought to be no strained effort, no suspense, no artificial ways of living, no "holier than thou" feeling, no separateness from any life of creation, no reason to misunderstand anyone or any movement and yet with childlike simplicity and with childlike grace we attain that state—the Critical-Certain-Stage.

*Cp. Prof. V. Ditfurths bestseller called 'Kinder des Weltalls', (Vgl.) Hamburg 1970.

Normally, a human being is awake for about sixteen hours each day. Then in 960 minutes, even if he were to think at a very low rate of say 20 (not thinks, but decodes coded impulses) thoughts per minute, we get 960×20=19,200 thoughts. The normal decoding rate is far greater and in between there are countless drifts. Taking a round figure of 19,000 we have the minimum score of 19,000 per day. Each decoded impulse is cardexed into its respective centre and, if corrective methods are brought out and applied, the rate falls to perhaps 10,000 which would in that case mean so much energy (19000—10000=9000) stored.

The correctives add immensively to the plus score and we find ourselves on the way to success. Similarly, the three-step rhythmic breathing would reduce our daily average of 25,920 breaths to a mere 17,280 per day besides lowering (due to the imposition of this rhythm) the decoding rate even further. Imagine what colossal saving in energy is thus brought about !

The incoming impulses, those practically unobservable power points, that reach us continually (instead of flaring up and burning away like highly inflammable gas) thereby turn into a powerful storehouse of vital force.

Finally, the most important point to grasp is the fact that one is to be convinced that these simple, commonplace and yet essential activities like eating, sleeping, sex, corrective methods, check of drifts and analysis are the stepping stones to real progress.

Take this thought for serious thinking, "How can I free myself from my own shadow ?"

Chapter III

UNDERSTANDING OF THE LAWS OF SPIRITUAL SUCCESS

"Some have abandoned home, some have abandoned heritage; but fruitless is all abiding place, *if thou hast not thy mind under subjection.*"

A rocket has to attain a certain speed in a certain direction; this is analogous to what we call in man the rate of resultant intensity or the flow of resultant intensity (or the movement of the Parameśvarī). They say, the speed required to break away from the gravitational pull of the Earth is 25,000 miles an hour. Analogically the equivalent we have in Yoga is two 'plus-Zenoga-Units'. If this speed is not attainable, the rocket must return to Earth after some time, due to gravity and would, in that case, (if not guided through atmosphere at reduced speed) burn out in the atmosphere due to the heat of friction. If the speed is great enough but not sufficient to break off and reach some target in our Universe, it will then orbit round our Earth impotently, may be for an eternity, or after a time be pulled back by our Earth.

In the same way, if a man cannot attain that rate of intensity he remains bound to the gravitational pull of life or comes back again and again to this flow of life, or lives his life impotently like a machine. The gravitational pull is the inherent property of Earth and the gravitational pull of life is also the inherent property of the flow of life which we in a human being call the life of inertia and pleasure or the line of least resistance !

We have as a race now become conscious of the gravitational pull of our Earth, the speed that is required to break away from such a pull, and are also aware of the results of immature attempts or insufficient speed to break away. In these days of such consciousness we ought to understand much better, and be able to work out much more easily, the internal resultant so that the immature and insufficient methods to break away from the pull of life be substituted by the better ones of Zenoga.

When a rocket has to develop such high speed care is taken to see that the material it is composed of stands the strain, even at critical speeds, and also of the heat created by friction when travelling through the atmosphere. One also takes care to see that the right type of fuel is made use of.

The corrective methods and the three-step rhythmic breathing, the care with which we select and create new 'material' for making it possible for a human being to attain that intensity to break off from the gravitational pull of life (for any intensity below the required intensity will fail to pull a human being away from the gravitational pull of the flow of life) is our 'material'.

Even so, should we go beyond that Critical-Certain-Stage, we have indeed gathered enough intensity to pull away from the gravitational pull of life, but we are as yet in that stage which we call the 'No Man's-Land' or pratyāhāra. We are now neither here nor there ! Let us also compare what should or would happen to man who would reach that Critical-Certain-Stage. He will indeed be free from the inherent pull of life. If he were now to shoot out, but as yet not being prepared with right knowledge to reach a certain destination and without a proper chart, he would not be able to land wherever he wants, and there is every chance that he will fly past his destination, or burn out or harm himself or be held in bondage elsewhere unconsciously; as yet he is unable to come back at will. However nice and good and high be this new found freedom or shall we say new found bondage ! Similarly the higher practices of dhāraṇā (concentration) and dhyāna (meditation) will enable man to pull away safely from the gravitational pull of the flow of life !

Take this thought for serious thinking, "Is the Supreme Creator, the God of our Universe ?" And if you should find this thought a little difficult think seriously on, "closing the gates of the body, drawing the forces of his mind into the heart and by the power of meditation, concentrating his vital energy in the brain one leaves the body with mind unmoved and filled with devotion; by the power of his meditation, gathering between his eyebrows his whole vital energy he attains the Supreme."

Chapter IV

THE GLAMOUR OF LIBERATION FROM BONDAGE TO THE EGO

> "Who is he that is wrapped in sleep, and who is he that is awake?
> What lake is that which continuously oozeth away?
> What is that which a man may offer in worship to the Lord?
> What is that supreme station to which thou wilt attain?"

"Alas! length of days doth more often make our sins the greater, than our lives the better! Oh! that we had spent but one day in this world thoroughly well!"

There are many who have earned the right of freedom from bondage from the flow of life. Many have bartered their newly earned freedom, for bondage on the astral and mental planes. But what are these new terms we are introducing? Are these areas somewhere, far away in our galaxy or in some other distant galaxy? Perhaps it is not exactly so! Perhaps our scientists will say that our astronauts have found no such areas existing!

It is to be noted that the sixth centre which we call the junior Managing Director is responsible for guiding the I. centre as well as for bringing about the internal harmony of centres. However, unassumingly, the 7th centre or the senior Managing Director keeps helping both the I. centre as well as the 'junior Managing Director' (or the 6th centre) who do not realise this fact and feel they are solely responsible for all progress. However, it so happens that after a time, the 7th centre (or the senior Managing Director) stops helping and the person crossing that Critical-Certain-Stage finds himself in or rather 'enters' that which we call the 'glamorous' stage of occult powers in yoga; the stage of early freedom from bondage, with insufficient intensity to break away from the pull of the flow of life and reach a destination ! Such a person feels that he has arrived and makes a show in external change of dress and speech and in many other ways, because the absolute knowledge and deep sobriety of the seventh centre is missing.

Some start a following or a school or an āśrama. Some get as by-products some lesser powers attendant on the junior Managing Director i.e. on attaining certain high intensity. These according to Yoga, are called Siddhis (=psychic powers) whilst those of the 7th centre are recognised as ATMAN-in-Itself. The former is a treacherous stage. All but a very few forget this warning and so are held as revolving satellites. If this new stage were the destination, it would be well and good but this new bondage is in a field not intended to hold us forever. The powers of the cellular-molecular and molecular planes are great but it means only exchanging one less equipped prison for a better equipped and more luxurious one. Compared to our cellular structure and awareness the molecular structure and awareness is indeed one of great freedom, and wonderful indeed, but it is only a station on the way not the destination or purpose of life and birth !

Should our destination be something else, and if we find a certain station on the way wonderful, we do not drop out of the transport and suddenly decide to stay at that station. If we do, it speaks of a weak mind and a life without plan or purpose. In any case, this stage is not what we have to reach ultimately and if we are sincere to the formula, "what is the purpose of life and birth" we shall not get trapped by such stations on the way and will continue going; however pleasant the stations on the way may be !

Most aspirants not only think that they have arrived but also that the junior Managing Director (the 6th centre) is the Chairman, while in fact he is even below the senior Managing Director (the 7th centre). Such persons describe these (on-the-way-stations) at great length, in prose and poetry, and the pupils that they find are also misled, though such aspirants be honest, for they firmly believe that they have now reached their destination. If the destination were so near and so easy of access then poor indeed is this entire creation and its purpose !

The glamour of this stage is so great that aspirants stay there for almost an eternity or till such time one informs them.

They then again realise the new bondage and make a fresh start.

In poetic language : "Yet although they enjoy the *spacious* glories of Paradise, nevertheless, *when their merit is exhausted*, they are born again into this world of mortals."

Should our aim be freedom from bondage, at no stage let our aim be relative, accepting anything less than continuous progress till absolute freedom is achieved. If this requires our efforts till the end of time and our waiting till the end of creation, falter not; do not accept, even out of exhaustion, anything less than asked for, worked for, aimed at ! We assure you that such unflinching devotion, such supreme duty to yourself is always respected and even suns and stars and galaxies give way if required to get out of your path so that you may progress; for instinctively all creation can sense this one supreme purpose or urge, though most of creation is unable to express it in as many words but will know by instinct a person who seeks freedom from *all* bondage !

Take this thought for serious thinking : "What is prayer ? How could it be made effective to work instantaneously ?"

CHAPTER V

YOGA SŪTRA IN THE LIGHT OF OUR UNDERSTANDING

> "Before the eyes can see they must be incapable of tears, before the ears can hear, they must have lost their sensitiveness, before the tongue can speak in the presence of the Masters, it must have lost the power to wound. Before the Soul can stand in the presence of the Masters, its feet must be washed in the blood of the heart".
>
> Light on the Path

We now begin the exposition of Yoga Sūtra based on our understanding, so far explained, of Zenoga.

Yoga is controlling the interplay of qualities of the centres I., E., S. and M., under the jurisdiction of Section *one* of the brain or mind. This 'Section' is known as Chitta. When this mind achieves rhythm of the centres and when it further develops the Sections 2 and 3 of mind our gross essence becomes fine essence. When this happens i.e. when rhythm is achieved, Section No. 2 of the brain is fully formed. It is then like the bottom of a lake which is clearly seen when there are no ripples.

Normally, before this rhythm is achieved, either the I., E., S. or M. centre predominates.

The activities of mind Sec. I are (i) experience, (ii) perversion, (iii) delusion, (iv) sleep, (v) recollection. Some of the activities are painful, others pleasurable.

Control of the activities by the corrective methods and self-analyses and three-step rhythmic breathing is essential. Practice is essential and should be steady and daily and over a long period. Long unremitting sincere practice develops Section No. 2 of mind completely.

Detachment is the inherent quality of this mind No. 2. The highest form of detachment is the absolute rhythm of the interplay of qualities of the centres of mind No. 1. When rhythm prevails in the centres, ignorance, anger, passion are replaced by purity of thought which is the inherent quality *of mind No.* 2. This is the greatest struggle, the greatest achievement, the greatest renunciation. This is brought about by corrective methods and three-step rhythmic breathing and proper habits of food and sleep.

The mind is pure, the form is pure, the relationship is pure, but though pure it is still a sentiment and all sentiment is weakness, bondage. A true yogī goes beyond this. Power of knowledge is great, the power of control of knowledge is greater. Spiritual life begins with control; one can get control by practice only. So long as mind is limited, the joy it can experience is limited. The purpose is to merge Section 1 of mind with the Section of mind No. 2 into the Section of mind No. 3 into the Section of mind No. 4; then one is able to function on the 2nd to 4th stages of cosmic consciousness. Then joy changes to "peace that passeth understanding" and is no longer limited. This is of course relatively speaking only.

The power of the material sphere is great, but that of the spiritual sphere is even greater. If one renounces occult powers he is safe; if not, one travels the path of rebirth over and over again.

Success is immediate where effort is intense. Zenoga-Units are also accumulated by devotion to an ideal but they are then seldom in proper proportion to the centres as required. Concentration is only possible by mind No. 2. But concentration is on some form, and form means desire, and desire means some kind of action. One must go beyond this.

The meditation of mind No. 3 is on 'Om' (= the Moon as God). Meditation on Om through mind No. 3 removes any obstacle. Pain, disease, doubt, sensual pleasures, etc. are obstacles. The mind attains peace by regular three-step rhythmic breathing. As you meditate, so you become. There is nothing which Section 4 of the mind cannot grasp. When the mind's activities are controlled (i.e. the activities of *all* the sections of mind), illumination of varied degrees prevails lasting for a few seconds or even up to a long period of years.

When this happens, this physical world seems superfluous i.e. the true understanding of creation and the purpose of life and birth and death become apparent and the perspective and values of life change.

This illumination however is with what is called 'seed'. This illumination being pure brings spiritual contentment. There is complete freedom from bondage. One appears to oneself, at this stage, almost as God incarnate.

However, all freedom from bondage is limited however vast and hence this kind of illumination is said to be with 'seed' (=the seeds of future eventual bondage).

In this condition intellect becomes pregnant with truth. This state brings direct knowledge. All religions spring through higher beings going through such stages.

When even this has been surpassed, seedless Samādhi is attained.

Austerity, study, devotion to God, constitutes practical yoga. This constitutes part I of our book. The aim is to attain illumination. The aim is to form and develop by corrective methods all the portions of mind Nos. 2, 3 and 4. The transfer of consciousness from a lower vehicle, into a higher is part of the great creation and evolutionary process. (The words lower and higher depict limitations of language.) All organs, limbs, brain and mind are vehicles as is the body also and the other bodies besides the physical, viz., cellular-molecular, molecular, and electronic i.e. the astral, mental, and causal bodies.

Ignorance is the cause while fear, desire and aversion are the effects of wrong practice. We have seen in Part I that decoding of incoming impulses leads to the decoding of thoughts at the rate of twelve per second. This encoding and decoding constitutes pure mind-energy. This mind-energy has a resultant intensity according to the interplay of the centres.

Ignorance of this fact leads to aversion, fear and desire of every kind. Aversion on the other hand is recoiling from pain. When corrective methods replace wrong methods and when the three-step rhythmic breathing replaces wrong breathing (which is the normal breathing of an average person), illumination results i.e. all the Sections Nos. 2 and 3 and even 4 of mind are developed with their peculiar inherent qualities and possibilities.

So long as the root is present, Karma remains and creates rebirth. So long as four plus Zenoga-Units are not accumulated, till then free-will in its higher form and potential is not possible. So long the resultant intensity goes to one of the thirty-one Stars* and returns rebirth is compulsory. However, after this stage, free-will is immense and birth on this planet is by choice only and for a special purpose only as, for instance, in the case of an Avatāra.

Every man has to struggle for himself i.e. if one man is able to liberate himself from the gravitational pull of life, it does not mean that all men today or in future will be automatically free and that a particular person has atoned for us all, however great the seeming sacrifice be !

When one is able to liberate himself the result is sevenfold: (i) true renunciation is understood, (ii) what is to be renounced is renounced, (iii) cause is separated from effect and the one is not mistaken for the other, (iv) one attains freedom from the solar system, (v) one is content, (vi) the limitations of the centres are dissolved, (vii) the purpose of life and birth on *this* planet is fulfilled.

Part I shows practical ways to the first four steps and by that time two Zenoga-Units are accumulated. In pratyāhāra a further two Zenoga-Units are accumulated by corrective methods and three-step rhythmic breathing.

By this time mind No. 2 is developed and so the inherent quality of mind No. 2 makes Dhāraṇā and Dhyāna possible. This developes mind No. 3 and the inherent quality of Samādhi is achieved. This leads to illumination and liberation from bondage as is understood on *this* planet. By the corrective methods no efforts are wasted, there are no life-long struggles and with effortless effort one proceeds along the path and with the development of mind No. 2 parapsychic powers or occult siddhis naturally accompany progress on the Path.

There are three nerves, the Idā, Piṅgalā and Suṣumnā, of special note. The Idā and Piṅgalā pass through either side of the spinal chord, but the Suṣumnā which runs between the two is normally blocked. *Not* until sub-section B of mind Section No. 2 is formed does this passage become clear. Not till the

***Explained later on in Appendix at the end of this book.**

passage is clear can anyone practise yoga; even the *elementary Yoga*. There are artificial methods to clear it which are harmful and should be avoided.

Part one of our book is therefore essential, for it aids in clearing this passage.

Attention fixed upon an object is Dhāraṇā. Union of mind and object is Dhyāna. Samādhi is that condition of illumination. Successful concentration is necessary for direct knowledge. At every step distractions lessen and control increases until the mind changes to the condition of control; when control prevails mind flows peacefully. Note the words "mind flows". The incoming coded impulses form a continuous incoming flow and the outgoing decoded thoughts form the outgoing flow. Before the corrective methods are put into practice, the interplay of the qualities of the centres i.e. the inner state of mind No. 1 is in a state of chaos, utter chaos. Corrective methods and three-step rhythmic breathing bring about harmony in the centres. Not only mind No. 1 is developed more fully but Sec. B of mind No. 2 is also formed in due course. Mind flows peacefully at this stage. Concentration is natural at that stage.

Mind No. 1 has the inherent quality to make pictures and to prevent it from doing so is impossible and if done is detrimental for it amounts to paralysis of the mind Section No. 1. Mind No. 2 has the inherent quality to concentrate. It cannot make fresh, ever changing pictures like mind No. 1. It can take any picture given by mind No. 1 and understand its meaning and purpose and in turn illuminate mind No. 1 which then becomes 'knowledge' for mind No. 1.

The simple process of closing mind No. 1, opening the Sub-section B of mind No. 2 and concentrating on the picture given by mind No. 1 is Dhāraṇā or the higher beginning of Yoga. Mind No. 1 is wonderful but that which is not in its jurisdiction should not be forced upon mind No. 1. Change the subject or picture for Sub-section B of the mind No. 2 and various different types of knowledge are apprehended, understood, and passed on to mind No. 1. This way one can know past, present, future, the inside of the body and distant stars. This is what sage Patañjali also says in his Yoga Sūtra.

These occult powers yield power and knowledge yet are

obstacles to illumination. When that stage is reached, when one can consciously propel resultant intensity and induce the essence to change its normal course, the resultant intensity gathers the inner essence of a planet or a person. This is what Patañjali wishes to convey in his Yoga Sūtra. This is an advanced stage and is made use of to gather knowledge but if overindulged in it creates obstacles to real illumination and progress. During this progress mind Section 3 is fully developed also and portion 4 of the mind is also, though only partly, developed.

Finally, by renouncing even these powers, the seed of bondage being destroyed, the Yogī attains liberation. Then follows the power to take any form big or small. The chief powers are (1) to take the smallest form, (ii) to take the biggest form, (iii) power to touch anything, (iv) power to control anything, (v) power to create anything, (vi) power to penetrate anything, (vii) power to bring about anything.

Powers are either revealed at birth, or acquired by medicinal herbs, or by repetition of sacred words, or through austerity or through illumination. When the yogī attains final discrimination, but renounces even that, he then attains the condition called rain-cloud of divinity. The whole process of discrimination is the elimination of all limitations; when that is attained, the process itself is to be eliminated, as a man who lights the fire throws away the match. Nothing remains then to hinder the natural outpouring of Divinity. Mind without impurity and impediment attains infinite knowledge. What is still worth knowing in this world, then becomes negligible. Changes from moment to moment come to an end, their purpose being fulfilled. All doubts are dissolved, the problem of life is solved, the man becomes forever free from bondage to this Earth or Sun or this Solar system and becomes an inter-planetary citizen as it were.

Take this thought for serious thinking :

"Thy duty binds thee. *From thine own nature has it arisen.* The duty that of itself falls to one's lot should not be abandoned, though it may have its defects. All acts are marred by defects, as fire is obscured by smoke."

CHAPTER VI

THE FIVE GOSPELS

(Spiritual Life according to Zenoga)

GOSPEL I

(THE SIXTY SECRET SACRED STEPS TO SALVATION)

1. OM ! we now begin the esoteric exposition of Yoga fit only for the initiated. The unrevealed secrets of Yoga, when taught by an absolutely competent Master (Avatāra), become transmuted to the Higher-Science of Zenoga.
2. The mystic union is achieved through the control of the waves of uncoded impulses flooding Sec. 1 of the brain or the 'mind-stuff' called : chitta.
3. When the means to Zenoga have been steadily practised and when Sec. 1 of the mind (chitta) has been re-educated by corrective methods and other practices as outlined in this book, Erleuchtung ensues leading one on to full illumination.
4. The eight steps of orthodox Yoga are : Yama, Niyama, Āsana, Prāṇāyāma, Pratyāhāra, Dhāraṇā, Dhyāna, Samādhi. Beyond the first four, which together constitute prāṇāyāma, it is not possible to go without putting into operation the corrective methods and other disciplines as explained in Part I of this book. Pratyāhāra is as we have seen the 'No Man's-Land' stage. Only after that stage are dhāraṇā i.e. concentration, dhyāna i.e. meditation and samādhi i.e. identification possible. This is done by Sec. 2, 3 and 4 of the mind respectively.
5. Yama is the ethical-moral aspect or the corrective methods and other disciplines which are to be followed as explained. Devotion to the Master is the highest ethic for it is the root of all virtue.
6. Yama constitutes universal duty and is irrespective of race, place, time, emergency and circumstances. One cannot even once take a holiday from the moral side of

life. To help to disseminate the LIGHT is the most universal duty bringing good karma.

7. Internal and external purification, contentment, fiery aspiration, spiritual reading and devotion to the feet of an Avatāra, constitute niyama. It should be noted once again that it is not enough if not followed by the corrective methods and other disciplines such as implicit obedience to the Guru.
8. When thoughts contrary to spiritual success are present there should be the cultivation of their opposite, i.e. minus resultant-intensity thoughts should by corrective methods be changed to *plus* resultant intensity. The implementation of the corrective methods is essential.
9. Contrary thoughts are in short those which create minus resultant-intensity. For this reason the opposite kind of thoughts must be cultivated i. e. thoughts creating plus resultant-intensity should be consciously cultivated. Minus resultant-intensity brings about pain only and is due to avidyā or ignorance of the law. Again we see the need of implementing corrective methods.
10. The Avatāras of yore explain or rather describe the effects of plus resultant-intensity. This is from one to fortyeight plus Zenoga-Units, and is described at length up to verse 14.
11. Internal and external disciplines produce repulsion to the original resultant patterns due to the vibrational tone of the plus Zenoga-Units; these patterns could be our own or those of someone else whom we have unconsciously and thoughtlessly imitated.
12. When the highest cosmic stage of the fourth Section of the mind is reached, there results: a quiet spirit, concentration, control of all organs and an ability to witness one's subtle essence in the kuṇḍalinī.
13. As a result of such perception and understanding, bliss is achieved.
14. Reaching or developing Sec. 4 of the mind brings out our presubtle essence.
15. Use of Sec. 4 of the mind results in a contact with the subtle essence.
16. Through Bhakti Yoga the 1st and 2nd stages of cosmic consciousness are reached as explained.

17. Then poise of the body and mind should be steady though easy.
18. This is possible by following the programme and the corrective methods and other disciplines as explained in this book.
19. When this is achieved, the pairs of the opposite, i.e. the functioning of Sec. 1 of the mind or chitta (i.e. the interplay of the qualities of the centres) no longer obstruct.
20. When the 'No Man's-Land' is crossed over, right control of prāṇa and proper inspiration and expiration follows, i.e. the whole art of prāṇāyāma becomes possible as one integral whole.
21. Right control of prāṇa impulses is external (before 'No Man's-Land') yet internal (after 'No Man's-Land') and motionless when the 3rd Section of the mind is being formed. It is subject to place, time and numbers (i.e. to plus resultant intensity) and could be protracted or brief.
22. There is a still higher or *fourth* stage (i.e. beyond Sec. 3 of the mind as stated above i.e. the fourth stage of Cosmic Consciousness) which transcends all other phases.
23. Through this (i.e. Secs. 2 and 3 of the mind or 1st and 2nd *Cosmic* stage) that which obscures the LIGHT (of illumination) is gradually removed.
24. The 2., 3., 4., Sections of the mind are prepared for concentration, meditation and Samādhi respectively.
25. Pratyāhāra is the 'No Man's-Land'. Corrective methods and other discipline are followed and so comes the balance within between the centres.
26. As a result of these means there follows the complete re-education (subjugation) of sense organs and of the mind stuff (chitta).
27. Concentration is the steadying of chitta or mind-stuff (i.e. Sec. 1 of the mind) and the opening of Sec. 2 of the mind. This is the beginning of dhāraṇā or concentration.
28. Further progress to Sec. 3 of the mind is in the same way and is called dhyāna or meditation.
29. Further progress to Sec. 4 of the mind in the same way is Samādhi or identification. Here the mind goes beyond forms and to the actual purpose behind all forms.

30. When Sections 2., 3., 4., of the mind are also made use of, the fourth stage of Cosmic Consciousness is achieved.
31. As a result of this, illumination follows.
32. This illumination is gradual. Very naturally the progress is slow.
33. The last three i.e. the stages of dhāraṇā, dhyāna, samādhi are possible only after the crossing over from that Critical-Certain-Stage (No Man's-Land) before which the first four steps have to be mastered.
34. Even the fourth (Cosmic Consciousness) stage of the fourth Section of the mind is external and one must go still further beyond. The 4th stage of Cosmic Consciousness though is free from all *human* limitations as we understand it for our Solar system.
35. The sequence of mental states is as follows : The mind reacts to that which is seen (in Sec. 1 of mind or chitta coded impulses create the interplay of the qualities of the centres). Then follows the moment of mind control (the disinfection chamber and the corrective methods are brought in). Then ensues a moment when the chitta (mind stuff) responds to both the factors (i.e. both to coded impulses and to decoded thoughts). Finally, this ceases to be essential (when, by disciplines, Sec. 2 of the mind is formed, the old method of Sec. 1 of the mind is not essential) and the perceiving consciousness has full sway and then Sec. 2 of the mind functions fully.
36. Through corrective methods and other disciplines, a proper habit is formed and there will eventuate a steadiness of spiritual perception.
37. When this is done Sec. 2 of the mind is developed and concentration is possible and the picture-forming habit of Sec. 1 of the mind is less and less indulged in.
38. When the rhythm between the centres is maintained and Sec. 2 of the mind functions, one-pointedness results.
39. Section 2 of the mind reveals the wonders of the internal and the external worlds.
40. This verse gives further description of what happens then. It is then possible on looking at an object to simultaneously know aspects, symbolic nature, characteristic and specific use—in short what is called spiritual reading.

41. The versatile psychic nature (i.e. Sec. 3 of the mind) and the thinking principle (i.e. Sec. 2 of the mind) when developed reveal the next stage of development on the ladder of spiritual evolution.
42. Section 3 of the mind reveals along with Sec. 2 and 1 of the mind the triple nature of every form.
43. Section 1 of the mind is in a confused state and understanding is not possible for that is not the nature of Sec. 1 of mind or chitta. When all the portions of the mind function, the subtle essence comprehends the form, the purpose and the key-note or sounds of all objects.
44. When the resultant-intensity and resultant patterns are consciously propelled and the essence separated from patterns, as is required, knowledge of previous incarnations becomes available; so also the thought-images in the minds of other people become visible. This should never be indulged in unnecessarily.
45. On the 1st and 2nd stages of Cosmic Consciousness, meditation excludes the tangible.
46. On attaining 3rd and 4th stages of Cosmic Consciousness occult powers are attained. It is difficult and even impossible to explain the processes of the working of these powers to a layman.
47. The resultant-intensity has long or short cycles depending on the central point of return. Knowledge also comes from signs as shown in the palms of one's hand.*
48. Experience (of the pairs of opposites) or the modifications of Sec. 1 of mind (chitta) prevents the subtle essence from distinguishing between ego and puruṣa (or spirit). The objective forms exist for the use of the spiritual man. Sec. 4 of the mind brings about the perception of spiritual nature.
49. As a result of this (refer § 48) the powers of clairvoyance, clair-audience, psychometry, telepathy and other powers arise producing intuitional knowledge.
50. These powers are obstacles to the highest spiritual realisation however fascinating they may be.

*This method is revealed in Appendix at the end of this book.

51. By liberation from bondage of the interplay of the qualities of the centres or through their weakening (i.e. by introducing the corrective methods and other disciplines), the creation of *plus* resultant-intensity and patterns follows, and a stage or a moment in time comes when it is possible to consciously propel the resultant-intensity as well as the patterns and by so deviating the essence away from fixed patterns of thought in which it is encaged one can experience any life and can even understand the mind of another by entering the other's body; and this knowledge is then transmitted to Sec. 1 of one's own mind. (See SAHER in "Das sonderbare Leben eines Fakirs", by Osborne in Henn Verlag 1971).

52. When the 1st and 2nd stage of Cosmic Consciousness is reached a stage arrives called discarnate i.e. freed from the modifications of the thinking modus. This is the state of illumination. Discarnate should not be misunderstood as free from limitations of the human body as here described.

53. By following the programme and disciplines over sufficiently long periods comes symmetry and compactness of form, balance of centres, poise of the mind and peace of the subtle essence. The kuṇḍalinī rises through the Master's grace.

54. Mastery over the senses, and over the constant play of the qualities of the centres, further develops Sec. 2 and 3 of the mind and meditation is made possible. Certain wrong qualities most natural to a human being are understood and even these harmful qualities have thus served their useful purpose.

55. When this happens, (refer § 54) then comes rapidity of action i.e. perception independent of the senses and the laborious working of the mere intellect.

56. The person reaches the 4th stage of Cosmic Consciousness and becomes 'omniscient' (by our human standards but that is a relative term). The distinction between soul and spirit must here be understood.

57. By freedom from bondage (of the interplay of the qualities of the centres) by a passionless attitude towards all powers

of Secs. 3 and 4 of the mind, one attains the condition of isolated unity.

58. There comes a certain natural repulsion or rejection of all allurements from all forms of being (within the radius of our planet and the star Canopus), even celestial-being; but the possibility of changing the resultant-intensity still remains.

59. Sec. 2 and 3 give intuitive knowledge and one is able to live in the eternal now.
The intuitive knowledge possible through the development of Sec. 2 and 3 should progress further and Sec. 4 of the mind should also be fully developed. Then a state of omniscience and omnipresence will be reached (of course relative in relation to a normal human being) and such a person is now able to live in the past and future as well as in the Eternal Now.

60. When the highest stage of Cosmic Consciousness is reached liberation from human form and its limitations takes place because now both physical and mental, inner and outer integral harmony of all centres has been achieved. This then is Zenoga: the theory and practice of finding immediately THAT which the rest of mankind will find through the slow and sluggish process of Evolution through countless reembodiments.

GOSPEL II

(THE TWENTY-FIVE SPIRITUAL SENTENCES)

1. Beyond, or rather after crossing over the 'No Man's-Land', Secs. 2., 3., and 4., of the mind begin to develop rapidly and so many of the obstacles formerly experienced by and through Sec. 1 are eliminated.
2. These are the interplays of the qualities of the centres or Sec. 1 of the mind and constitute hindrances through avidyā meaning ignorance of the law.
3. We have clearly seen that it is avidyā, (i.e. ignorance of the law) and not sin or crime which is at the root of all human problems.
4. Avidyā is the perception of Sec. 1 of the mind through the running or continuous interplay of the qualities of the centres. In the absence of the corrective methods, 'dis-infection chamber', the three-step rhythmic breathing and other disciplines that which is perceived by Sec. 1 of the mind is bound to be all-confusing.
5. In the absence of the development of Secs. 2., 3., and 4., of the mind, the wonders of the inner, the psychic and the cosmic worlds are not known and not knowing enough this Sec. 1 of the mind one arrives at incorrect conclusions as is quite natural.
6. Desire is the effect of the interplay of the qualities of the centres of Sec. 1 of the mind or chitta.
7. Hate is nothing but a peculiar interplay of the qualities of the centres of Sec. 1 of the mind or chitta.
8. As long as Secs. 2., 3., 4. of the mind are not formed and the technique of closing Sec. 1 of the mind during their respective process is not practised, it is natural for any human being to be attached to the physical world of form in its various fascinating ways. However learned the man, he is still helpless under these circumstances, for worldly knowledge or technical knowledge by itself does not make man free.
9. These can be realised and then they automatically remove

the play of qualities of the Sec. 1 of the mind; then Sec. 2 of the mind will help us enormously. Herein also help the corrective methods.

10. Meditation or concentration is possible for Secs. 2., 3., and 4. of the mind only, and so these activities of the interplay of centres and the processes of different Secs. of the mind cannot simultaneously take place; i.e. either Sec. 1 of the mind i.e. chitta is closed and silenced or Secs. 2., 3., and 4. of the mind remain closed.

11. Reaction is to the coded impulses; i.e. decoded thoughts are either expressed or unexpressed, or suppressed and constitute pure mind-energy, this is what we should call 'Karma' and not the later desire which follows this pure mind-energy state nor the action which follows upon such desire which then is actual Karma. This creates resultant-intensity which must go to its source and return. Depending on the length of cycle the fruition will take place either in this life or in some later life.

12. So long as the necessary Zenoga-Units in their proper proportions are not gathered and the 4th stage of Cosmic Consciousness has not been reached, so long remains the bondage. In some manner or other it is in this human form in our Solar system and on this earth (=Reincarnation).

13. Good and evil have no meaning excepting that the resultant-intensity is plus or minus i.e. the interplay of the qualities of the centres does lead one towards the Zenoga plus units or does lead one away from it to minus. That which leads towards it is good and that which leads away from it is evil in descriptive language.

14. All states in human form below the highest and fourth stage of Cosmic Consciousness exercise so much limitation and hence are 'painful' in some manner.* These states result from the limitation of either of the Secs. 1., 2., or 3. of the mind and can be described as producing consequences, anxieties and impressions.

15. The greatest promise to man from God or Nature is that he is given free-will which he can use wisely so that the

*** This is what Buddha means by his axiom : "All life is suffering". This has nothing to do with pessimism.**

pain (due because of the accumulation of minus resultant-intensity in the past) can be warded off by corrective methods, by the 'disinfection chamber', by the three-step rhythmic breathing, and such other disciplines as explained in this book. This creates plus Zenoga-Units consciously which automatically prevent pain from reaching us.

16. All knowledge based on the interplay of the qualities of the centre of Sec. 1 of the mind or chitta is incorrect and is avidyā and thus gives us a 'false' impression.
17. That which is exclusively known through Sec. 1 of the mind (chitta) has the interplay of the qualities of either I., E. or S. centre, i.e. coded impulses received from sense organs and then decoded. Proper use of corrective methods will eventually give us liberation; i.e. these centres themselves become the stepping stones for eventul liberation when corrective methods and other disciplines (relating to them) are introduced. The same chitta then becomes the cause of liberation.
18. The division of the interplay of the qualities is fourfold as expressed.
19. Our subtle essence at the fourth stage of Cosmic Consciousness makes use of Sec. 4 of the mind yet before that stage, it is content to view through whatever Section of the mind which may happen to be developed at that time.
20. All that exists is to be used to serve the 'Chairman', i.e. the Ātman or the Lord within.
21. The man who has reached the 4th stage of Cosmic Consciousness may not take a human form in our universe even if he so chooses; whilst for those below that stage it is essential and compelling according to karmic law. Avatāras are an exception to all rules and almost all Laws.
22. The association of the subtle essence is usually with the Secs. below the 4th Sec. of the mind and thus that which those Sections of the mind perceive produces an understanding (through Sec. 1 of the mind) of the nature of that which is perceived and likewise of the perceiver.
23. This stage is not free from a certain sense of avidyā. One has to go beyond and to the highest cosmic stage.
24. One can and should go up to and beyond the 4th Sec. of mind and therefore, up to and beyond the highest

stage of Cosmic Consciousness, (the highest possible within the radius from here to star Canopus) this is for a human being the Great Liberation.

25. The state of bondage of the last kind is overcome through perfectly proportionate accumulation of Zenoga-Units. The Illumination so achieved is sevenfold and is attained progressively.

GOSPEL III

MYSTERIES OF THE HIGHER GRADES OF INITIATION

1. When the highest goal is achieved or accomplished, one knows himself as he is in reality i.e. one understands how it is possible to function with the whole brain or mind. This union is achieved through the understanding of Sec. 3 and then passing it on to mind 4 i.e. going beyond the psychic nature of Sec. 3 and of course the complete understanding by Sec. 1 (the Chitta or 'mind-stuff' that constantly forms pictures), i.e. where the interplay of the qualities of the centres is in harmony.
   Mind is one and not many. Only different Sections of the brain or mind have different characteristics and each Section is unconscious or unaware of the other except when the whole brain or mind is developed (i.e. when even the 4th Sec. of mind is developed). When all the Sections become conscious of each other, the mind becomes and acts as one sequential whole.
2. Till such mystic union of all seven centres in all the four Sections of the mind is attained, one remains in a state conforming to the vagaries of the various Sections of the mind. For all Sections except the 4th or highest contain ultimately only the modifications of their respective centres; that is to say : one remains chained to whatever thought-impulses are ruling the mind at the moment.
3. The first or lowest Section of the mind we may call : Sec. 1 of the mind or, in this case even, brain. This Sec. 1 experiences various vicissitudes, all subject to pleasure and pain. One could name at least five such modifications (=Bewegungen der inner-seelischen Welt).
4. Till this is attained one is either conscious of mind Sections 1, 2 or 3 or the interplay of the qualities of the centres of Sec. 1 or the memory of psychic powers in Sec. 3. These are all but modifications ultimately of the mind as such.

5. The mind states of Section 1 or chitta are five and are subject to pleasure or pain, they are painful or not painful.
6. These modifications are : (i) correct knowledge, (ii) incorrect knowledge, (iii) fancy, (iv) passivity (sleep) and (iv) memory.
7. The basis of correct knowledge is a proper use of corrective methods and bringing about a balance among the centres.
8. Incorrect knowledge is a result of the interplay of the first four centres of mind (Section 1) and of not developing and making use of the other Sections of mind (such as 2, 3, and 4); and so one gathers incorrect knowledge only.
9. Section 1 of mind alone can perceive what often amounts only to fancy.
10. Sleep is an important state of being for gaining proper knowledge if Sections 2, 3 and 4 are developed. Sleep is brought about through the fatigue imposed by the constant picture-forming of Section 1 or by its leakages.
11. Memory is a 'quality' (=Errungenschaft) of Sec. 3 of the mind and is very deep and far reaching. Yet if Sec. 3 is not developed memory in its instructive sense is not possible i.e. the knowledge of past births is not possible.
12. The control of these modifications or states of the internal organ (Section 1 of the mind or chitta) is to be brought about through non-attachment; tireless endeavour is through corrective methods and rhythmic breathing.
13. Tireless endeavour is the constant effort to restrain the modifications of the chitta i.e. the constant conscious efforts at each coded impulse into decoded thought, to subject the same to the corrective methods and 'disinfection chamber', thus changing the possibilities of minus resultant-intensity to *plus* resultant-intensity.
14. If one were constantly to take care to put into operation corrective methods and change minus resultant to *plus* resultant-intensity, then the steadiness of the Sec. 1 of mind follows i.e. Section 1 of the mind develops Subsection B. of Section 2 which in turn develops Sec. 3 of mind and this again in turn develops Sec. 4 and with it the whole MIND.
15. Non-attachment is the functioning of mind Sec. 4.

16. The result of such non-attachment results in an exact knowledge of spiritual Being when liberated from the interplay of the qualities of chitta or Sec. 1 of the mind.
17. The consciousness of an object is attained by concentration on its fourfold nature i.e. the form through examination (by Sec. 1 of mind), the quality through discriminative participation (by Sec. 2 of mind), the purpose through (Sec. 3 of mind) and soul through identification (by Sec. 4 of mind). Normally a person does not go beyond the interplay of chitta or Sec. 1 of the mind.
18. A further stage of Samādhi is achieved when the chitta i.e. Sec. 1 of the mind is responsive only to the subjective impressions of Sec. 4 of the mind.
19. The Samādhi just described above passes not beyond the bounds of the phenomenal world, it passes not beyond the 'gods' or those concerned with the other worlds. This Samādhi is the 1st and 2nd stage of Cosmic Consciousness. The resultant-intensity in Zenoga-Units is not in proper proportion and so it reaches certain stars and suns but then returns to Earth (as explained) through celestial influences. When this is so, Samādhi is of an inferior type.
20. Other Yogīs achieve Samādhi and arrive at discrimination of pure spirit through belief, followed by energy, memory, meditation and right perception. By corrective methods, rhythmic breathing and other disciplines, the passing over to Sec. 4 of the mind is achieved and the 3rd and 4th stages of Cosmic Consciousness is reached.
21. The attainment of this state (of spiritual consciousness) is rapid for those whose resultant-intensity is in the proper proportion of plus Zenoga-Units.
22. Mobility, intellect, emotion or vitality; the balance of plus Zenoga-Units in them all is the sure way to create real free-will.

GOSPEL IV

THE HOLY CONCORDAT

1. If 'God' be Light,
   and
   if all material objects without a single exception are nothing but condensations of that radiant energy of Light,
   then 'God' is omnipresent.
2. There is only one reason why you are here on earth, and that is to find the true Spiritual-Self, the Ātman or true inner-being. Unless you do find this you will be compelled to re-incarnate again and again, and suffer until you do find IT.
3. By quieting body and mind, we prepare the conditions in which Infinite-Spirit speaks to us and manifests itself. Our effort to do this is a form of worship, and God will come in that great silence. HE cannot come if we are too busy thinking of personal problems.
   If we make an effort to silence the mind in the way shown by Zenoga, that means we are beginning to forget a purely personal (egoistical) life. The ego is nothing but the sum of all thoughts in the mind.
   Where there are no thoughts there can be no ego. The silencing of thinking is, therefore, the same as eliminating the ego.
   "Be still and know that 'I' am God."
   i.e. : that the 'I' is linked to God through the Ātman.
4. Before one can begin to worship 'God' one must be able to forget one's self; and before one can do that : one must learn how to control thoughts and silence Section 1 of the brain.
5. When the Master sees that you are making sufficient effort HE will come to you and you will gradually begin to feel His presence.
6. You will have increasing worrylessness of the personal life and increasing moments of divine stillness, and slowly you feel that within that Silence there is a Higher Power

called grace descending upon you. That is the test of true worship—the sense that you are being taken up by a higher power.

7. In that moment when you feel that you are being taken up by a Higher Power you must not resist, let this Power take you wherever it wills. It will not take you to any place, but it will take you out of your ego-prison.
8. Should this experience come to you, do not be afraid to let yourself go. What is there to fear?* You may feel that you are going to vanish into spacelessness, that there is even danger of death. Even if there were danger of death, it would be worth dying for such a revelation. But you will not die; this is a temporary experience on the way to deathlessness.
9. Through Zenoga we must find 'God' as *being*—as something which we *are*.

   Each of us is a Ray of God. To know God is to *be* God not to think of God. To think implies duality, the relationship of one who thinks and that which is thought, but to *be* implies no relationship whatsoever, only the fusion of the ray with the Sun. This is the highest state of spiritual unity to which man can attain; that is why the existentialist Philosophy of Heidegger emphasises BEING above all else.
10. The transfer of consciousness from Sec. 1 of the mind (chitta) to Secs. 2, 3, and 4 is evolution. Spiritual education is not the accumulation of knowledge or even cumulative knowledge. Progress is done rapidly by corrective methods and other disciplines. This is part of the great creative and evolutionary process constantly going on and so the prophets of doom may rest at ease.
11. The corrective methods and other disciplines are not the true causes of this transfer of consciousness but they serve to remove obstacles i.e. they serve to develop Secs. 2., 3., and 4. of the mind.
12. Interplay of the qualities of the centres of Sec. 1 of the mind (chitta) creates the "I am" notion of surface consciousness.

* Vide, Saher, Indische Weisheit und das Abendland, Meisenheim/Guru 1965, S : 218, Anmesh : 23.

13. Consciousness is one harmonious whole whether of the Section of mind 1, 2, 3, or 4. Yet the surface consciousness or chitta (Sec. 1 of the mind) produces the varied forms of the many.
14. Among the forms which consciousness assumes only that which is the result of Sec. 4 is free from latent Karma.
15. The activities of the liberated soul are free from the interplay of the qualities of the centres of Sec. 1 of the mind. Those of other people below the 4th stage of Cosmic Consciousness are of three kinds i.e. due to Sec. 1, 2, and 3 of the mind.
16. From these three kinds of Karma or pure mind-energy the states of the three centres I., E. and S. emerge; those forms which are necessary for the fruition of karmic effects now emerge.
17. This is worth serious study. There is identity of relation between memory and the karmic effect producing a new cause even when separated in time and place. So long as Sec. 3 of the mind is not developed, the deep memory records are not opened consciously (except by some artificial means, hypnosis or drugs etc.). But if opened by conscious development of Sec. 3 of the mind, one can see certain relations existing between effects and causes. As the memory records are opened then though one may now find himself in completely different circumstances (separated by time and place) one realises how the law of Karma works.
18. Till conscious efforts are not used, till the corrective methods and other disciplines are not put into conscious operation, man lives (and must live) in the interplay of the qualities of the centres of Sec. 1 of the mind however educated he may be. However happy a person may be with Sec. 1 of the mind a day will dawn when change for the better will be sought after by him.
19. Sages explain how it all works. Only when finally Sec. 4 of the mind is developed fully do things cease to attract or repel.
20. Māyā only means the less permanent and the less essential. The promise holds latent seeds of future quality and it is up to us to see to that.

21. The interplay of the qualities of the centres I., E. and S. colour all characteristics whether latent or patent.
22. As long as this interplay of qualities of the centres goes on without the corrective methods and other disciplines so long is this manifestation of the objective forms necessary !
23. These two, i.e. consciousness and form are distinct and separate. (Though form may be similar, the consciousness may function on different levels of being.) All human beings for example have the same potential within them but most of them function on the various grades of consciousness of Sec. 1 of the mind. Some function on the various grades of consciousness of Sec. 2 of the mind. A few function on the various grades of consciousness of Sec. 3 of the mind. Rare people function on the various grades of Sec. 4 of the mind. No one (except a Mahā-Avatāra) can function beyond the fourth stage of Cosmic Consciousness on this earth while in human form. Beyond that no form is required of a human being nor is rebirth necessary in *our* Solar system.
24. The chitta (or Sec. 1 of the mind) with the interplay of the qualities of centres causes māyā.
25. All cognition depends on the stage of consciousness; and hence also all interpretation of life as presented by God or Nature and as is understood by an individual.
26. Our subtle essence is called the Lord of the mind (whole mind) and is aware of the activities of all the four Sections of the mind. Yet it has to function *through* that Section of the mind which happens to be developed and so we must wait till full development of all Sections takes place. Such is the Law.
27. All Sections of the mind (including the fourth) are not the source of illumination for it is seen or cognised by the "Lord of the mind".
28. Sec. 4 of the mind can understand the other Sections of the mind yet not itself, just as chitta or Sec. 1 of the mind cannot understand itself but only be understood by Sec. 4 of the mind. Our subtle essence can in turn understand all the four Sections of the mind. (It is understood that for the limitation of language we speak of 'four' Sections of the mind, it is in fact but *one* mind 1, 2, 3, and 4 are

merely the four Sections of the one whole mind). At no stage are these to be misunderstood as different minds.

29. We cannot go beyond the fourth Section of the mind when in human form. By the time that stage in reached it is unnecessary to have a still higher mind even if we have to function further; (i.e. actually we discard the thought of a second separate mind), for human existence would on the contrary tend to confusion instead of clarifying the matter; for if mind after mind were to exist, it would become too confused to understand the higher aspects beyond the 4th Cosmic Consciousness stage.

30. When all that is revealed by the consciousness of Sec. 4 of the mind with the help of our subtle essence, is conveyed to Sec. 1 of the mind to be translated in understandable language, it becomes the consciousness of Self. But it is the subtle essence, the Lord of the mind, who ultimately conveys the higher aspects and only after the 4th Section of the mind is developed.

31. Then illumination and conscious understanding follow as a matter of course.

32. Sec. 1 of the mind has (only on this physical plane) to grasp what is cognised by Sec. 2, 3 and 4 of the mind; this it can do with the help of the subtle (Kuṇḍalinī) essence. It is the unifying agent and draws knowledge of illumination on to the physical plane.

33. The person who can consciously shut out anyone of the four Sections of the mind at will and consciously propel resultant-intensity and thought patterns *knows*, and knows truly.

34. With the passage of time such a person moves to greater illumination; on the way he discriminates and understands the *true* nature of all created things.

35. Ages of wrong habits of Sec. 1 of the mind will retain a natural tendency to continue the interplay of the qualities of its centres and so even a very wise man makes mistakes even now at this 'higher' stage; such is the mind of man.

36. Whenever what is stated in § 35 above happens, the same steps are to be taken; viz. correct methods, disinfection chamber, and three-step rhythmic breathing and the like.

37. A person moves towards the highest consciousness without

any motive, except for the sake of being a human being, and because he is a human being he cannot help living that way of life. He will then be able to go even beyond the fourth stage of Cosmic Consciousness and enter the fifth Kingdom of Nature as a purely spiritual being.

38. When this stage is reached, existence in human form on earth or in the Solar system is not necessary unless voluntarily and consciously taken as in the case of Avatāras.

39. When the resultant thought-patterns are corrected and also reduced and when the resultant-intensity is in proper proportions of plus Zenoga-Units, when corrective methods and three-step rhythmic breathing becomes natural and other disciplines are inculcated, the astral, mental and causal bodies (sheathes) are developed. Naught remains for him to do.

40. The interplay of the qualities of the centres ceases, for they have served their purpose and man has been so re-educated that he goes beyond to accumulate fresh experience elsewhere; for richer existence beyond the star Canopus.

41. When this becomes possible, a person functions on a faster-than-light plane and in human terms he is simultaneously aware of the present, past and future. Time is visible as it ever was and ever will be, because all eternity is visible i.e. has a new perspective (and the tape-recorded type of knowledge or Sec. 1 of mind ceases to give the false impression of a moving cinema film) as he now understands time rightly.

42. When this state of isolated unity exists, chitta (or Sec. 1 of the mind) is completely at rest. Even Secs. 2 and 3 of the mind do not interfere and Sec. 4 of the mind *alone* functions and its mechanics are quite different especially from those of Sec. 1 of the mind. But now the subtle essence needs nothing. The pure spiritual or Cosmic Consciousness of the fourth cosmic stage prevails. Our subtle essence exists seemingly alone as Divinity-in-itself. A ray of the Light has returned to its source in the Light. That is 'salvation' which word is made up of two other words meaning 'safe' and 'return' = the safe return.* This is the holy concordat between you as pure essence and the LIGHT.

*In Chinese the term for "Salvation" is = the return [to] home.

GOSPEL V

DEVOTION TO AVATARA SURPASSES ALL

1. By intense devotion to an Avatara knowledge of the Avataras is gained.
2. An Avatara is the universal essence of Being untouched by limitations, free from Karma and desire and is even beyond the fourth stage of mind i.e. even beyond the stage of the fully developed brain and mind. Then one learns and is guided by the Super-Cosmic-Mind only.
3. In the MAHA-AVATARA, all Avataras unite to form his person as Master on Earth; the germ of all knowledge expands into infinity. This infinity is relative with respect to human consciousness. It is the consciousness above the 4th stage of Cosmic-Consciousness.
4. The MAHA-AVATARA, being unlimited by time conditions, is the teacher of the fourth Section of the mind or those whose minds are already fully developed and so are called 'primeval Lords' or Avataras. In some cases HE teaches even ordinary mortals.
5. The name of Avatara is Om (= God-is-the-Moon). When this stage is reached the human language, mind, understanding and reason are superseded. That is why people cannot understand 'Om' or 'Moon' rationally.
6. Unless the stage beyond 'No Man's-Land' is reached the true pronouncement of Om usually remains as a mere sound and serves no true purpose !
7. All obstacles cease to exist once the 'No Man's-Land' is crossed and the other side reached. That is initiation in its higher stages.
8. Obstacles to soul-cognition are bodily disability, mental inertia, wrong questioning, carelessness, laziness, lack of dispassion, erroneous perception, inability to achieve concentration and failure to hold the meditative attitude when achieved. These are the interplay of qualities of the centres of Sec. 1 of the mind and are due to absence of corrective methods, disinfection chamber and the three-step rhythmic breathing.

9. Pain, despair, misplaced bodily activity and wrong direction (or control) of the life currents are the result of the obstacles in the lower psychic nature; i.e. : when rhythmic breathing is not followed Sec. 2 of the mind is not formed.
10. To overcome the obstacles and their accompaniments, the intense application to some one truth (i.e. some form of yoga) is required, i.e. the methods as shown in Part I of this book.
11. The corrective methods as well as the creating of thoughts having 'plus resultant intensity' are essential.
12. The peace of the chitta is also brought about by the regulation of prāṇa i.e. by 24 hours rhythmic breathing and corrective methods; for prāṇa is Impulse-in-itself and the science of the control of all impulses is explained at length in this book.
13. Section 2 of mind is able to concentrate provided the technique of closing Sec. 1 of mind is understood and practised.
14. Section 2 of mind with the aid of Sec. 4 of the mind can meditate. The knowledge thus gained brings peace. Section 1 of the mind should be closed during this process.
15. The interplay of the qualities of the centres in Sec. 1 of mind are reduced by corrective methods, disinfection chamber, the three-step rhythmic breathing and thus the chitta is made more stabilised by re-education on these lines.
16. The state of dreaming whether awake, or in sleep or in trance is the plane of Sec. 3 of the mind in its less advanced state. When by proper practice and technique Sec. 3 of the mind is controlled and the psychic nature is thereby also kept under control great knowledge of the psychic world is gained. Chitta i.e. Sec. 1 of the mind experiences peace i.e. freedom from the interplay of the qualities of the centres.
17. Through intense bhakti or prayer or love of God, is also brought about a paralysis of the interplay of qualities in Sec. 1 of the mind and hence a sort of peace is enjoyed. For higher progress this alone may not prove sufficient unless an Avatara helps.

18. When Zenoga-Units are gathered in any proportion the person is able to propel the resultant-intensity and the resulting thought-patterns and can persuade his subtle essence to separate from the gross body and can experience any life from the atom to the infinitely great within the venue of the star Canopus.
19. When Secs. 2, 3, and 4 of the mind are developed and when the technique of closing Sec. 1 of the mind during the process of concentration or meditation is practised, modifications of the chitta or mind-stuff are no longer possible. The Secs. 2, 3, and 4 of the mind give knowledge and bring about the stage of identity on other planes. The methods of gaining knowledge on other planes differ completely from the methods of gaining knowledge on the physical plane i.e. it is not by learning and memory but by intuition and identifying.
20. As we have seen, reason or judicial reasoning is one of the qualities of Sec. 2 of the mind on the physical plane.
21. This is the technique of Sec. 3 of the mind on the psychic plane. The cosmos is regulated by one energy only and that is the undifferentiated power of MIND. Reflect on this.
22. The techniques change, the gross essence to the subtle and in turn the subtle essence into pure spiritual being. These changes are called pradhana. By it we learn to handle the one cosmic energy mentioned in § 21.
23. As we have seen, all these are just on-the-way-stations and not the destination itself which is very far beyond these. Thus meditation and even identification (a poor substitute for the word Samādhi) is 'with seed'; that which is with seed remains gross, however subtle. Liberation is, however, now very near and the initiated aspirant seldom falls back into bondage.
24. When the chitta or the mind stuff or the interplay of the qualities of the centres are so re-educated that plus Zenoga-Units are gathered in the proper proportions, the 4th stage of Cosmic Consciousness is reached. This is the farthest a person can go in human form on the physical plane.
25. For human consciousness, the truth revealed here is abso-

lute; that stage considered by human standards is the highest.

26. This perception is unique and Sec. 1 of the mind has no jurisdiction over it i.e. the qualities of each Section of the mind are completely different and as such, that which Sec. 4 of the mind reveals, Sec. 1 of the mind cannot reveal or even understand.

27. When we realise that even this state i.e. the 4th stage of Cosmic Consciousness is not the ultimate state and we go beyond it, then from our human standpoint we reach the state of pure Samādhi i.e. freedom from human limitations of all kinds and freedom from birth on this or any planet in our Solar system. We are then taken to where the Avatara normally dwells as in his home. Spiritual Evolution means returning home; slowly and painfully through repeated reincarnations—or instantly through Zenoga and the grace of the Masters of whom the total is designated as: MAHA-AVATARA.

RECAPITULATION

The area of the brain can be divided into several portions, and these can be placed under the jurisdiction of four main sections of the brain. Each Section of the brain has its own 'mind' and thus we may also say: four sections of the mind.

The centres I., E., S., M., comprise the first portion of the brain: this is mind Section one.

The In. centre is the second portion or mind Section two.

What we call 'the junior managing director' or sixth centre is the third portion or mind Section three.

The 'senior managing director' or seventh centre is the fourth portion or mind Section four.

The routine work of portions three and four i.e. mind Sections 3 and 4 is carried out by the In. centre or second portion of the mind; Section 2, so to say.

All conscious reactions of pleasure or pain, the range of human emotions and patterns, are registered (i.e. coded impulses decoded into thoughts) by the I., E., S., and M. centres. These four centres, along with their working, form what we call our waking mind, or consciousness, or 'normal' consciousness; Section 1, so to say.

Certain agitations, certain subtle movements, certain giving-off of rays, certain striking of notes, certain creation of intensity, a "certain something" is the 'mind' of each of the four Sections. Normally there is very little reaction in Sections 3 and 4. Only in a few cases is there a possibility of mind Sections 3 and 4 being active in human beings.

Sec. 1 keeps our contact with the physical world and makes us aware of physical things i.e. our body, its condition of health or ill health, the world around, our environment, and the other kingdoms of Nature. Because of this Section of the brain and its activity we are aware of the world we live in, through the interplay of the qualities of the four centres. We, therefore, call this portion of the brain or mind Section 1: the 'conscious' mind. Actually, the word 'conscious' is misleading. We can tabulate as under:

(1) Section one makes us aware of the external physical world, i.e. all creation. Its weapons are reasoning (not reason), logic, common sense. It is 'subconscious' in relation (unless developed and corelated) to the other three centres.

(2) Section two, makes us aware of the inner functions of the body over which we have no control because we are normally in Sec. 1. It is 'sub-conscious' to the external physical world but conscious of the other two Sections; viz. 3 and 4. Its weapons are intuition and reason.

(3) Section three is the so-called 'super-conscious' mind. It makes us aware of our past, present and future which is an enchanting but treacherous world. Unconscious to the former two and the fourth, though fully conscious on its own plane, its weapon is its ability to function on a 'higher' (molecular) plane.

(4) Section four is the Cosmic-Consciousness and makes us aware of the causes behind all other worlds and the reasons of their existence; the beginning and the ultimate end, in relation to man and this world. It is conscious on all planes and in all the worlds related to man—and even the previous three Sections of the minds are included in it. It is able to function on the electronic as well as molecular planes that is its starting point and it is aware by direct perception or 'spiritual reading' of all that goes on in cosmos.

The four portions of the brain or 'minds' can be compared to an auditor, engineer, doctor and a lawyer. These are just what they are and each abides by its own profession, each wonderful in its respective field and quite unsuited in the other fields; of course, the only exception is Section 4 which remains supreme in all fields.

The important functions of digestion, breathing, blood circulation, beating of the heart, movement of the diaphram etc. are in the jurisdiction of brain Section two. There are two sub-divisions of this Section:—

(a) : One sub-section is already developed at birth.

(b) : the other portion is to be developed consciously by all human beings. The above mentioned physio-biological functions are looked after by sub-section (a).

All coded impulses and the decoded thoughts therefrom

have a distinct pattern. These patterns are stored, filed, indexed, registered and maintained, i.e. all memory from birth to death as well as the memory of the final resultant intensity (='death') going to the source and returning (= 're-birth'), all are stored in the mind through movements of such 'resultant intensity' on the molecular plane. The conscious mind cannot remain aware of these activities but draws on this part of the mind for assistance.

Movements on the molecular and the electronic planes are under the guidance of mind Section four. All the four minds are conscious simultaneously of all the activities related to their own sphere but not aware of each other, except in the case of Section 4.

These are different spheres of jurisdiction (or technical qualities with different resultant intensities) and we should not class one as superior or inferior to the other; or one as conscious and the other as unconscious; one as animal and the other as divine and so forth. Nor should we consider these four Sections of the brain or mind as separate entities but only as portions of "one stupendous whole" called : MIND.

These four Sections are doing their duty whether pleasant or unpleasant. "Do thy duty however humble. That is better than the duty of another however pleasant. For to do the duty of another however noble is fraught with danger."

The cells within the body, the different portions of the brain, human beings, our planet earth, and all creation must evolve. Sooner or later they ultimately reach that state of cosmic consciousness required by the Divine Plan; but how soon or how late is our choice ?

As these cells evolve within a living body they are shifted from one section of the mind, or one portion of the brain, to the other; just as evolved man is shifted from planet to planet or star to star in keeping with his evolution ?

We have just studied the four different Sections and their spheres of activity. Section 3 of the mind we may call the 'junior managing director' and Section 4 the 'senior managing director'. When a person has developed his Section 4 and thus reached a high stage of cosmic consciousness, his 'senior managing director' (Sec. 4) calls in the CHAIRMAN, or in theological terminology: God.

It is a fact that this 'Chairman of the Board' within one human being is the same Chairman within all other human beings. The Chairman is the common chairman but whenever presiding at a particular meeting he is the Chairman of that particular Board? This is the Divine in man. When man reaches the highest stage of Cosmic-Consciousness the senior managing director hands over the reins of control to the Chairman just as earlier the junior managing director handed them over to the senior managing director. The Chairman does not preside at a meeting before this state has been reached.

The 'senior managing director' is also our real SELF (not ego) and works through the fourth Section or rather all the four Sections of the mind. In other words, it means that a sufficient number of cells in us have evolved to justify this Section No. 4. If mind Section 4 is not present then Cosmic-Consciousness is as impossible as sight to a creature whose eyes have not been formed.

Man must evolve—man must consciously evolve—man must consciously strive with corrective methods to bring this to fruition. Add to this the love of God, add to this either prayers or japa or meditation or any yoga or any other practice of a religion that you are inclined to and then it will be possible. The highest stage of Cosmic-Consciousness is an initiation into a new dimension of Being.

This Cosmic-Consciousness enables us to function at will in any state of Being almost anywhere.

When the cells in the human body from that portion of the brain called Section 1 and 2 evolve sufficiently to form Sec. 3 then only is it possible for the patterns and the 'resultant intensity' to separate; either in sleep, or consciously when awake in order to visit the source of the resultant intensity. Such 'occult' experiences or 'astral' experiences are possible for Sec. 3 yet it is treacherous ground so we call it the false Yoga of 'glamour'.

Here one can demonstrate a sort of superiority over the average man by the show of certain powers. We have to strive to go beyond this stage into the realm of the 4th Section by constant corrective methods and 'disinfection' practices along with the rest of the programme. Then we reach the highest stage of Cosmic-Consciousness; the stage we call Yoga without glamour. The end can only be reached by real hard work upon ourself, which begins with that Critical Certain Stage as a human being on this planet.

Section 2 is created when cells in the human body (brain) have evolved far enough to form Section 2. Then a person is able to function within himself. His focus changes from the outside world to the inside world. The vibrations of life change, the perspective of life changes and man becomes 'sober'. *He knows for the first time that he does not know* ! He begins to learn ! But Sections 2, 3 and 4 cannot be formed if the cells in Section 1 of the brain have not sufficiently evolved to form Section 2 and so on. For this purpose the most imperative steps are the corrective methods, the disinfection chamber, changing of the minus 'resultant intensity' to plus resultant, the forming of psychic reserves, reaching that Critical-Certain-Stage and going beyond to the stage called 'No Man's-Land' through the help of the three step rhythmic breathing.

It is therefore clear that:

(i) Man below that Critical-Certain-Stage functions with Sec. 1, and the necessary sub-section (a) of Sec. 2; very limitedly formed, is his Sec.3; Section 4 is out of question.

(ii) Please note that a small part of Sec. 2 [i.e. sub-section (a)] is already formed by Nature to make the instinctive centre function automatically; yet the rest of Sec. 2 is to be formed consciously. The first part [sub-section (a)] enables a person to function in the world consciously and with the help of this sub-section to fulfill unconscious functions within his body such as digestion, breathing etc.

(iii) It follows therefore, that a large portion of the human brain is not used at all. Where the cells are still in the process of development we can 'see' their movements; we would see something akin to a nebulae in the heavens where future Solar systems are in the process of being born ages hence. Therefore, for an average person, 80% of his brain is not even formed but is merely in the *process* of being formed.

Sec. 1 of the brain has areas marked out for different faculties. One of the many faculties of Sec. 1 is metaphysical. We have seen that the cells when they evolve sufficiently in Sec. 1, begin to form Section 2 and so on. We would like to clarify that to form Section 2, cells which have evolved sufficiently in Sec., 1 (i.e. in that portion of the brain) are transferred and their place is filled by fresh ones. The transfer of such cells to form Section 2 is possible especially when this particular portion is related to this particular faculty of Sec. 1; this is also possible from other faculties *conjointly* with this particular faculty.

It is, therefore, not essential for the development of cells of Section 2 (or development of mind Sec. 2) to go through academic education. In fact, academic education if not conjoined to this faculty of metaphysics or higher arts, may never develop the cells in Sec. 1 for the benefit of Sections 2, 3, and 4. Thus a very brilliant individual may remain so or be born again and again as a brilliant individual according to the resultant intensity—yet Sections 2, 3, and 4 will have very little chance of formation without which real *evolution* is hardly possible i.e. the evolution of being free to use free will judiciously.

Yet how great is Section 1! We must never forget this fact. We should never demean this part of the mind. We must never forget that this is the mind that ultimately makes Sec. 2, 3 and 4 possible. In our ecstacy of reaching Sec. 3 we forget the spade work of our Sec. 1 and call it the 'lower' mind or the 'lower self', or the 'animal mind' or the ego. Walt Whitman realised this when he rebukes those temporarily having a glimpse through Sec. 3 of mind: "Therefore, I believe in you my Soul....the other 'I' must not abase itself to 'you' and 'you' must not be abased to the other". Unfortunately either Sec. 1 tyrannises (whenever it is supreme) the other Sections which, are then in a rudimentary state or when another Section is supreme it makes Sec. 1 look wretched or, in other words, it (in turn) now tyrannizes. In either case this should not happen; if it does, it proves that the experience of being able to function with higher Sections is but recently and sporadically found. Opinions are then hastily expressed in poetic and profuse language condemning or belittling the state, work and prestige of Sec. 1.

Who has not known men of great intellectual prowess who were petty, mean, cavilling, vain, psychopaths who lived wretched ulcer-ridden lives and died long before their time from one of the psychosomatic diseases. Hence a man of great intellectual development, without a corresponding development of the *total* personality, may well be a highly dangerous, mechanical, and amoral robot.

Who would then prefer, if once the re-education of the mind takes place, to ever indulge in or be a party to the inside mismanagement ! We all see the need of inner correctives and imposition of proper management. In all cases there is an introduction of a programme of administration, which is well-meaning, yet often it all goes over the heads of the aspirants, or the methods are found not to be practical in our usual daily life; or so it seems.

In whatever we have stated there is no strained effort, no suspense, no artificial ways of living, no "holier than thou" feeling, no separateness from any life or creation, no reason to misunderstand anyone or any movement and yet with childlike simplicity and with childlike grace we attain that state—the Critical-Certain-Stage.

Normally, a human being is awake for sixteen hours, each day. Thus in 960 minutes [even if he thinks at the low rate of 20 thoughts per minute (not thinks but *decodes* coded impulses)], we get 960 $\times$20 = 19,200 thoughts. The actual decoding rate is far greater and in-between there are also countless drifts. Taking a round figure we get a minimum score of 19,000. Each decoded impulse is cardexed into its respective centre. If now corrective methods are brought about and applied, the rate could fall to perhaps 10,000 which would, in the first instance, mean so much energy (19,000–10.000 = 9,000) saved and stored away for future use.

The correctives add immensely to our plus score and we find ourselves on the Way. This very life, which otherwise seems a mockery, becomes the base for triumphant operations !

Similarly, the three step rhythmic breathing would reduce the 25,920 daily breaths to 17,280 per day and lowering still further (due to the imposition of this rhythm), the decoding rate. Imagine what colossal saving in energy is brought about !

The incoming impulses, those practically unobservable power points that reach us continually, instead of flaring up and burning away like a highly inflammable gas, turn into a powerful storehouse of vital force thereby ?

Finally, the most important point to grasp is the fact that one is to be convinced that these simple, common-place and yet essential activities like eating, sleeping, sex, corrective methods, check of drifts and analysis are the stepping stones to real progress.

Take this thought for serious thinking, "How can I free myself from my own shadow ?"

APPENDIX I

A Few Questions Answered.

Q. 1 What is resultant intensity in terms of Yoga?

A. 1 The Kundalini is sleeping above the Kanda, dispensing liberation to yogis and bondage to fools. He who knows that, knows yoga.

Kundalini is a man's basic resultant intensity; minus intensities resulting in bondage, high plus resulting in liberation. Through purified desire and sanctified emotion he provides those stable vibrations. The cultivation of emotional tranquility is one of the first steps. Further, when the body is purified and its energies rightly directed (parameshwari passing up the Sushumna nāḍī) and when rhythm is achieved (by three-step rhythmic breathing) then life becomes radiant.

Q. 2 What exactly is meant by pranayama?

A. 2 The steps necessary for the achievement of yoga are :

1) yama, 2) niyama, 3) asana, 4) pranayama, 5) pratyahara, 6) dharana, 7) dhyana, 8) samadhi

The first four *and not only the fourth step* is pranayama proper. Breath alone has very little to do with it, though the art of breathing is one of the means of bringing the "prana" under control, i.e., energy or nerve impulse. It can well be called the art of control of the nerve impulses; for the real object of pranayama is to control the nerve impulses and nerve centres.

Prana is Impulse. Vayu is a current of impulses. The sympathetic nervous system and the para-sympathetic, or the autonomic nervous system, have the ability to carry impulses. Currents received from within the body or from outside the body either coming from other human beings or from other terrestrial or cosmic sources, or from, (1) food and drink, (2)breathing, and (3) sensations of sound, touch, sight and smell, are converted into incoming coded impulses or out-going decoded thoughts.

Pranayama therefore signifies the control of energy, i.e. the impulses of the automatic nervous system and the numerous activities of the body caused by them. It prevents disposition or dissipation of energy and directs it along a particular channel. It means the controlling of impulses received as well as the directing of energy thus received.

The autonomic nervous system has two sets of fibres, afferent and efferent, i.e., the first stops expiration and produces inspiration and the second does the reverse. These fibres are excited to action by the alternative collapse and distention of the air vesicles of the lungs where the vagus terminations are situated.

Pranayama, is then in effect a process of bringing under control the autonomic nervous system over which normally, we have no control. Mistakenly pranayama is regarded as regulation of breath alone. Pranayama is the art, or technique of the control of the impulses by the help of many factors, of which, one such factor is breathing.

Q. 3. There be some one particular overpowering weakness in each individual against which all attempts at control fail. Is there no remedy for such a crushing weakness? Can you suggest something else besides what you offer in your book?

A. 3. The breath (or air current) flows in a healthy person (established in perfect yoga) from the left and right nostril *alternatively* for equal durations of one thousand and eighty breaths, for each nostril.

In a healthy person, not established in yoga, it alternates every 1700 to 1800 breaths, i.e., the duration is equal but the number of breaths being more than in the above case. A healthy person is healthy physically, mentally, emotionally and sexually. *Whenever the left nostril flows the right ceases and vice versa.* The rhythmic and balanced formula of the centres as we have seen is 5:2:2:1 for the four centres I. E. S. and M. of Sec. 1 of the mind.

The right nostril stands for the intellectual centre, the

left for the emotional, sex and moving, i.e., when the right nostril flows the intellectual centre is clear, active and tense. When the left flows it is dull, confused or even dominated.

About 1,700 to 1,800 breaths of a normal persons take about one and half hours or ninety minutes. This means that for ninety minutes the flow will be first in the left and then the right (and vice versa). Whenever the flow is in the left the emotional or sex impulse would overpower or dominate the intellectual, and more of the emotional sex and moving coded impulses are received and registered. This ninety minutes of flow is divided into 36 minutes of emotion, thirtysix minutes of sex and eighteen minutes of moving, but there are no water-tight compartments and it is not divided for first thirty-six minutes, second thirty-six minutes and third eighteen minutes. The impulses reach these centres in mixed timing but the total coded impulses received give the total time for each centre accordingly. When impulses reach the Moving centre the movement could be mental or physical.

However, as the average person has the more common ratio of 2:4:8:2 the right flows for twenty-two and half minutes only, the emotional for forty-five minutes, sex for ninety minutes and moving for only twenty-two and half minutes as explained above.

This is the total flow of coded impulses to the respective centres per every three hours duration, and for most part of the day the intellectual centre is dull, confused and dominated. The person with 5:2:2:1 ratio will be able even when the left is flowing to keep the intellectual clear and undominated which in case of 2:4:8:2 ratio is not possible. It also means therefore that the whole body is more negatively charged, and all the ill health symptoms of various types are also resultant thereon. The further away this irregularity of breath is from the normal, will be denoted the malady a person would suffer, whether intellectual, emotional, sex or moving.

Even in sleep our dreams are dependent on the flow of breath from a particular nostril, its duration and the centre concerned. Perhaps medical opinion may or may not agree, but one should accustom oneself to sleeping on the left side so that the right nostril may have the greater flow.

The unbalanced flow from the left nostril creates high minus resultant intensity due to overactive conditions of the emotional, sex and moving centre and such a person is therefore prone to anger, sex, depression, strained nerves, and inferiority complex.

Can one blow the breath out through the mouth and simultaneously be able to drink also? Natural laws bring about obvious and definite results. Can one therefore have a predominantly left nostril flow and yet have a high plus intensity of thought ? It will be learnt from experience that whenever an overpowering weakness is predominant then predominance of flow will be in the left nostril. Whenever a malady or disease is oppressive the left nostril will be active out of proportion as explained. What is the remedy therefore ? To wait till the rhythm of 5:2:2:1 is established would take a long time. Three-step rhythmic breathing and corrective methods will also take their own time to be understood, mastered and then to be effective. But kind Nature and God have always provided for the sincere some means to be made use of. We suggest that you block the left nostril for the first 15-20 weeks between 1 and 2 p.m. in the afternoon with plain sterilized cotton.

When told to block the nostril one should not feel uneasy. No person on earth can breathe through both the nostrils. We always breathe through one at a time.

However if this blocking with cotton is uncomfortable, the plug can be replaced every ten or fifteen minutes during the specified time. One gets used to this after a few days. Then slowly increase the time after the first 15-20 weeks from 12.30 p.m. to 14.30 p.m. After about five weeks further increase this time from 12 noon to 15 p.m. In the meantime proper methods and disciplines as outlined will slowly bring about the 5:2:2:1 rhythm in the body. Further to these three hours, add the evening hours. After five weeks, block also in the evening from 8-9 p.m. After five further weeks, block from 7.30

to 9.30 p.m. and after further five weeks, block 7 to 10 p.m. Neither is this blocking uncomfortable nor is the blocking visible, if the plug is fine and light and small. It is also very beneficial to carry a fairly heavy book, tightly held in the left armpit.

Q. 4 What are the Vayu-nadis and describe them broadly ?

A. 4. The important Vayu-nadis are (1) Ida (2) Pingala (3) Sushumna (4) Gandhari (5) Hastijihva (6) Pusha (7) Yashasvini (8) Alambusha (9) Kushu (10) Sankalini. Numbers (1) and (2) stand for breathing and smell; (3) and (4) are for the eyes or seeing, (5) and (6) are for the ears or hearing; (7) and (8) for mouth and tongue, for taste and speech, (9) and (10) are for the penis and the perineum and a network between them for touch, i.e., they govern our five senses.

Vayu means a current of impulses or flow of impulses. These impulses as we have seen earlier could be physical, chemical, electrical, radio-active, magnetic, cosmic and coming through food and drink, breathing and sensations of sound, smell, touch and hearing, etc. Whenever by proper three-step breathing and other disciplines the rhythm 5:2:2:1 is established, Sec. 2, 3 and 4 are developed. Even the complete formation of mind Sec. 2 is sufficient to make Sec. 3 of the mind active. Forming of Secs. 3 and 4 clears the way and high plus intensity flows through unobstructed and brings about, or rather makes it possible for the co-relation and proper operation of Sections 2, 3 and 4 of the mind. This in turn brings decoded thought forms and other valuable knowledge and wisdom from the Sections 2, 3 and 4 to the intellectual centre of Section 1.

These Vayu nadis, in short comprise the sympathetic and the para-sympathetic nervous system, i.e., the autonomic nervous system. The control of impulses with three-step rhythmic breathing and other corrective methods will play an increasingly important part in our existence in the future. If for example the nadis Ida and Pingala (1) and (2) are for breathing and smell, why do they take their origin in the Muladhara Chakra and twist round the spinal column and end in the left and right nostrils respectively ?

Meditate on this ?

Muladhara Chakra is the pelvic plexus of the sympathetic system. Through this plexus the sympathetic makes complete relationship with the spinal cord, where it joins the brain. At the tail-end both sympathetic trunks end in the pelvic plexus.

The nadi Sushumna passes through the spinal cord. It originates inside the sacrum. It runs up the spine and pierces the base of the skull and joins the Brahma Chakra or cerebrum. This nadi as it ascends and reaches the level of the larynx divides itself into two—an anterior and a posterior.

The anterior goes towards the ajna chakra the *plexus of command* (between and behind the eyebrows and so reaches Sec. 2 of the mind—and joins the brahma-randhra or cavity in the brain.

The posterior passes from behind the skull (= reaches Sec. 3) and joins Brahma-randhra. It is this posterior position which is to be developed by the student of Yoga. The various powers as described by Pantanjali in his Yoga Sutra are the powers of Section 3 of the mind, and this when formed completely, is capable of demonstrating all that has been enumerated in the Yoga Sutra. By constant control of the working of these sympathetic cords, it is possible to put a stop to the Katabolic activities of the body, i.e., suspend the general wear and tear of the tissues of the vital organs and the whole body in general. This control should begin with the Ida and Pingala nadis, (the three-step rhythmic breathing) which form a connecting link between the pre-vertebral plexuses of the sympathetic system and the spinal cord. The reader will realise the importance of the th ee-step rhythmic breathing, corrective methods, 'disinfectant chamber', disciplines in food, drink, sleep, sex and finally the formation of Sec. 2, 3 and 4 of the mind; and the ultimate possibility thereby of functioning through the molecular and electronic bodies on the molecular and electronic planes.

Q. 5. What are the important chakras and give a short description?

A. 5. The important chakras or plexuses are : (1) Muladhara (Pelvic), (2) Swadhisthana, (hypogastric), (3) Kundali (solar), (4)Anahata (cardiac), (5) Kantha Vishuddhi (pharyngal) (6) Aįna (neaso.)

Each chakra or centre has its fixed resultant intensity according to natural laws which are in a fixed ratio to each other. (This is described in yoga as 'petals' of the chakra and designated with letters of the Sanskrit alphabet). However, seldom does a human being have the resultant intensity required in each chakra or plexus. The scriptures have given them the names of ruling deities.

The resultant intensity of a chakra or plexus is this 'deity' and exerts an inhibitory influence through a subsidiary nerve centre in the spinal cord and controls unconsciously (= Instinctive centre) the activities of the organs excited by fibres of the sympathetic plexuses. The names of the 'presiding deities' (= the resultant intensity of each centre) are, (1) Dakini (2) Rakini, (3) Lakhini, (4) Kakini, (5) Shakini, (6) Hakini.

They are excited by the resultant intensity of the entire person which is then the Kuṇḍalinī or the basic resultant intensity of a being. It is therefore said that the excitement of all the chakras takes place always through the Kundalini. *To put it crudely, it is the agitator of consciousness.* The creative impetus and the cosmic impulses are communicated through the Kundalini and in turn to the various chakras or centres and they in turn excite the organs and nerves and the relevant portions in the grey matter *and so our desires are born*—from the desires come action, and from action, reaction or what is termed "fruits of action" and the whole chain is forged on man.

Q. 6. Has prāṇāyāma any effect on concentration or dharana?

A. 6 We have noted that prāṇa is impulse and prāṇāyāma is the science of control of impulses. By corrective methods, three-step rhythmic breathing and by establishing a kind of check called 'disinfection chamber' the art of pranayama or the art of controlling impulses begins. When in due course, 5:2:2:1 rhythm is established and Sec. 2 is activated, prāṇāyāma is achieved. When this is done, the mind stuff or chitta (=Sec. 1) is not necessarily made to do the impossible practices of dhāraṇā or concentration, i.e., is not made to stop forming pictures or associate different pictures but is made to create high plus intensities. The steadier part of Section 2 of the mind (or Sec. 2 B)is then able to function which in its turn can easily hold one picture at a time almost indefinitely.

Q. 7. Is Kuṇḍalinī, a very important nerve like Vagus ? And if not, what is it ?

A. 7. All nerves of the sympathetic and para-sympathetic (i.e. the autonomic nervous system) have to abide by their rules, i.e., carry impulses both ways. Some may be more important and some less. The Vagus may be the most important, *but Kuṇḍalinī is not a nerve, it is a force, it is Parameshwari*, i.e., a great force. A nerve is a vehicle for conducting blood or force (energy) or impulse. Vagus could be the nerve for the Parameshwari to flow through, i.e., for the basic resultant intensity to flow but Vagus is a nerve only and Kuṇḍalinī is Shakti or psychic energy. Shakti when it is very high plus or minus, forces the way up the Sushumna. If not high, it is sleeping or coiled, i.e., goes up the Ida and Pingala and we call this 'sleeping Kuṇḍalinī' a low resultant intensity. When it is high it is called 'awakened Kuṇḍalinī' or high resultant intensity. *The Vagi are two important vehicles for conducting such forces, i.e., plus or minus high intensities.*

The resultant intensity is a mighty but potential force for better or worse. The word "coiled or sleeping" meaning wise or dangerous, describes eloquently the power of high resultant intensity either plus or minus to free a person from bondage or to enslave him. In the case of the average human being this force is a mere trickle. It can be gathered into hundreds of thousands of units of force and then that force can symbolically break open all doors and locks anywhere. Knowledge of the laws would act automatically.

Q. 8. Can there be manifested interference with normal functions of the Vagus or the sympathetic or para sympathetic, i.e., the autonomic nervous system ?

A. 8. The only visible interference with the normal functions of the Vagus or autonomic nervous system is either by means of certain mild poisons or certain medical agents, in short chemicals with psychoelastic effects. Such chemical effects of drugs may be duplicated by :

1. holding the breath for abnormally long duration,
2. prolonged fasts,
3. rhythmic three-step breathing,
4. corrective methods,
5. by thoughts of a particular nature of intense resultant intensity.

All these provoke the resultant intensity and so create voluntary control. Indirectly, through a change in resultant intensity this can be brought about.

Q. 9. What relationship can be established between an impulse and the art of three-step rhythmic breathing ?

A. 9. Prāṇāyāma though it denotes the science of control of impulses is generally understood as the science of control of breath. Let us recapitulate. Prāṇa is impulse or energy. All visible and invisible happenings in the universe are under the influence of cosmic impulses. The activities of the human body (including chitta or the mind stuff or Sec. 1) forming a part of the whole mind automatically come under its control and this cosmic prāṇa (=impulses) *as it functions in the body is named variously*. There are chemical, physical, electrical and radio-active impulses, coming from the cosmos, all of which the autonomic nervous system receives, relays, transmits to and from the brain (the coded impulses to decoded thoughts =task of Sec. 1).

Q. 10. What stimulation or inhibition can breath have on an impulse for better or worse ? Cannot this relationship create high or low, plus or minus resultant intensity ?

Can it not therefore lead from sleeping Kuṇḍalinī to the awakened Kuṇḍalinī ? Or is it all a play of words or shall we dare and verify ?

A. 10. In the process of prāṇāyāma, prāṇa is said to be generated with the intaking of breath. It is an impulse going to the brain and nerve centre located in the body and is therefore an afferent impulse. This is a case of vayu. Apana-vayu on the other hand is generated by the exhaling process in the performance of prāṇayāma and is an impulse which travels away from the brain or nerve centre. It is therefore an efferent impulse. The junction of the afferent (prāṇa) and the efferent (apana) impulses is said to be formed by vyana-vayu. The function of the vyana-vayu is to transfer the prana influence or impulses to the apana impulse. Therefore vyana-vayu is a reflex impulse.

When this reflex impulse starts from the brain, the energy of the prāṇa impulse is transferred through the apana impulse to the Skeletol muscles of the body and movement results. When this reflex impulse starts from the plexuses of the sympathetic, it controls the accumulating effect produced by the prana and apana impulses in the organs supplied by that particular plexus without producing any conscious sensations.

When this unconscious act is to be made conscious, the accelerating action of the organ sends a vyana (reflex) impulse to the spinal cord which ascends the posterior part of the Brahma Randhra, where the thalmus is situated and finally reaches the cortex of the brain where consciousness is manifested.

This ascending acceleratory impulse is called Udana. When the udana impulse reaches the cortex, it stimulates it to start a controlling or inhibiting impulse back to the excited organs which started the vyana impulse. This is an efferent impulse from the centre of the brain and it equipoises or controls the excited organ and is called a samana. This impulse is made to pass through the parasympathetic portions which have their nuclei in the midbrain and the bulb.

It must be noted that though the autonomic nervous

system is to a large degree, autonomous, there is still a dependence upon and a close relationship with the central nervous system.

We have seen earlier that the efferent and afferent fibres when excited to action by the alternate collapse and distention of air vesicles of the lungs, stop expiration and produce inspiration and vice versa. To this breathing, if we impose the three-step rhythmic breathing which is 'all-purpose', (with other disciplines) it brings us to the technique of prāṇāyāma. Anyone honestly following and cultivating this three-step rhythmic breathing (with other disciplines) will perceive, or rather feel, subtle changes taking place in his nervous system and a further development of higher faculties takes place after prāṇāyāma is attained. This nervous system to a certain extent is independent of the central nervous system. All the three sets of ganglia comprising the sympathetic chain, with strands connecting them together, ultimately gain connection with the spinal nerves and pass through them and the blood vessels. In fact stimulation of sympathetic or of para-sympathetic fibres causes inhibition to the other.

The brain is not the beginning but the end of all nerves, where the sum of all impulses or impressions of the nerves is stored up, filed and indexed. The brain is therefore the lotus of a thousand petals and these petals surround the cavity which is also known as the Brahma Randhra chakra. On the shores of this cavity are arranged the 'four brains' or rather the four sections of the brain each of which touch the shores of this cavity.

Q. 11. Is it true that when the Kuṇḍalinī is awakened the Yogi manifests supernatural powers?

A. 11. It is said that the resurrection of the soul from the grave of untruths becomes an actual fact. Health is also supposed to be a gift of the Kuṇḍalinī. Kuṇḍalinī is the mother of joy, of sweet rest, of sleep, faith and wisdom. The 'resultant intensity' as we understand it is 'Kuṇḍalinī'and the Yoga schools understand it perhaps otherwise. Till it is a minimum half-zenoga unit (plus or minus) it is said to be asleep or coiled, i.e., twists through Iḍā and Piṅgalā. When it is a minimum one Zenoga unit it awakens from sleep or moves up, i.e., consciousness progresses and reaches the heart centre.

When two Zenoga units are gathered it reaches the throat centre, when three Zenoga units are gathered it reaches the Ājñā centre and when four Zenoga units are gathered it reaches the Brahma chakra but in this case only if the centres are in the right ratio : the 5:2:2:1 ratio. Otherwise the Yogi's concentration is permanently centred in the heart, throat or Ājñā chakra but never can reach the Brahma centre. The Sushumnā nāḍī is used in all cases once one Zenoga unit is gathered and inhibition of other impulses is brought about and the Samādhi (with seed) stage is reached.

When the Yogi reaches the heart centre he works through Sec. 2 of his mind; when he reaches the Ājñā chakra he uses Sec. 3. Only when he reaches the Brahma centre does he function through Sec. 4 and consequently in or through all the four Sections of the mind. *Till a person is able to function in Sec.* 4, *he can function merely in one Section of mind at a time. But when he can function in Sec.* 4 *he can function simultaneously in all the four Sections.*

When the Yogi reaches the heart centre he works through a cellular-molecular body. When the Yogi reaches the Ājñā chakra he functions through the molecular body and when the Yogi reaches the Brahma chakra he functions through the electronic body. The centre where all residual sensations are, as it were, stored up, is called the mūlādhāra chakra (at the base of the spinal cord, near rectum) and the coiled up energy of actions is Kuṇḍalinī, (the coiled up). All explanations about the shakti could as well be applied to the autonomic nervous system. The static or anabolic power is the para-sympathetic (i.e., plus resultant intensity) portion of it and the dynamic or catabolic power is the sympathetic (i.e., minus resultant intensity) portion of it. The ventrical cavity in the brain is the seat of Brahma. The passage to that cavity is the narrow spane at the lower end of the fourth ventricle in the brain. This communicates the ventricles of the brain with the channel in the spinal cord and the subarachnoid space. The Kuṇḍalinī thus guards important openings in the cerebro-spinal nervous system.

Further it will be seen that the Kuṇḍalinī extends from the brain to the mūlādhāra chakra and is divided into two parts by the Kulakundali which rests on the lower end of the spinal cord. Kulakuṇḍalī is, therefore, the resultant pattern in conjunction with the resultant intensity. It is the cavity which is guarded by six doors in the grey matter and the Kuṇḍalinī is the only force (resultant intensity) that can open them. It is here that the unruly Chitta or the 'mind stuff' is captured and made steady by the processes of prāṇāyāma. It is only when the mind and the prāṇa *act as two conflicting entities* that they run riot and keep the Soul in bondage to māyā.

Q. 12. Are you trying to present a pet new theory of your own?

A. 12. Truth is eternal and very simple. It is able to be grasped by a child and yet it can evade the scholar and the very learned. Being eternal, what was said and taught ages ago before our times is taught again in our times and will be repeated ages later, only the language will change. The Gītā says: "This indispensable philosophy I taught to Vivasvān, the founder of the Solar Dynasty; Vivasvān gave it to Manu the Lawgiver and Manu to King Ikshvāku. The Divine Kings knew it, for it was their tradition. Thereafter a long time later, at last it was forgotten. It is this same ancient truth that I have now revealed to thee, since thou art my devotee and my friend. It is the Supreme Secret, oh Arjuna." Does it therefore follow that it all falls on deaf ears? No. But there are three reasons, that make the same eternal truth appear different so that man seldom grasps it.

i. The advanced souls who from time to time expressed this truth, expounded *that aspect only* which was capable of being understood by the people around them.

ii. More important, it is but too true that simple statements of truth are brushed aside as too elementary by the masses who deem it not deep enough to impress them and no thought is given to such statements.

iii. Our hands and feet are as tied, our eyes are blindfolded and our mind is as if under hypnosis due to our daily wrong habits of thought, eating, sleep, sex and other habits. The simple way to break this hypnotic spell is not consciously followed or practised, because these steps unfortunately seem too simple. Overeating and eating at odd times, oversleeping and sleeping at wrong hours agitate the S. and E. centres and dull the I. centre. So too does incorrect breathing. Try to operate these and other simple steps as shown and progress is certain.

Q. 13. Please clarify the so-called four Sections of the brain.

A. 13. There are four Sections of the brain. The first Section has the propensity of creating forms and making pictures; very rapid pictures to understand life's expressions and movement. It can never focus attention for more than a split second. *It is not supposed to do otherwise by Nature ! If this quality of this Section of the brain were not operative as it is, life as commonly understood in this physical cellular world would be impossible to experience.*

It is the world of cellular beings. Normally, 99% of humanity does not go beyond this Section of the brain. And what is worse, they either cannot or will not make use of more than 20% even of this Section. This Section of the brain is the realm of accumulated facts collected over ages and improved by re-use and yet this world (the world we can experience through Section 1) is magnificent and its knowledge and consciousness capable of being very vast. In this Section man is aware of time and distance by virtue of moving pictures, their speed and distance from each other. *This Section of the brain is purely intellectual and has no bearing on the moral, wisdom or spiritual side of a human being* ! This Section controls the four centres for normal operation, viz., Intellectual, Emotional, Sex and Moving.

Section 2 of the brain has two sub-sections: (a) takes care of the internal very vital functions of the body like breathing, movement of diaphragm, heart, circulation, pulse, digestion, excretion, sleep, etc.

(b) The second sub-section has the special ability to take one thought or picture at a time (as sent by the I. centre of Sec. 1) for deeper study and to learn the purpose and find the proper answer to the problem or question presented. If that quality of this sub-section of the brain were not operative all our inventions and so-called inspired creations in art, music, poetry, etc., would never be possible. (Even though this contact by the intellectual centre of Sec. 1 with Sec. B of Sec. 2 is unconscious). *This sub-section of the brain gives moral aspects and true values to life.* This sub-section of the brain is not operative (consciously) in 99% of humanity today. This is the world of cellular-molecular beings.

The third Section of the brain has the ability to understand the purely molecular world. It is in direct contrast to Sec. 1 of the brain, with the result that people living in either Sec. 1 or 3 find each other's world meaningless and unreal, even non-existing and their pursuits vain and illusory; but to themselves they find their world true, forthright and practical. Time and space as understood by Sec. 1 cease to exist for Sec. 3. It is however also true that people who live in Sec. 3 live in a world of extreme glamour—glamour in the sense that being able to function and understand the molecular world, their powers in the physical world are also great. Being able to operate with higher laws, great is their temptation to use or misuse them. They appear in our world as saints, prophets, or miracle workers.

The fourth Section of the brain has the ability of Section 1, 2, and 3 put together—and much more. It is the electronic world and at will the Yogi is able to function in any or all Sections of the brain. The new dimensions of consciousness and power due to an understanding of all laws is great *and never misused.* Such a person is almost a god on earth. No Section of the brain can be or should be called conscious or subconscious or super-conscious. *Each Section is fully conscious within its own domain though The consciousness of the I. centre of Sec. 1 may not be aware* and hence the misleading term 'sub-conscious'. *Sec. 4 is a very distant scene.* Do not be in a hurry. Practise step by step. The road is long and even with the fastest mode of travel, we shall require quite some time to reach the journey's end.

Q. 14. What happens, when the Soul is freed from bondage to Māyā ?

A. 14. The Soul, freed from the control of prāṇa (impulses), chitta (mind stuff or play of the first four centres of Sec. 1), and vāsanās (minus resultant intensity) lies in the Brahma chakra, the Cerebrum. That state is supposed to be the state of Nirvikalpa or seedless Samādhi by which the Yogi gets in tune with the Infinite and escapes rebirths. This is only possible when the art of control of impulses (prāṇāyāma) including the rhythmic three-step breathing and other processes as outlined, like corrective methods are perfected and four or even more plus Zenoga units of resultant intensity have been gathered. Thus the Yogi reaches the state which is called Samādhi.

When this high plus intensity is sent out with whatever sets of resultant intensity patterns to the central revolving point in the universe, the resultant patterns are not able to keep up with the high resultant intensity's speed and rate of vibration and, therefore, separate or fall out and are dissipated (i.e. are absorbed by lesser equivalent patterns), the resultant intensity thus returning to the Yogi then achieves the Samādhi state for him.

Q. 15. What is the benefit of high plus intensity ?

A. 15. Resultant intensity is the Kuṇḍalinī but it must be high to be awake. We have studied till now the effects of such awakened intensity. According to certain cosmic laws, if the resultant intensity be high, it automatically cuts off all cosmic impulses (prāṇa) reaching us from outside the human body from any source further below a certain octave and it therefore insulates and insures ourselves from a certain range of damaging, violent cosmic impulses thrown out and circulated by unfortunate beings. This automatically guards the five prāṇas in the body with their relevant centres—our whole being is automatically made safe. In turn our reactions (i.e., decoded thoughts to incoming coded impulses) to the higher and nobler cosmic impulses are high and noble (which up to now went over our heads as our resultant intensity was too low to reach these higher impulses) *and it is then easier to live well and be good than otherwise which is a contradictory condition with people having low plus or worse, minus resultant intensities.* And all this happens without use of so-called will power.

Q. 16. What according to you is the disinfectant chamber?

A. 16. The Thalamus is the highest reflex centre in the brain and as all impressions ascend to it, it is called Udāna-Prāṇa. The Yogi, by a conscious control over the Udāna-prāṇa, suppresses all incoming and outgoing sensations in it and such suppression is necessary to prevent distraction of mind. The Udāna-Prāṇa is the controlling switch of the disinfectant chamber. However, no actual suppression as such or will control as such is needed or is done or is even possible. The authors of such statements are perhaps not able to verify by personal experience. But this is done by regular processes of correction methods, three-step rhythmic breathing, with the art of control of impulses and with such disciplines the switch is made operative. And then Udāna-Prāṇa starts functioning for all incoming coded impulses from all known or unknown sources and the decoded thoughts are sent out. The basic resultant intensity forms the envelope around the body we call the disinfectant chamber. The Thalamus is the switch that operates this envelope we call disinfection chamber.

Q. 17. Is Bandha a link between the art of control of impulses and the art of rhythmic breathing ?

A. 17. The practising of certain bandhas are recommended, the important ones being (1) mūla bandha (2) jalandhara bandha (3) uḍḍīyāna bandha : during the process of breathing each complete breath.

1) The mūla bandha is to be practised with the intake of breath. In this the centre of the pariniyum is firmly pressed by the heel of the left foot (the body resting on that heel) and the left leg is placed over the right. The hands rest on the knees. The full inhalation (Puralea) is done when this is completed. It should not be tried without the help of a competent teacher.
2) The retention of breath is practised. (Kumbhlea) the head is bent forward and the chin is made to press firmly against the root of the neck. This is Jalandhara bandha. Same advice.
3) After this is done the breath is exhaled (Rechalea) the navel drawn up and the abdomen drawn in. This is Uḍḍīyāna bandha. In one prāṇāyāma or complete breath all the three bandhas are practised.
The effect of these bandhas on the autonomic nervous system is supposed to be like this: In the Kula bandha the pressure of the heel stimulates the pelvic plexus (mūlādhāra) to action and blocks the downward outgoing efferent impulses. The upward ascending impulses ascend through the svādhiṣthāna and maṇipūra chakras, the hypogastric and solar plexuses respectively. When the plexuses are stimulated there occurs an inhibition of the organs supplied by the sympathetic fibres from the plexuses. Consequent upon these disturbances of the catabolic activity of the sympathetic system there occurs a general circulatory and respiratory disturbance. This automatically excites the Kuṇḍalinī. The efferent impulses travel upward towards the medula.
The Jalandhara bandha prevents these efferent impulses from reaching the medula. It directs downward the afferent impulses generated by the inhalation of the breath. This afferent impulse (prāṇa vāyu) meets the efferent impulse (apāna vāyu) generated by the mūlādhāra chakra, in the region of the anus. We have seen earlier that when these prāṇa and apāna impulses meet, the meeting is manifested by internal sounds. These two impulses stimulate the endings of the vagi nerves, generating a reflex impulse (vyāna vāyu) which in turn produces an ascending impulse; the Udāna Vāyu goes

through the posterior portion of the spinal cord during the Uḍḍīyāna bandha. This bandha prevents the Ud¯na impulse from descending. The Udāna therefore rises by relays to the cortex of the brain and transmits the impressions through its nerve endings and the mind, through the medium of Brahma Randhra chakra. The brain thus becomes conscious of its functions. By constant practice with these a Yogi slowly gets control over the Kuṇḍalinī. This conscious control does not last long. The Kuṇḍalinī tries to resist this interference and begins to move in and out of her abode in the medula. This in western physiology is termed "the Vagus escape".

Q. 18. What is the Randhra?

A. 18. Randhra is the inter-communicating tunnel or cavity of the four Sections or ventricles of the brain and is continuous with the central canal of the spinal cord. This cavity is constantly secreting a fluid called the 'Nectar of Life' or the cerebro-spinal fluid. This has a deeper meaning and science may not understand it for some centuries to come.

Q. 19. Is there a simple way to know whether a person is ruled by the 2:4:8:2 ratio or is more and more advanced towards the 5:2:2:1 ratio?

A. 19. There are many physical tests and ways to know this. The most dependable is the human palm in this respect. The palm of the right hand of a person of either sex is an unmistaken proof of this. In the palm are the important lines of (1) head, or depicting the I. centre, (2) heart, or depicting the E. centre and (3) Life, or depicting the energy flow of vitality or the S. centre.

The lines (1) and (2) or of head and heart run horizontal more or less parallel across the palm from below the base of the index finger towards and below the base of the small finger.

In case of 5:2:2:1 ratio these two lines will run parallel like two railway lines laid with care and attention. When the ratio 2:4:8:2 is prevalent these two lines show a wider gulf between them either at the ending or at the beginning or at certain other places along both the lines. Of the lines (1) and (2) the one above or higher up is the heart* line and the lower is the head** line. To show that there is proper rhythm and control of this line over the other, there is, between these two lines, a *cross* about mid-way between these two lines showing proper inter-communication.

The head line meets the life line in the beginning. The life line† flows round what is called in palmistry the mount of *Venus*, depicting *vitality*. If this mount is well formed and the life line running round it is long then it shows a vigorous flow of life (sex) held under proper control. The base of the index finger has what is called the mount of *Jupiter* and is held in great veneration as depicting balance, judgement, success and noble qualities. Therefore it is worthwhile that the line of heart should take its source from the centre of the mount of Jupiter so that it gives the person concerned fine, noble emotions. Opposite to the mount of Venus is the mount of Moon★ and right above it far up below the base of the little finger is the mount of *Mercury* but between them both is the mount of Upper *Mars* denoting harmony, bravery, fighting ability for a righteous cause, the noble soldier and general in contrast to the cruel, despotic soldier and therefore it is well that the line of Head to end touching this mount for *the person concerned is engaged in a terrible war with himself deep within.* The thumb (the only pointer according to Darwin's theory of evolution, the placing of which makes man distinct from the ape) should be supple, flexible and able to bend backwards, denoting a character of flexibility or rather tolerance and we have noted before in this book that those who can tolerate can hope and those who can hope could be compassionate. Should the line of heart curve off to either the long finger or droop and join the head line the emotions are not

*=E. Centre
**=I. Centre
†=S. Centre
★ Astrological Moon, not to be confused with the Moon as Divinity.

controlled and dominate the I Centre. Should the line of head at its ending drop and fall towards the mount of moon (explained above) then the intellectual centre is dominated by S. centres.

Q. 20. What if the age be advanced or the body and mind has already grown stiff for any particular technique or methods or if the desire to fight back has withered, is there then no hope ?

A. 20. We would like to answer this question at length, but we would rather quote here those beautiful lines which express the thought from the Gītā which is in reply to a similar question asked by Arjuna.

Krishna :

"Cling thou to Me (=Avatāra)
Clasp Me, with heart and mind so shall thou dwell
Surely with me on high. But if thy thought drops
from such height; if thou be'st weak to set
Body and Soul upon Me constantly.
Despair not, give me lower service. Seek
to reach Me worshipping with steadfast Will,
And if thou canst not worship steadfastly
Work for Me, toil in works pleasing to Me.
For he that laboureth right for love of Me
Shall finally attain, but if in this
Thy faint heart fails, bring me thy failure. *Find
Refuge in Me. Let fruits of labour go,*
Renouncing all for Me with lowliest heart
So shalt thou come; for, though to know is more
Than diligence, yet worship better is
Than knowing, and renouncing better still.
Near to renunciation—very near
Resideth Eternal Peace.

Q. 21. How useful or how important are āsanas (postures) and which of these do you recommend ?

A. 21. The āsanas or postures are enumerated hereafter. The most important point to remember today is that of all the teachers, schools, and ashrams explaining and teaching these yogic āsanas, not even 2% know and understand what they are doing and asking their pupils to do and for what purpose. This means that 98% of all those who are engaged in yogic āsana do it incorrectly or thoughtlessly and it is like the blind leading the blind. The second point to remember is that each āsana has four distinct effects.

Each student must ask his teacher what exactly is the fourfold effect of a particular āsana he or she may have been asked to follow. These if not understood would be harmful and dangerous. We shall later enumerate these fourfold effects. The third point to remember is that these āsanas were taught in ancient India ages ago and by now Nature has made the human frame much more sensitive and some of these āsanas if indulged in would seriously harm rather than heal.

We would request the reader to rather abstain from than indulge in āsanas. We shall also recommend a few that would be very mild and are necessary for healing the daily wear and tear of the body, the toning of nerves, silencing of centres as an aid in our programme of construction and re-education.

The fourfold effects of āsanas are :

1. Remedying of certain physical ailments.
2. Gaining control of certain nerve centres.
3. Keeping in abeyance the overpowering effects of the play of qualities of the S. and E. centres.
4. The most important of all :—Closing Sec. 1 of the brain while opening Sec. 2 temporarily and passing a certain thought or problem (to be analysed) from Sec. 1 to Sec. 2. Also : to await the receipt of an intuitive solution by opening Sec. 1 again thus transferring the solution or insight gained to the I. centre of Sec. 1 and then closing Sec. 2 again.

The point to remember is that all āsanas lose their meaning and are positively harmful if not accompanied by three-step rhythmic breathing. Before beginning an āsana, we should relax and practise three-step rhythmic breathing. Then take a thought or a problem and simply state it silently to yourself. Now begin the āsana otherwise the Sec. 2 although opened will not be able to receive anything useful and the opportunity will be wasted. Another point to remember is the time limit. Any āsana to be useful should not be practiced or continued for more than 108 breaths (= one mala of rhythmic breathing . *Even if there be miles and miles of atmosphere, we can take in only a little measure of air. Even if there be a feast spread before us we can eat only a certain measure.* In the same way even if it be possible to keep to an āsana for hours on end the best is to be satisfied with a fixed measure and the fixed and *maximum measure* is one mala or 108 rhythmic breaths and no more. Excess in all forms is bad and never so anywhere than when indulged in any of these āsanas. Anywhere between 54 and 108 rhythmic breaths duration is justifiable; anywhere between 36 and 54 rhythmic breaths is good. Anywhere between 24 and 36 rhythmic breaths is satisfactory and gives great benefit and satisfaction.

Let us now explain how the fourfold effect takes place, and why three-step rhythmic breathing is essential and why a particular thought or problem has to be thought out. Whenever we begin an āsana, if it is done correctly, it will have control over a certain nerve centre. This when it continues for 12 to 24 rhythmic breaths is able temporarily to shut down the E. and S. centres. Whenever E. and S. centres of Section 1 are shut (even temporarily), Sec. 2 of the brain automatically opens. If you have already a thought, or problem in the I. Sec. 1 centre this is passed on to or Sec. 2 of the brain which then analyses it and gives an intuitive solution. One may continue this practice for 12 to 24 more rhythmic breaths and the maximum should be 54. Now relax the pressure a little on the nerve centre and Sec. 2 will send the solution to the I. centre and Sec. 2 will close by itself. *If there be no thought kept ready, the last struggling thought of the I. centre will pass on to Sec. 2 and this could be a harmful thought for all we know.* Then no sooner Sec. 2 supersedes the normal functions of Section 1, than all the four centres are subdued. Then the āsanas must stop for its purpose is served.

Supposing you argue that nothing is wrong even if the āsana is continued and Sec. 2 is kept open for a longer time. It may be 'nice' to concentrate longer. Please note that breathing is good and deep breathing is better but holding the breath long is harmful because in three seconds (at the maximum) all the oxygen content of the lungs is burnt up. Similarly Sec. 2 can find a solution to a problem or can think on a thought in a maximum of 54 rhythmic breaths.*

Therefore to hold an āsana longer is futile. *It may satisfy one's ego but does nothing beyond that.* More important is the fact that we begin the āsana correctly and in the first 12 to 24 rhythmic breaths shut off the E. and S. centres through the control of certain nerve centres.

(b) Pass on the thought or the problem to Sec. 2 which opens automatically by shutting the E. and S. centres; because the door which opens one, closes the other and vice versa. This can be continued for 54 breaths. (c) To relax the pressure a little. This technique of relaxing the pressure on the nerve centre is difficult and must be shown properly by a competent teacher. Then the solution to the problem or the thought is sent back to the I. centre of Sec. 1, and Sec. 2 shuts off. This takes about 12 to 24 rhythmic breaths.

After the āsana is over, relax pressure and continue the three-step rhythmic breathing for about two minutes. Please note that without mastering the three-step rhythmic breathing an āsana is of only a little value; for a proper control of the nerve centre is essential to secure this.

Human beings still think that: the Absolute has no other responsibility than ourselves and that we are so great and advanced that nothing less than the Absolute must incarnate ! † Shall we not at least now, give up this school-boy thought and accept that in creation we are too far down the line of evolution

*Never try to solve more than ONE problem at a time. Simultaneous mixing of problems or questions is called MISJOINDER—and is very, very harmful.

†He alone, whom we call 'rational' (=modern man), has a habit to be pleased with nothing unless blessed with all . He thinks himself high Heavens' peculiar care; to be made happy on Earth at all costs and later on even immortal.

and therefore usually a much smaller Entity (an Avatāra instead of Mahāvatāra) incarnates to guide us ! May we be forgiven if we have hurt anyone's feelings.

If there were but *one* world, peopled by beings, for every million universes then there would be more worlds peopled by beings in entire creation than there are living creatures of all grades on our planet !! Of these billions of worlds peopled by beings there are some who are far *behind* in evolution and there are others far *advanced* in evolution, and so much more advanced as to baffle our imagination. There is nothing 'supernatural' in all this and what to us may appear as 'supernatural' only obeys other *higher* laws. When the fourth Section of the mind is developed (Cosmic Consciousness) we will understand even these laws.

There have been some who have had glimpses of the cosmic consciousness and have seen some of the laws operative there, but the duration of their stay being short, they have felt, on experiencing again the normal physical consciousness, that either this physical experience is false or the other world is false. When such people get repeated glimpses of cosmic consciousness they are convinced that there is another state which is superior to ours and they verify in many ways its superiority over our normal consciousness along with its superiority over usual consciousness with its limitations.

"He was in tears and was emotionally carried away." So too are those who get glimpses of the first stage of cosmic consciousness; they are in ecstacy and call all else Māyā.

We also know that after long struggle and search the young Gautama became the Buddha.* He then gave the Eightfold Noble Path and the Four-fold Noble Truth. He, then, without tears in his eyes could say :

1) There is suffering;
2) There is a cause of suffering;
3) This suffering can be removed;
4) There is a way to remove that cause of suffering.

He did not say (like an ostrich putting its head in the sand) that there is no pain and, all is Māyā, because He had by now lingered long enough on the second, third and even fourth

*Vide SAHER, Happiness and Immortality, London 1970.

stage of the cosmic consciousness, and having more clearly understood was not in a mighty hurry to say that this world is all Māyā. He was born of Māyā, that he was convinced of, for she happened to be his mother !

If we can only study and understand the episodes of such lives like Gautama, Jesus and others,* we would definitely understand more clearly and then one would not, parrot-like, repeat what somebody else has said or written.

Now a time comes when a person gets the first glimpse of cosmic consciousness; at least the first stage of it. This is called "grace" by many; and normally we say "when grace descends".

When by daily corrective methods the resultant intensity reaches two plus Zenoga units this intensity of the resultant brings about a state we call Vision. This is the state in which a general clearing or cleansing precedes all other activities; a cleansing of all unwanted stored-up thought patterns ! This is done by corrective methods over a sufficiently long period and the patterns are changed and reduced by the interplay of different qualities. The rate of rotation of the patterns drops simultaneously with the reduction in the number of patterns and the rocketing force of intensity which is not quite so high is able to throw the entire set of patterns outside into space and propel them to the source with similar intensity; just as it happens at death. This, if brought about by unconscious efforts or misguided efforts, makes the person unconscious or throws him into a state of trance. Such an experience without diminishing the number of patterns or correcting the patterns is also brought about by drugs like L.S.D. and breathing, in which the breath is held for a very long time.

However, in all these cases one is in a partial or complete trance and experiences a temporary artificial freedom from the limitations of the physical body or 'bondage'. This creates another type of bondage or slavery viz. addiction to drugs or to wrong breathing. Even after spending one hundred thousand lives in this manner one would not be advanced even a step further and there is here not the slightest hope of progress.

There can be no negative spiritual states, nor unconscious spiritual stages. A spiritual state is a state of pure-consciousness

*: like Mani, Milarepa, Maharshi Ramana, Zarathustra etc.

where uncontrolled trance has no place ! If the resultant intensity is minus and if the propelling is artificially brought about, it would propel the patterns as well as the intensity to the 'planet' having that minus resultant intensity. No minus resultant can teach wisdom or make one wiser or better. *On the contrary* the minus resultant brings the attendant diseases from the 'planet' concerned on the way back to that person.

The only temporary compensation is the false sense of freedom from bondage (temporarily) till the minus resultant of the person concerned is propelled to leave and return to the body. For this very damaging result, the reader is requested to keep away from all alcoholic drinks, drugs, so-called tranquilisers, so-called Yoga breathing exercises or so-called postures and breathing.

The more the number of times the resultant intensity (along with its patterns) is propelled away from the body in an artificial manner as many times it contacts its source and as many times one gets an imaginary freedom from bondage. The terrible reaction of such 'enjoyment' is obvious !

(1) The waste of time in terms not of one life time but many.
(2) The inherent nature of repetition of patterns will force this artificial state; i.e. another added slavery is enforced and a wrong habit inculcated.
(3) It may become with passage of time so overpowering that one may be forced to put aside normal work (along with all sense of morals) and, in spite of inner unwillingness, be dragged to the artificial 'enjoyment' of so-called release from bondage.
(4) It weakens the I. centre by aiding the E. and S. centres and very soon the I. centre is permanently frustrated.
(5) When death approaches, one's resultant intensity is a very large minus !
(6) The propelling of minus resultant intensity amounts to frequent visits to the source i.e. the 'planet' concerned and the bringing of misery.

Let us now examine in this light the *plus* Zenoga units. What is required is the harmonising plus unit of all centres; there are also Zenoga units which are excellent in themselves yet not plus units in a harmonising proportion to the centres.

In order to acquire a plus 'Zenoga-unit' one must have the

following total of rotations of vibrations :—in the :

I.	Centre	75,000,000,000 R.o.V.*
E.	Centre	30,000,000,000
S.	Centre	30,000,000,000
M.	Centre	15,000,000,000
		150,000,000,000 = one Z. Unit.

The M. Centre has a huge score of 15,000,000,000 though it is the smallest of the four centres' score.

It, therefore, conclusively requires one to be active and not to be a hermit. Otherwise there can be no opportunity to gather plus intensity for this centre in order to neutralise the minus intensity. This is possible and progress of other centres is also possible whilst facing the normal problems of life.

The second important centre is the S. Centre. The big plus score of 30,000,000,000 again requires one not to lead a life of abstinance only. It is not the ignorance of this urge that is required, it is the knowing and proper understanding of this urge and then putting it to constructive and better use that creates a *plus* resultant out of a minus resultant and so increases the score to that which is required.

The third centre is the E. Centre and the plus score of 30,000,000,000 requires a harmonising and understanding of all the shades of emotion and merely a single octave of the emotions does not lead to an all-round, balanced personality.

Finally, there is the I. Centre with the highest score of 75,000,000,000 or equal to the added score of the other three centres thus creating a perfect balance. This is comparable to a balance-beam with one arm longer and the other scale heavier.

The score of the M. and S. Centres makes it imperative for a person to live a normal worldly life; to meet the waywardness of these centres and create a plus intensity for the I. Centre requires an active, intelligent and honest mind, which ultimately leads one to higher and yet higher stages.

The divergent paths leading to different spiritual destinations is by virtue of the qualities inherent in those paths. Un-

*Rotation of Vibrations, for short R.o.V.

fortunately this is also the inherent quality of the aspirant or his inherent resultant intensity ! These different paths (in the absence of proper corrective methods) are sought after by persons with different resultant intensities just as different resultant intensities also seek different planets as their source. Different metals have different melting points depending on their basic resultant intensity; just as flowers and fruits have different fragrance and colours or food values, depending on their basic resultant intensity. Life, consciousness, resultant intensity and thought patterns are in all creation. It may be, that the pulsation of life is in some cases so slow as to be imperceptible; it may be that consciousness is so simple as not to impinge on our awareness; the resultant intensity may be so concealed as to mislead us into believing it to be the 'quality' of that substance. And thought patterns may be so deeply buried (or though on the surface may be so faint) as to require the help of the most powerful analysis. Yet patterns are sometimes visible and resultant intensity is traceable. Life and consciousness in all creation remain yet to be accepted by man. Yet man suspects life and consciousness to be inert even in 'lifeless' substances.

Nevertheless life, consciousness, patterns and resultant intensity could be so intense and the patterns so re-arranged that in comparison to the highly evolved beings even the *best of human kind would be so much inert matter in comparison* ! But that advanced state of consciousness does not accept the idea of inert matter in creation.

There is no reason to believe that man is not changing and that his consciousness is not fast developing. We have selected a few planets and a few suns totalling in all thirty-one out of the myriads within a 600 light years radius. It is just to show that these have direct relations to our world.*

There are very many similar races of men, there are very many advanced types and there are very many resembling man as he was when he was an ape-man on earth. These worlds are far away and their resultant intensity in some cases has not reached us like the light of some planets. We see certain positions in the galaxy that took place hundreds of thousands of years ago and some 20,000 to 50,000 years ago. All these can be read as the past, present and future by reading the resultant intensity

*See Appendix IV

as it reaches us. Let us consider only those thirty-one 'planets' (suns, stars and moons) which have a certain range of intensity for man upto the 4th Cosmic stage, i.e. when even Sec. 4 of his mind is opened.

The practices and methods are not the true causes of the expansion of consciousness but they serve to remove obstacles or 'minus' resultant intensities.

Now let us take, as anology, the case of a rocket. When the rocket carrying the satellite is on the launching pad it resembles a person much below that Critical Certain Stage who does wish to exercise free will in the way one ought to, or, as one who feels it is not possible to exercise free will at all. At the next stage the person decides to make use of the corrective methods, analysis, the disinfection chamber and the rest. It resembles the rocket getting ready for the flight with all items checked sufficient fuel and the final release button ready.

It may not get free from the gravitational pull if there is something wrong with the proper methods of launching. Before the rocket leaves the launching pad it knows that there is some pull of gravitation which is responsible for its position on Earth. Then it realises that it can hope to be free because someone (scientist) knows the proper methods and has decided to make the start.

No sooner it is launched (i.e. we begin to keep the rhythm of the centres) than it experiences in fact what it always suspected,—that terrific gravitational pull. It climbs and continues to climb and the gravitational pull keeps on pulling. It must first free itself from the inherent pull of the planet. The gravitational force is a good force for keeping all of us as we are, but to the rocket, during its efforts to progress, it is a pull, on obstruction, an evil force, a devil ! Frustration or despondency at this stage would mean not only zero resultant intensity (for it will not land again on our planet) but will mean even a high minus resultant intensity for it will break to pieces, or burn out and be useless for another effort. That is why we warn against all sense of despondency once having accepted or resolved to strive upwards.

Before a person knows of its possibility, that person is below that Critical-Certain-Stage. When someone shows us the methods, we decide to make the attempt. No sooner is the attempt made than the pull (=inertia) is experienced! This pull is the inherent pull of the flow of life which is a good force, for it is essential like gravitation. It is through this pull alone that man ultimately (by exercising proper methods) reaches that Critical-Certain-Stage. This 'pull' brings about results of the past thought patterns indulged in, to settle some of the 'outstanding account' before the person becomes free. This will add character and sincerity to the person if he honestly keeps his progress in mind. God is the source that suggests the desire for freedom. The hint may come through a prophet, or a sage, a saint, or a wise man or any religion, or philosophy or theosophy or some school or ashrama or book or person, or even through a fool; for God or Nature have always desired that all creatures be free, that they make use of free will in time and space and accumulate wisdom. It is not the wish of God to see men remaining stuck in the mud.

Why must we live in a state of such colossal contradictions? Man is not an animal, man is not a machine, man is not an incapable creature for the simple reason that even mathematically it is possible to gather that momentum, to gain that speed, which counters the inherent pull of the flow of life! Now what does happen to the rocket which escapes the gravitational pull?

Suppose it has 100 miles per hour more than the speed required say of 25,000 m.p.h. as the escape speed; this is added to that 100 odd extra speed left. That great force of gravitational pull which to the rocket is an 'evil' force or devil obstructing its efforts and progress is now its 'friend' because it never was an evil force! This reminds us of that anecdote from Sir Walter Raleigh's life. "If thy faint heart fails thee, never rise at all". Let us, therefore, take this simple rhyme seriously. A person has not to have a "faint heart" and all is well and will be well.

Take this thought for serious thinking: "Seek in the heart the source of evil and expunge it. It lives fruitfully in the heart of the devoted desciple, as well as in the heart of the man of desire. Only the strong can kill it out. The weak must wait for its growth, its fruition, its death. And it is a plant that lives and increases throughout the ages".

APPENDIX II

PRACTICAL EXERCISES

Sincere students will experience many difficulties, some will find getting up early difficult, some will find the three-step breathing difficult and some will find the one meal formula difficult and some will find it difficult to subdue sex. Our entire inner life depends on the adjustment or balance between the centres. On our internal harmony will depend our outer life of balance and peace or one of non-balance and worries.

In Africa, in the Congo, only 120 miles apart from each other on the equator are two spots; one of eternal molten spots of lava lake and the other of eternal snows. So are centres within man. The cold, high, snow-clad peaks of the I. centre are very near the eternal molten lava lakes of the S. and E. centres. Just as, compared to the whole size of Africa, 120 miles is a very short distance, so compared to the size of man, the distance between the centres is a very short distance indeed. But were the cold, high, snow-clad mountains to gradually lose their height and were to become smaller and smaller and finally come to the level of the molten lava lakes of the E. and S. centres, we can imagine what would happen.

We therefore realise that: 1. the most important work is to practise, read and study those portions of the book which clarify the centres. Carry on daily with the diagnosis of the weaknesses as explained. Take up these weaknesses one by one and apply the corrective methods. The weaknesses thus listed should not include, getting up late, over-eating, over-sex-indulgence, for they are first to be taken in hand before any other weakness is even listed. Correctives should be applied first. This programme continues over twelve to eighteen months and simultaneously the 'one meal a day' habit is established; 11 p.m. to 5 a.m. sleeping hours are established; the three-step rhythmic breathing is mastered and the E. centre's re-education exercises are attended to unfailingly.

We also set aside a five minute period to visualise the colour pink. See it emanate as a ray from in-between the eyes and see it proceed on its forward journey to a distance of two feet in front of you on the level of the eyes. Increase this distance slowly, increasing by about six inches, but see it pointedly clear as emanating and reaching that distance. At the end of five minutes, slowly but completely withdraw it to its source. In the beginning do it for ten seconds. Increase it by ten seconds and 15 centimetres every week till you reach a distance of one metre, in front of you for a duration of 5 minutes. After that continue without increasing distance or time.

In the same way visualise a blue ray. This ray emanates from the top of the head and if extended ten feet would meet the pink ray at that point. The incline is two centimetres in a metre. As in the previous case, increase time and distance till the final distance of one metre is reached.

In the same way visualise a yellow (yellow which is tinged with gold or yellow-gold) ray emanating from the heart and extended in front of you so that on reaching the distance of one metre can meet the same spot as the pink and blue rays. The rising incline in this case could be 35 centimetres in a metre. The time and length can be increased as in the previous two cases.

These three exercises are separate exercises each lasting for five minutes at the maximum. In between each exercise of this nature, relax or do some other exercise as shown later.

In the following exercises continue the three-step rhythmic breathing. Sit on the floor, legs in front, bend as far as possible, from the hips but without experiencing discomfort and try to touch the toes. Keep the knees straight. Progress by a centimetre towards the toes each week till the fingers of the hand touch the toes of the feet. Begin with ten seconds increasing by five seconds every week. Maximum five minutes.

Stand with legs apart 60 centimetres or so depending on your height. Hands at back supporting the lower spine on each side of the spinal cord. Bend forward and exhale. Breathe in as you make half circle at the hips either to the left or right and breathe out at the other half circular movement till you reach the position of origin. Repeat in the opposite direction. Increase by one movement in each direction every fortnight. Maximum should be ten movements in each direction. Do not alternate in your movements, just in one direction all the movements and then in the opposite direction.

Kneel on floor. Bend forward and touch the top of the head to the floor (preferably do this on a carpet). Keep hands locked behind the back and take the weight of the body on the head. The knees and head apart as much as is comfortable. Slowly reduce this distance. Begin with ten seconds increase by five seconds every week. Maximum two minutes. Decrease the distance between head and knees by a centimetre every month but do not bring the knees and head so close that the full weight is not felt at the top of the head.

Lie flat on the back on the floor. Hands stretched behind your head. Rise to touch toes, breathe out, come to original position and breathe in, lift both the legs and bring them over the head; breathe out, lower legs and come to the original position and breathe in. This is one movement. Increase by one movement every week. Maximum fifteen complete movements. The first step of rhythmic breathing is to be practised along with this exercise.

Exercise for the eyes : To be done without glasses and without straining. Keep this book on a level with the eyes, whether standing or sitting about a metre away. Do not move the head or neck. Only the eye-balls should move aside drawing an imaginary circle without jerks or backward, hesitant movements.

Without glasses, from a distance of 35 centimetres, read the type readable without glasses. Take the morning paper which has many different sizes. Read for one minute a particular size. For one minute look out of the window to a distant object without straining. Repeat. Five movements. In- crease by one movement every week. Maximum ten movements.

Make pendulum movements with your eyeballs, the weight being on the level of the eyes standing or sitting. Swing the 'pendulum' (without glasses) and without moving the head or neck, keep the eyes on the pendulum till it comes to a rest.

At night, move from a lighted room to a dark room and see the objects in each room closely, without glasses. Repeat five times.

When all the exercises are over, press the eyes closed, tight and open them. Repeat three times.

Exercises for nerves : Put a small dot mark that can be seen without glasses on the mirror on a level with the eyes when sitting. Look into the mirror without glasses and try to keep the mark exactly between the eyebrows in the reflected image in the mirror. Observe how much the body swings and how much attention is needed to keep it steady. Maximum to begin with, one minute. Increase by one minute every fortnight till the maximum time of five minutes is reached.

Relax in an armchair. Continue the three-step rhythmic breathing. There should be no movement from head to foot. Begin for one minute. Increase by one minute every fortnight. Maximum time five minutes.

Sit near a mirror. Look into your own eyes, both eyes, (you will find it easier to look into one of them at a time). Continue three-step rhythmic breathing. There should be no movement from head to foot. Begin with one minute. Increase by one minute every fortnight. Maximum time five minutes; (the eyes should not blink).

When you get up in the morning, the first thing you should do is to take a glass of water, ordinary and cool, if possible, not refrigerated water.

At night, gargle deep in the throat with warm water with some salt in it.

Be not over anxious for results. If you are sincere, results must come and will come. Do not be anxious to meet a Master or Guru, for let us assure you that you could not be half as anxious as he is to meet you; but first you must cross that critical certain stage. It is only then that he can meet you for however anxious he may be to meet you (or you are to meet him) he cannot meet you on your grounds—it is imperative that you meet him on his grounds.

To begin with take up a subject and in some half hour daily allotted for this mental exercise think on that subject and note carefully all the drifts. Keep a diary. Make summaries every week. Make analyses of all these summaries at the end of the first three months. Note the weaknesses that they convey in order of magnitude. Take up corrective methods and then along the lines shown have your own creative method drawn up. Check up every three months for quarterly analysis. Simultaneously start the sleep reducing method and sleep only from 11 p.m. to 5 a.m. by your local time. Simultaneously reduce the food intake in quantity and also in frequency, till you take only one mid-day meal every 24 hours. Check up twenty or thirty times a day in which centre you are.

Simultaneously adopt the three-step rhythmic breathing. Master it one step at a time till you can do it for 24 hours at 12 rhythmic breaths a minute. Employ simultaneously corrective methods when breathing during some half hour of the day. Employ also the corrective methods whilst eating. Be very moderate in sex. Keep to good and constructive reading if you have time. Learn the proper way to issue commands through the I. centre to take care of the E. and S. centres. Study this book carefully. Read and re-read the book. Watch that the 2:4:8:2 ratio of the centres is slowly changing to 5:2:2:1. Keep the purpose of Life and birth constantly before you during the whole day. Check up frequently during the day to see that you have not lost sight of that purpose for anything that is done, however nice and satisfactory, which is not fulfilling that purpose *is a drift.*

Whenever a person reaches a total equivalent of four plus Zenoga units, the formations and functioning of Sec. 3 and 4 of the mind enables him to understand and act in a manner so different as to surprise a person living only with Sec. 1 of the mind. The grace and love of God can never be understood with Sec. 1 of the mind. It is not intelligence that is necessary. It is the different rates of intensity of Sec. 1, 2, 3 and 4 of the mind that make it possible to understand and see and feel intensities that are equivalent to higher frequencies.

The intensity of the flow of God's love and grace is not possible of comprehension by Sec. 1 of the mind because its sensitivity lies beyond, and only Sec. 2 of the mind begins to sense it; Sec. 3 of the mind begins to comprehend it. Grace of God and the flow of God's love is *not* therefore the *arbitrary* moment and movement or decision of God to favour a particular person but it is the awareness during the evolution of man, brought about by man himself by his constant progress. We must say that a certain amount of discipline is required, but discipline should be understood as reasoned living and not mere regimentation.

Till such time as one has decided to remain indifferent

to one's possible progress and freedom from bondage to thought patterns, till such time can the patterns be expected to repeat themselves along with the effects attendant on such patterns. These in turn become causes to bring about certain results which mistakenly come to be called destiny or Karma.

If God or Nature were anxious to keep man in bondage as amplified by all literature or philosophy then God or Nature would not from time to time request the Avatāras (=advanced sons of mankind) to remind (and remind forcibly) others, who have not yet decided to exercise their free will in a proper manner, to reach that Critical-Certain-Stage !

Many religions are based on Bhakti or devotion, for unless the E. Centre is taken into account it would not result in plus resultant intensity.

The stage of Bhakti helps; by using methodical corrective methods we wipe out the minus resultant intensity and quickly build up a plus resultant intensity. The only limitation is that the plus resultant is basically emotional and thus has no rounded personality. The law permits two plus zenoga units whether balanced as required or whether belonging to one centre only to reach No Man's-Land and four plus zenoga units to go beyond the No Man's -Land. The Law does not permit accumulation of four (and over) plus zenoga units of a single centre. From here onwards the aspirant who has already reached a very high stage of Bhakti realises his one-sided development, and consciously takes birth again with objectives clearly defined. Such persons then prefer the life of the ordinary householder because herein one gets a natural chance to build a balanced plus *resultant intensity*. Whatever the score of the E. Centre it must be redistributed in proper proportion over the other three Centres. It is essential not to miss this supreme opportunity of living correctly as a householder and with corrective methods to proceed forward !

Those who follow the different techniques of Yoga build up a plus resultant intensity for one of the centres. In Rāja Yoga is advocated a greater balance. But the finest possibility of balance is practice of Rāja Yoga techniques living as a householder.

The table is as follows

Different Yoga Systems :	I. Centre :	E. Centre :	S. Centre :	M. Centre:
1. General Yoga	2000	4000	Nil	150,000,000,00
2. Bhakti Yoga	50,000,000,000	100,000,000,000	4000	2000
3. Jñāna Yoga	150,000,000,000	2000	2000	2000
4. Rāja Yoga	70,000,000,000	50,000,000,000	30,000,000,000	6000
5. Karma Yoga	40,000,000,000	45,000,000,000	35,000,000,000	30,000,000,00
6. ZENOGA (Yoga-Practice as explained in this book)	75,000 000,000	30,000,000,000	30,000,000,000	15,000,000,00

(Adjusted to the main centre or to any one centre)

From the above it is evident that in the case of 1, 2 and 3 the M. or the E. or the I. centre respectively does predominate completely and annihilates the possibility of the other respective centres to express themselves. In the case of 4 and 5 we note that there is no harmonious balance between the centres. In No. 6 (zenoga) the I. centre perfectly balances the other three and neither side can predominate and any alliance with the I. centre is not to be feared nor the complete alliance between E., S. and M. Centres is not to be feared by the I. Centre. The much needed balance is reflected in the balanced palm of the hand and the parallel lines of the 'Heart' and 'Head' in the palm. The great stumbling block in the way of man's orderly development is that when he is preoccupied with things spiritual he tends to neglect other functions by means of which he must bring the spiritual down to earth. It is apparant that ZENOGA or Yoga of intensity of centres gives the required balance and is the most easy to practise inasmuch as the coded impulses which are here decoded are consciously treated in the disinfection chamber with the corrective methods. In the normal flow of life, with the normal pull of the flow of life, there are chances that some great Emotional or Sexual outburst (even very few times a year) may seriously hamper or retard or lessen the plus resultant intensity. Besides, the corrective methods are administered not in any artificial condition as in the case of Bhakti, Jñāna or Haṭha Yoga but in the actual life of daily living in this world.

We say 'artificial' conditions because in Bhakti the person has taken upon himself a somewhat restricted life and therefore finds that the flow of the coded impulses of 120 per second is also more or less restricted to a particular channel. In Jñana Yoga, the person is deep in study and has in different ways also a 'restricted' life and, therefore, the flow of the coded impulses is again more or less in a particular channel. In Haṭha Yoga practices, the emphasis is entirely on postures and breathing and so once again we see that the flow of life is restricted and the flow of coded messages is also restricted to certain particular channels only. In Rāja Yoga though a person may be leading a normal life it is possible that certain 'restrictions' on life i.e. on the natural flow of life of a householder arise. When it comes to the life of a householder with the natural and unrestricted way of life, with the normal 'pull' of the flow of life he acquires the best way to the great solution of the question whether man is a machine with no free will or a human being with free will which he can use in all matters; and thus can create consciously his own circumstances as the master of his destiny. That is ZENOGA.

We also find that Karma is not action nor is it merely the solely Yoga of cause and effect. *If Karma is action it certainly is not the* cause which brings about an effect. It is already the effect of the main cause ! The main cause is the decoding of coded impulses, the state of the four centres and their management.

Whenever the proportions are unbalanced we have the intellectual Will or emotional or Bhakti Will, or the Haṭha or Physical Will, or Sex or artistic Will, or with minus. So, intensities the brute Will. When the total two Zenoga units are gathered at one centre, it becomes either a genius or a monster functioning in that *direction depending* on whether the intensity is plus or minus.

From this we note that this very life, this daily life of ours, this humdrum life of ours, this life we so easily condemn, this life which is routine, this life which is full of care, this life from which we would run away, this life which is so common-place, this life in which we do not even wish to discuss so-called far-away thoughts is in fact the most wonderful gift imaginable for it enables our progress to spiritual salvation combined with unfailing happiness.

The flame of a candle will not be steady where there is wind. The inherent qualities of the flame are (i) to give light, (ii) to flicker with the wind and (iii) with violent wind to go out completely. To steady this flame there are two ways : (i) put it in a quiet place free from wind; (ii) cover it and make a lamp which will regulate the wind and prevent it from flickering or going out.

If we take the former course, the flame will be steady as long as it remains there. Even if it were to remain there for a thousand years yet brought out into the open it will be subject to all the reactions of wind and could be blown out. It cannot even form a habit in those thousand years to be steady, for it is not its inherent quality to be steady. The light in that sheltered place is useless for you (however steady it may be there) whenever you need it in the open.

So is Sec. 1 of our mind. It has as its inherent qualities (1) to give 'light' i.e. cognize, (2) to move or flicker with the incoming coded impulses and decoded thoughts. To steady this Sec. 1 there are two ways: (1) to put it in a quiet place free from all incoming coded impulses, i.e. to select the life of a hermit, (2) to cover it like a lamp which regulates the wind and prevents from flickering or going out and be of use to us wherever we may be.

If we take the former course, Sec. 1 will be steady as long as it will remain there. If it were to remain there for a thousand years and if brought out into the 'open' world it will be subject to all the reactions of the incoming coded impulses and decoded thoughts. Sec. 1 cannot form a habit even in that millenium to be steady for it is not its inherent nature to be steady. The sheltered life is useless however steady the mind there could be; for life there is restricted.

If we take the other course, Sec. 1 will be steadier and useful in the life of the world. For Sec. 1 is now no more merely Sec. 1 ; it has developed contact with Sec. 2 i.e. has become like a lantern whose inherent quality is steadiness. The corrective methods, the disinfection chamber, the three-step rhythmic breathing, the change of habits of sleep, food, drink, etc. form the lantern.

Can we concentrate and how best to do this. We have noted that impulses impinge on our brain (in the respective spots or centres) at the rate of 120 per each pulse beat, and after decoding, natural selectivity and rejection, the decoded rate drops to 12 per each pulse beat. Science will certainly be able to verify this with sensitive instruments. These 12 decoded thoughts for each pulse beat create a kind of 'internal traffic'. These 12 decoded thoughts for each pulse beat start off internal messages and communications between the centres of Sec. 1. This heavy traffic keeps the nerves (= nāḍīs) congested like city roads at peak traffic hours.

There are also 'crossings' and important traffic 'junctions'. The traffic 'jam' is enormous at certain periods and at certain places. Such internal conditions create certain pathological conditions. Taking sedatives or pills or drugs does no good, though apparently they seem to reduce the pains attendant on such traffic jams. Should we study well such symptoms, we shall know from the traffic the 'patterns' or the trend of our thoughts. There are hundreds and thousands of such patterns and we add to them each day and each hour and these we play-back on our mental tape recorder from time to time. We play these patterns at different speeds and like gears we can adjust to different speeds though unlike our gears not to any speed. Twelve thoughts per each pulse beat is a high rate indeed, but such is the rate in an average person. How can we reduce this rate? What are the methods? It is very common for people to say, "I spend one hour each morning in concentration" or "I meditate each morning for one hour". We do not understand what they actually mean. There are prolonged drifts and quick drifts of the mind and still quicker interruptions which we are never able to notice because of their suddenness and great speed.

We do realise, that with our physical eyes open, we see pictures, clear lifeless pictures moving, and we honestly think that those in the pictures, really move, how much more so can invisible drifts and quick interruptions befool us! There are certain limitations inherent in the physical senses.

Thoughts are of such a tenacity that we cannot command them by our will to disappear. This would amount to sweeping a room clear of darkness with a broom. If we ever actually try to command thoughts by our will the result would be similar to the story of the king Canute and his attempt to turn the tide. We have noted the sorry state of the I. centre due to the use of will in the absence of right methods of issuing commands.

Of the 120 impulses reaching the various centres in the brain, it should be noted that it will depend on the ratio of centres, i.e. in a person with 2:4:8:2 ratio these 120 impulses will reach the respective centres in the same ratio and in case of a person with 5:2:2:1 the 120 impulses will reach the respective centres in that ratio only. So we realise that: (1) without analysis of our drifts, (2) without knowing the plus and minus resultant intensity of our centres, (3) without introducing the corrective methods, it is impossible to get any plus resultant intensity. Without collecting one Zenoga unit it is not possible to function with Sec. 2 and interconnect it with the I. centre of Sec. 1.

Till then concentration even in its rudimentary stage is not possible. Hence what is concentration and how is it done? Concentration is a single and smaller step to meditation; how can we meditate? To hold one thought for one pulse beat exclusively forms the beginning of concentration practice. Resolutions should not be made lightly, for every time we fail we become weaker and accumulate minus resultant intensity.

From the 'traffic' between the four centres and added to this, the traffic of the In. centre (No. 5 in Sec. 2), we get fifteen major junctions. There are certain pathological symptoms attendant on these fifteen junctions and one hundred and eight smaller crossings of this 'traffic'.

The incoming impulses and outgoing decoded thoughts take a certain form. Further, the incoming coded impulses have their speed in relation to the intensity of the centres concerned and to which they reach. According to their speed they race through the nerves from the coding centre to the decoding and back. In decoding and on translating these decoded thoughts to action, the relevant organs, senses, limbs are made use of.

However, it is not possible to apply corrective methods at that high speed of incoming coded impulses or even at the rate of decoded thoughts. What is then the solution? The ancient sages found the answer after long observations, and a sure method of helping the sincere aspirant was evolved. Thought, they visualised, must be confronted by "something" which should be equally subtle as the thought, the strength being in the intensity of that something. They found that in breathing, man had a certain rhythm. They found that the movements of the diaphram, the heart and the lungs like the movements of the planets had certain rhythm and ratio and balance, the whole creating some divine music. One thing is certain, that our breathing could be made more rhythmic and the timings could be improved.

The breathing rate of a normal person is 18-20 breaths per minute. There is no regularity of this rate for the breathing is faster or slower during the day or night or from day to day and this change is not consciously brought about. The practice of three step rhythmic breathing brings this rate down and keeps it constant at 12 per minute. This breathing when mastered and imposed for twenty-four hours a day, slows appreciably the decoding rate of the centres and this is brought about without using any physical will.

There are some who practise control of the vital energy and govern the subtle forces of Prāṇa and Apāna, thereby transforming their Prāṇa unto Apāna, or their Apāna unto Prāna.

Concentration is the art of controlling the impulses. These impulses are received from (1) food and drink (2) breathing (3) the sensations of sound smell, touch and sight. We have also noted the corrective methods for each. Sincere adherence to the methods and techniques shown would bring a person to the verge of the Critical-Certain-Stage. An important step is Pratyāhāra. The first four steps bring one to the bank of a river. Then there is the river and then there is the other bank. On the other bank is the master waiting for the sincere disciple to come. The disciple has after a long journey come to the bank of the river. The river we call the 'No Man's-Land' or the fifth step or Pratyāhāra.

Man has a certain pattern of behaviour. These patterns are hundreds of thousands. Thereafter, no two human beings seem to behave similarly or are similar. These patterns, however many they may be, are limited and therefore, it is possible to mathematically code these patterns, index them, and file them. After such methodical arrangement, it is like feeding a computer with certain data and expecting a certain answer: Yet, we may not damage the dignity of man nor his divinity by reducing him to a machine however complex by expounding a new theory of man being like a machine. Mathematically, however, it is clear, that these patterns if fed into a suitable machine will create certain effects. These patterns therefore, create certain behaviour or actions on the physical plane i.e. coded impulses are decoded into thought and actions. These actions are considered by man himself in a different manner or rather he looks upon these actions as inevitable and as forced results i.e. man interprets these actions as effects (which in turn become a cause), of the mental or psychological patterns which are fed into this so-called fine 'machine' as if by some 'Higher Power'.

Some view this as incorrect. The 'machine' has the liberty and has the freedom to feed in whatever patterns it would like and so control the results i.e. actions on the physical plane and therefore the results attendant thereon. There is yet another aspect where it is claimed that man is not like a computer of a high order but is actually free from all these mental or psychological patterns. He can create something new always and be responsible for it.

There are yet some more human beings who feel that there is a 'higher Power' that feeds in the patterns as this Power would divinely wish and therefore man will act according to the desire of the Divine Being; that man cannot match his will against that of the Divine Being. The consolation is, that if we accept the Divine Choice or Divine will of the Divine Being for all time to come, we shall be idling at peace in some wonderland called Heaven. Hell therefore is the price of revolt? There is yet another group that claims man is God himself, and the Supreme Architect. This leaves the whole world today as it was yesterday—in doubt. What is true? We have seen that man has also the ability to carry out functions which the advanced techniques of science today cannot match. In carrying out certain activities like breathing, which is not possible for man to do consciously, there is a method laid down for internal administration which is left to the higher centres of Sec. 1 of the brain to carry out.

To describe further; suppose we ask a friend to stand at the door and prevent certain types of persons from coming in. Your friend is sincerely helping in keeping these people out, but is himself held in bondage in attendance at the door and cannot peacefully come in and be with you. This 'friend' is like your mind within, the 'other people' are the types of impulses you want to keep out; so your mind remains engaged full-time in trying to keep these impulses from coming in i.e. instead of the bondage of indulgence of certain thoughts, you piously engage yourself in the bondage of preventing these impulses from coming in?

Sincere aspirants have found to their dismay that no sooner an attempt is made for a 'better life' than, as if from some unknown quarter of the mind, a host of thoughts rush in to suffocate this noble urge; and the aspirant is astounded that such a host of vicious thoughts ever existed within him. Some piously believe that the Lord is putting him or her to "test", never suspecting the strength of the E. and S. centres and the hundreds of thousands of thought patterns all stored within, as well as the I. centre's unmethodical approach to the whole problem ! Taking refuge in repeating a mantra or holy name or visualising a holy face might not always help in carrying out our daily life, for our mind cannot properly dwell upon both the subjects simultaneously and no sooner is the mind left to handle the worldly life, than it plays its own tricks with a venegence.

So, by putting the teachings of this book into operation, one is able to put into operation all the steps needed for the art of control of incoming impulses. Sincere practice will bring one to the verge of that Critical-Certain-Stage which forms one bank of the river. Just as a river has two banks, so the flowing river of life has also two banks. One side of the bank is the life of the aspirant (below and up to that Critical-Certain-Stage)—on the other bank, is the higher, spiritual stage of the goal of life. Crossing the river is essential in order to go over to the other side. When in the river we can decide where we shall land on the other side. This river of life is normally a very turbulent river. Crossing from one bank to another one would need a good boat and a skilful boatman. We do not normally carry a boat on our heads in expectation of having to cross a river. But on coming to the river, we needs must search for a boatsman with a boat. We can neither search for nor find a boatsman before coming to the river.

A rocket to be free from the gravitational pull of the Earth has to develop a certain speed or intensity and for a rocket to escape the gravitational pull of the Sun, the intensity or speed required would be many times more. Is this gravitational pull a devil ? Is this gravitational pull of the Earth or the Sun a smaller or bigger devil ? Is the inherent gravitational pull of the flow of life a devil ? Is such gravitational pull in an ordinary aspirant and in a Christ or a Buddha a smaller or bigger devil ? Even supposing it is a devil, how is it that till this time i.e. till the day we decide to pull off we did not realise that it was a devil for it would amount to saying that America did not exist till Columbus or Amerigo de Vispuze discovered it ? The inherent pull of the flow of life is the force that counters our efforts to be free from it, and very naturally so. We have for a long time been very friendly and in line with the same flow of life and now that we have decided to break off, naturally the parting hurts and there is even a natural tendency to hold on. This can happen between any two living beings—the bond of long association. The advanced sons of man are past this No Man's-Land and are high up on the other side. They have already overcome the 'gravitational pull' but, let us say, are still 'satellites' of the Sun. They realise their new bondage and now seek release from that. The pull is however far too intense, but these wonderful demi-gods are equal to the task. In figurative language this pull from outside is a mighty devil with great powers and the things he can offer or the weapons with which he can oppose are tempting and awful from our point of view.

The 'No Man's-Land' or pratyāhāra is the stage where an aspirant has to add two plus Zenoga units to the two already accumulated. Pratyāhāra is, therefore, a stage sufficiently long for the sincere aspirant who can continue with the methods till his rhythmic three-step breathing is perfected. The decoded thought rate keeps on diminishing till it reaches one hundred pulse beats for decoding one coded impulse. The ground is prepared for the next and very important stage of dhāraṇā (concentration), dhyāna (meditation) and samādhi (identification) i.e. the proper use of Sec. 2 of the mind which is now developed completely. This is done of course under guidance of a teacher (= Master) which the aspirant is sure to find on coming to the verge of that Critical-Certain-Stage.

On this stage, i.e. stage of pratyāhāra occurs the two-fold change :—

(1) The stage of concentration is reached or the stage where for one thousand pulse beats one coded impulse is decoded and held exclusively. This means that the energy normally wasted in decoding 12x1000 = 12,000 thoughts is preserved and the intensity of that one decoding resultant is multiplied by 12,000. This makes it possible to create intense plus resultant intensity for every 1000 pulse beats.

This charges the whole body and the important reaction resulting from such intense charging is the separating of the cellular-molecular and the molecular bodies i.e. the physical or purely cellular body (with its functions) from the higher molecular body.

(2) The intensity is high enough to break away from the inherent pull of the flow of life. To reach this stage and be able to separate these bodies and to be able to function in them separately, therefore, is the important work of this stage of pratyāhāra. For this very important stage, a master arrives to guide the sincere aspirant if he has practised all that has been shown regularly.

If he should be lucky enough to find an AVATĀRA as his Master he need in fact be compelled to do nothing at all—for in this case all worry is superfluous.

APPENDIX III

CELESTIAL INFLUENCE OR INTENSITIES OF CELESTIAL BODIES

> "The ignorant think of an Avatāra who is the unmanifested spirit as if He were really in human form. They do not understand that His supreme nature is changeless and most excellent."
>
> —*Gītā*

The planets of our solar system and their approximate size and distances from the sun are well known to all. Normally the MOON should not be considered as an independent planet by itself but as God himself. As the MOON is very close to the Earth it has therefore enormous occult influence and we can consider it as divine-in-itself. Actually the Sun and Moon are called luminaries because they shine and disperse light. Other planets have moons also and Jupiter is said to be a miniature solar system complete. In each case where a planet has a moon or moons we should consider it as one single influence together with that particular planet and not separate. Though such ordinary moons may have a considerable influence on the planet concerned, they have in relation to our Earth (due to distance) a joint, single influence.

Our Earth has no importance as a celestial influence but the North and South shadows, i.e. North and South magnetic fields have. They are important for certain effects. We can safely say that these are the known astral influences in our Solar system, known even to orthodox astrology. The group of astroids are not taken into account here.

Out and beyond our Solar system (and about twenty light years away) is the double or biniary star, SIRIUS. Of the two parts of this double star, one is bright and the other is dark. The bright is bigger and twenty-five times as bright as our Sun (and has two and half times the mass of the Sun). The dark one is smaller and is composed of matter nearly 50,000 (fifty thousand) times heavier than water (and has five-sixth of the mass of the Sun) though only 24,000 miles in diameter.

Zenoga considers the effects of these two as extremely powerful and so they cannot be left out of our final calculations. It is around the biniary star Sirius that our Sun with its planets is orbiting once in every 25,000 years, so forming the circle of the greater Zodiac.

Between fifty to seventy light years away (out and beyond our Solar system) is the first group of five important stars each about hundred to two hundred times brighter than our Sun and possessing a definite astrosophical influence.

Between seventy to two hundred light years away and beyond our Milky Way is the second group of seven important stars, each about two hundred to five hundred times brighter than our Sun and they have even more influence.

Between two thousand to five thousand light years away out and beyond our Super-Cluster is the third group of six important stars each thousands of times brighter than our Sun and having still more influence. The giant Canopus for example is about one hundred thousand times brighter than our Sun. We feel therefore that unless the effects of these nineteen additional Stars (or suns) is not included, astrology as practised is not accurate and the calculations though seemingly correct (without further taking into account the above nineteen stars) gives as an incomplete picture. The total thirty-one heavenly bodies (including the North and South shadows) have each a certain resultant intensity with its own maximum and minimum. *Due to this resultant intensity, they have a peculiar spiritual quality which determines the rate at which we evolve.*

Whenever we say 'influence' we mean the final sum total of all the influences or all the resultant-intensities plus or minus. That which increases, is plus (and 'positive' or 'good') and that which decreases is minus ('negative' or 'bad').

Each resultant intensity has certain inherent qualities like colour, texture, speed, disease, metals, chemicals, etc. Each human being is likewise influenced by celestial influences according to Astrosophy.

The resultant-intensities of persons with coinciding maximum/minimum ranges, reach the planet or the Star concerned and return to Earth. The thirty-one astrosophical bodies between them cover a wide range. This indicates either :

(1) the state of affairs prevalent in a person

(2) the celestial body with which the person has affinity at any given moment.

Of these, fourteen types are major resultant-intensity types and besides these the remaining minor types are meant for ordinary people.

Those beyond the SIRIUS twin-star we denote by simple alphabetical letters and with minus and plus signs for resultant intensity. Let us take the plus Stars from the *three groups** beyond SIRIUS. In the first group (let us call this first group of stars the 'a' group) there is one positive or plus star i.e. the first or nearest to us in that group. One negative or minus star i.e. furtherest in distance. The remaining three in between are neutrals in the sense that they give their intensity the 'colour' (or plus or minus effect) of the other predominating Star. Similar to the M. centre (in Sec. 1 of our brain) which always joins the stronger side (whether plus or minus) in the group-conflict of the three I., E., and S. centres.

Group of Stars : (b)

In the *second* group there are three positive or plus stars, three negative or minus stars and one neutral star; i.e. 1st, 2nd, 3rd are plus, 4th, 5th and 6th are minus and the seventh (= furthest away from us) is neutral.

Group of Stars : (c)

In the *third* group there are two positive or plus stars and two negative or minus stars and one neutral i.e. 1st and last are plus, 2nd and 3rd are minus, and the fourth is neutral.

Now let us first give reference to all the positive stars of all the *three* groups. In all they are six, so let us name them as A, B, C, D, E, F; and there are six minus so let us name them H, I, J, K, L, M; and there are in all five neutrals and we can name them as V, W, X, Y, and Z.

The bright star of biniary SIRIUS (which is positive in influence or plus) we may designate as G. The dark star of biniary SIRIUS (which being negative or minus) be called N. Therefore the seven Positives are viz. A, B, C, D, E, F, G and the seven Negatives are viz. H, I, J, K, L, M, N.
G. and N. include both parts of the biniary star SIRIUS, bright and dark (positive and negative).

* Thus we have group (a), group (b) and group (c).

We can further classify the above as follows :

The seven very high plus resultant intensities in relation to human centres :

1. Maximum plus rotations of the I. centre with those of the M. centre = A
2. Maximum plus rotations of the E. centre with those of the M. centre = B
3. Maximum plus rotations of the S. centre with those of the M. centre = C
4. Maximum plus rotations of the I. centre with those of the E. centre = D
5. Maximum plus rotations of the I. centre with those of the S. centre = E
6. Maximum plus rotations of the E. centre with those of the S. centre. = F
7. Maximum plus rotations of the I. centre with those of the E., S., and M. centres = G

The seven other very high minus resultant intensities in relation to human centres :

8. Maximum minus rotations of the I. centre together with those of the M. centre = H
9. Maximum minus rotations of the E. centre together with those of the M. centre = I
10. Maximum minus rotations of the S. centre together with those of the M. centre = J
11. Maximum minus rotations of the I. centre together with those of the E. centre = K
12. Maximum minus rotations of the I. centre together with those of the S. centre = L
13. Maximum minus rotations of the E. centre together with those of the S. centre = M
14. Maximum minus rotations of the I. centre together with those of the E., S., and M. centres = N

Let us not believe implicitly all that our astronomers have to say regarding our planets and stars, for the simple reason that our observations through telescopes of those celestial bodies are modified or altered by Nature's distorting outer-space, and unknown rays give us at times completely falsified pictures! Nevertheless, much good work has been done, only that it is not enough to be dependable. The planets, including our Earth, let us describe briefly.

The seven important plus resultant intensities as we have seen are:

1. Plus intensities of the I. centre
   +M. centre = A
2. Plus intensities of the E. centre
   +M. centre = B
3. Plus intensities of the S. centre
   +M. centre = C
4. Plus intensities of the I. centre
   +E. centre = D
5. Plus intensities of the I. centre
   +S. centre = E
6. Plus intensities of the E. centre
   +S. centre = F
7. Plus intensities of the I. centre
   +E., S., and M. centres = G

These are the important types and the first three are pure types. But not in the sense of clean or holy but pure inasmuch as they are unmixed types. The plus resultant intensity can be equivalent to two or four plus Zenoga units.

The 7 other important high minus intensities are:

8. Minus intensities of the I. centre plus the minus intensities of the M. centre = H
9. Minus intensities of the E. centre plus the minus intensities of the M. centre = I
10. Minus intensities of the S. centre plus the minus intensities of the M. centre = J
11. Minus intensities of the I. centre plus the minus intensities of the E. centre = K
12. Minus intensities of the I. centre plus the minus intensities of the S. centre = L
13. Minus intensities of the E. centre plus the minus intensities of the S. centre = M
14. Minus intensities of the I. centre plus the minus intensities of the E., S., and M. centres = N

The minus resultant intensity can be equivalent from two to four minus Zenoga units.

From the foregoing we note the fourteen most powerful types of human personalities with very high plus or minus intensities. They are ruled by the fourteen positive and negative stars besides our planets and luminaries. These fourteen govern the most powerful fourteen types of people on Earth. Our Sun with its family of planets also revolves round a central point (ust as all planets including the Earth revolve round the Sun) and like the Earth circles one complete orbit in about 25,000 years and so is in each house of the greater circle or Zodiac for about 2108 years. Our Earth completes its round in 365 1/4 days and we have our twelve months or the smaller circle or zodiac. Our Sun with all the planets revolves round the star SIRIUS which for our Solar system is the central point. This central point is composed of two stars (binary) viz. the bright and dark or the very high positive and the very high negative as we have noted earlier. It follows therefore that all that exists in the Solar system cannot be free from auspicious and inauspicious days; the positive or good, and the negative or bad influences basically. Our Earth is neutral but some of the planets are positive and negative in which case the influence varies from higher positive to lesser negative and from higher negative to lesser positive. Our Earth though neutral has intense magnetic and electrically charged north and south zones known as 'Shadows of the Earth'. These zones have a force equivalent to minus 25,000 rising to +25,000 resultant intensity. The other planets have their respective resultant intensity as follows :

		Intensity
1 & 2 :	*Earth* : Neutral but the areas of extreme South and North magnetic fields or 'shadows' we denote by + ES and — ES	+ 25,000 —25,000
3 :	*Moon*	+35,000 to — 40,000
4 :	*Mercury* (a purely 'plus' planet)	+ 50,000
5 :	*Venus* (a purely 'minus' planet)	—05 000

		Intensity	
6 :	*Mars*	+ 75,000 to — 75,000	
7 :	*Jupiter* (a purely 'plus' planet)	+ 1,00,000	
8 :	*Saturn* (purely minus)		—1,00,000
9 :	*Uranus* (purely plus)	+ 75,000	
10 :	*Neptune* (purely minus)		— 75,000
11 :	*Pluto*	+ 10,000 to — 10,000	
12 :	*SUN*	half a plus Zenoga unit	

90% to 95% of humanity having their intensities within this range are firmly governed and affected by the above planets and react to them accordingly. Rarely do the influences of the other 19 stars come in and then we witness the ruling personalities, for such persons are the 'ruling types' who make history, civilization, culture, religion, or bring about misery, wars, destruction; peace or chaos, scientific progress or dictatorship by the help of science etc. etc. We shall describe briefly these fourteen important types; as five of them are neutral we shall only give their intensities. Then we shall also examine the intensities of the planets including the luminaries, Sun and Moon, who rule the average type of individual everywhere.

I (A) :

The I. and M. centres are at a high plus (between half to one Zenoga-Unit each) and the E. and S. centres a few thousand each only i.e. the I. and M. is at a 150,000,000,000 plus each which equals one Zenoga-Unit and therefore practically amounts to inhibiting the other centres. Such a person is intellectually obsessed. He has an immense ego, can be easily insulted or befriended by praise, pays no attention to details, yet sometimes shows an unnecessary attention to trifles. Prone to be very eccentric. Is a genius but purely intellectual and literary. Could be a great mathematician, astronomer, biologist, research student of the atom and a fine linguist or scholar having command over several languages. The poor development of the E. centre deprives such a person of real warmth or gratitude. The poor development of the S. centre makes this person over-pragmatic or materialistic with a sceptical approach to God, Soul and similar Spiritual subjects.

2 (*B*) :

The E. centre and the M. are at high plus intensity; half to one Zenoga-Units each while the S. centre is at a low of a few thousand only and the I. centre not much better. Highly emotional people; fanatics in all walks of life, people who think they are always right and sincerely believe it. To whatever they do they attach all emotional vigour. Such people could also be dangerous because they tolerate no opposition, though basically good and well meaning. Great social workers, religious leaders are typical. The S. centre not being high, energy is not brought in to bear on the pressing problems but only on whatever 'appeals' most; they do what is considered right, are selfless, and do not exploit situations for their own advantage. They appear to be heartless in their dealings at some times and over-tender at others.

3 (*C*) :

The S. centre and M. centre are at high plus intensity (between half to one Zenoga-Units each) and the E. and I. centres at a low of a few thousand only. Students of medicine who grasp more by intuition than by laborious methods; very intelligent and engrossed in research in biology. Geniuses in the field of medicine and biology. The I. though in comparison to S. centre seems low but is quite satisfactory. The E. being low, such a person is not warm-hearted and can be eccentric; could be impractical in life, rather absent-minded but adept in many other branches of science. Could often be like Dr. Jekyb and Mr. Hyde, having a split personality.

4 (*I'*) :

This is a fine combination. The genius plus the artist, unlike the preceding unmixed types, which are really undesirable because they could be fanatics or eccentrics due to their one-sided development. These are the people who give the world something new in every field. The E. and I. centres are each half to one plus Zenoga-Units and the M. centre has a plus of a few thousand while the S. centre has a few thousand more. These people have their own rhythm and are very pleasing and fascinating. The great sculptors, painters, musicians, poets and writers; the designers, the publicity people with extremely new ideas, the fashion creation artists (not the counterfeit type). The philosophers and theologians though not of the arm-chair class. They are not impractical or misfits in the world of action and earn great honours in whatever fields they engage themselves. They are usually (though of-course *not* always) born in April.

5 (*E*) :

This is another rare combination which does not fail to leave behind a permanent mark of greatness. The I. centre is brought to the S. centre while the S. centre is sublimated (sex as sex is not known). Sex as sex is wholly absent and is the pure creative genius especially in architecture. The Taj Mahal at Agra (India), the famous Cathedrals, Mosques and Temples and stupendous achievements like the Pyramids and Sphinx are examples, also the modern bridges, dams, underground tunnels and canals like the Suez and the Panama. All wonderful works both modern and ancient. The I. and S. centres are each half to one (plus) Zenoga-Unit and M. has a few thousand plus intensities and E. a few thousand more. Not cold, but indifferent; not aloof but prefer to be occupied by their own thoughts! —Introspective.

6 (*F*) :

This is a potentially dangerous combination, but as in no centre the intensity is high minus the danger is not acute; otherwise it would be devastating as we shall examine later on. The S. and E. centres have each half to one Zenoga-Unit and M. is a few thousand 'plus' but, the I. is a few thousands more *minus*. These people shake the world to its foundations. All world conquerers, founders of empires and dynasties, pioneers and travellers, and voyagers like Columbus and Dr. Livingstone conquerers of the class of Caesar, Napolean, Alexander. Founders like William

I and men like Drake, Sir Walter Raleigh. Could be deeply religious and, if the I. centre is not minus, could produce men like Martin Luther. Usually the intensities are tinged by a little minus of the I. centre.

7 (*G*) :

Such people lead fine lives and do great honour to mankind. The resultant intensities are over four plus Zenoga-Units. The first four centres are almost in the 5:2:2:1 ratio and hence they produce our saints. These people are able to function on the molecular plane and to a certain extent on the electronic plane as well. These are the advanced souls who fill up day by day the angelic kingdom in Nature and who are immersed in prayer and are in the God-intoxicated state and are also in possession of great occult powers. They have earned free-will in all matters and such free-will is safe in their hands. Here the only imperfection is that their salvation is not yet perfect for which they strive hard and finally proceed to the ideal stage.

7 (*G*) (*a*) :

These people are able to function freely on the molecular plane and to a great extent on the electronic plane. Their molecular bodies are completely formed and their electronic bodies are also partly formed. The Sec. 3 of their mind is fully formed and Sec. 4 is also functioning. They can transcend many of the physical laws. Some long cycles of return of past minus resultant intensity left over brings over diseases and pain into their lives; of course in their present advanced stage they welcome it and do not feel the pain arising from it. Such persons are rare and work quietly all the world over in every country and are born in all ages and are aware of each other. They are also called Masters.

7 (*G*) (*b*) :

These are still greater lives and perhaps the highest stage in which man can function on this earth in his physical body and the centres work in the ratio of 5:2:2:1 and are high in plus Zenoga-Units. Such are the prophets or Avatāras. They can function on the physical, dellular-molecular, molecular, and electronic planes freely. They can also function simultaneously in them and make use of Sections 1, 2, 3 and 4 of the mind simultaneously. They can transcend the physical laws and also the laws of the Solar system. Whenever they manipulate the laws prevalent in inter-solar-planes, we on earth are amazed and interpret their functioning as miracles. They are able to exercise all laws of the electronic plane and make these laws precipitate results on the physical plane ,and can precipitate them much faster, i.e. give faster results because of the inherent immense speed of the electronic plane.

They create their own circumstances and fulfil their destiny but they do so *as if* they accept a destiny over which they have no control. They are free from the gravitational pull of life on this earth. Such persons can be truly called Earth's representatives in the inter-planatary and inter-solar realms.

The first six types have a total of one to two Zenoga-Units and are persons who stand on the brink of that Critical-Certain-Stage. These are the great ones who make our history, our literature, our science, our architecture, and mould our thoughts in thousand and one different ways. They appear as children of destiny and seem to be born for great events. They have a great personality with hypnotic effects on others. But, as they have not yet crossed the 'No Man's-Land' as yet they have no equilibrium in their Zenoga-Units. Thus all such great men are actually 'small' men ! They do not or are not able to use their free-will on all occasions for good or otherwise, though seemingly they parade on the stage of our world as if they are masters of their destiny. Actually they make fatal mistakes and take fatal decisions which undo them in the end. They forget frequently that they have not crossed the 'No Man's-Land' and when they forget this, they turn away from their mission and we see the end of such 'great lives when minus intensity makes an entry. The seventh is a graded stage of candidatio master, master, and the prophet stage.

8 (*H*) :

This is exactly the opposite of 1 (A).A great master criminal who believes in quick thinking and quick moving. Suffering from an immense ego (which is very natural because he is highly intelligent), he thinks he has good reasons to bear a grudge against his nation, or his nation's head or government or against a great industrial combine, and he will apply immense energy to make very quick movements from place to place in order to enlist help or support for his cause or to defeat his adversary. Never noble in defeat and even more ignoble in triumph! His ego, unbending pride, worship of self, are the main weaknesses from which arise many other weaknesses such as torturing his rivals and adversaries. A dangerous enemy and an unreliable friend. The I. and M. centres each have half to one *minus* Zenoga-Unit, the E. centre a few thousand minus and the S. has a few minus thousands more.

9 (*I*) :

This is exactly the opposite of 2 (B). The E. and the M. centres are high *minus* half to one Zenoga-Units each and the S. at a low of few thousand minus intensity and the I. a few thousand *minus* more. Highly emotional and fanatical great persecutors and like those whose motto is "revenge is sweet". All religious persecutions are directly due to such people all over the world. Not the least bit truly religious themselves, they take an animal delight in persecution; even in their political persecutions it is equally true that they are no more patriotic than others but their fierce nature gives them the tendency to mislead.

10 (*J*):

This is exactly the opposite of 3 (C). The S. centre and the M. is at high *minus* (between half to one Zenoga-Unit) and the E. at a low few thousand whereas the I. centre has a few thousand minus intensities more. These are horrible people. They trade in sex and debase young boys and girls and divert them to the wrong path of drug addiction. They do immense damage all over the world. Never are they satisfied in their baser sex instincts and stop at nothing. What they are capable of and what they do, is not possible to describe in a book like this.

11 (*K*) :

This is exactly the opposite of 4 (D). This is a fearful combination. The genius plus the beast! The I. and the E. centres are each half to one *minus* Zenoga-Units and the M. has a few thousand minus and the S. even more minus intensities. Lower types of emotions, added to ego, unbending pride, worship of self. Here we have a dreadful personality, but perhaps for reasons best known to God, such people are allowed to work devastation on mankind to fulfil mass resultant karma of peoples and nations. They have criminal tendencies, are master international crooks. They Subdue other people and make them carry out their sinister plans for self-glorification. They exploit national and international situations.

12 (*L*) :

This is exactly the opposite of 5 (E). These are pure criminals of all types, are very intelligent and often belong to learned faculties. The I. and S. centres are each half to one *minus* Zenoga-Units and the M. has a few thousand *minus* intensities and the E. centre even more so. Murder and sex is more common to them than is eating and sleeping to ordinary men. They have no scruples.

13 (*M*) :

This is exactly the opposite of 6 (F). This is a terrible combination. We have those who deal in narcotics, tranquilisers, opium, illegal distillation, circulation of sex and pornographic nude pictures, or production and printing of nude pictures, printing and circulation of all subversive activities which undermine the goodness of man and his moral fibre. Sex and emotions are introduced through dance and music which sway the lower, animal passions of men and women, especially the young who are in the age of puberty (or teenagers) and we say that today this is spreading like wild-fire in all countries. Such a person is like the atom; he can destroy utterly but like the atom if harnessed (as in atoms for peace) he would usher in the golden age. This is the golden opportunity in our age for all nations of the world today. The whole world is under this combination and should understand the opportunity. Instead of going down under its pressure and becoming slaves man could become real superman. The E. and S. centres are each half to one *minus* Zenoga-Units, the M. has a few thousand minus and the I. a few thousand minus intensities more.

14 (*N*) :

This is exactly the opposite of 7 (G), (a) and (b) in varying grades. The total minus Zenoga-Units are over two minus and all the four centres are very active. The meanest, basest, moral cowards; and if history be true, then we have the Gestapo Chiefs, Aurangzeb who did not hesitate to act as he felt best against his father and his own brothers as well as towards others. Reckless people like Hitler and Stalin, dreadful people like Atila the Hun, the plotters of Pearl Harbour. Rulers who were debauched; Jenghis Khan and his treatment of foes; the reverse of evolution in every age. If these people had a plus combination instead of a minus they would have been the pride of the human race. They cannot do good even by mistake. Very selfish and heartless, nothing is too evil for them in order to fulfil their ends. The only redeeming feature is their cowardice, otherwise they would do much greater evil ! They pretend to lead a religious life and hide behind this mask many awful characteristics. They have great magnetic and hypnotic powers.

The remaining five neutrals have the natural resultant maximum-minimum intensity of their own but like clear glass take the colour that is visible; or more like the M. centre which merely adds to the final score and makes it more minus or more plus as the case may be. Their intensities and tendencies to influence centres is also shown; as these are neutrals, their intensities are shown as from minus to plus, minimum to maximum.

V	±	half to one Zenoga-Unit	I. and M.
W	±	upto half to one Zenoga-Unit	E. and M.
X	±	between half to one Zenoga-Unit	S. and E.
Y	±	between one to one-and-half Zenoga-Units	S. and M.
Z	±	upto one-and-half Zenoga-Units	I., S., M., and E.

From this we find that :

I	1 (A) and 8H are equal and opposite to group a of the stars	
II	2 (B) and 9I are equal and opposite to group b	,,
III	3 (C) and 10J are equal and opposite to group b	,,
IV	4 (D) and 11K are equal and opposite to group b	,,
V	5 (E) and 12L are equal and opposite to group c	,,
VI	6 (F) and 13M are equal and opposite to group c	,,
VII	7G and 14N are equal and opposite to Star (a & b) Sirius biniary Star	

This gives us *seven* clear twin streams of energies of vibrations of two diametrically opposite types reciprocal to each other containing high magnetic, electric, cosmic, and radio-active currents which sweep the whole galaxy; i.e. galaxy in which our solar system is one of the billions. This galaxy is 60,000 light years in diameter and 10,000 light years in 'depth' that is to say: like a coin horizontally placed but slightly tilting.

The reader might question how only a few suns within a small distance from our Earth could be responsible for these seven twin streams of energies which pervade the whole galaxy. It is not so. It is the other way round. Right from the depth of the galaxy and beyond there rise these seven twin streams of energies typically the same in their effects as enumerated above but highly concentrated. The deeper we go in the galaxy the more potent is the concentration of the force of these vibrations of intensities.

There are *seven* principal centres in the galaxy which step down the intense resultant intensity of these twin streams lower and lower. At the present stage these streams find the centres of distribution in the suns we have roughly indicated. Let us call these the *outer* centres of distribution. No human being is able to take or absorb these twin seven streams of force even in their next higher intensities. These twin seven-streams of force are *further* much reduced in intensity by those centres which are *within* our Solar system; these *seven* points of distribution we call the *inner* centres of distribution. They redistribute in such a way that even average people can absorb those seven twin streams of energies of force from the planets. Aspirants of Zenoga beyond the Critical-Certain-Stage can absorb directly from the *outer* points of distribution. The *inner* points of redistribution are :

1. Our Sun in relation to Sirius the biniary star.
2. The MOON in relation to group (a) positive and negative.
3. Mercury & Venus in relation to group (b) positive and negative.
4. Earth's S. & N. magnetic fields to group (b) positive and negative.
5. Neptune & Uranus in relation to group (b) positive and negative.
6. Mars & Pluto in relation to group (c) positive and negative.
7. Jupiter & Saturn in relation to group (c) positive and negative.

There is a much greater, hidden, and unknown esoteric meaning in these seven twin streams of energy of force than meets the eye. They feed our Sun and in turn are able to feed us and so they feed many other far-away Suns which in their turn feed their systems of planets. Man is not alone in this vast creation nor is he conscious of all in cosmos. These streams of force of energy are able to revitalize a being if known methods are followed and in fact do sustain the molecular and the electronic bodies.

In the *Gita* (Chapter XI) the Cosmic-Mind gives a glimpse to *Arjuna* of the molecular and electronic planes and the understanding of God at that stage but *Arjuna* (in his amazement not being able to understand) blurts out in his own language and understanding :

> "Could a hundred thousand suns blaze forth together it would be but a faint reflection of the radiance of the Cosmic-Mind. O ! Almighty God ! I see in Thee the powers of Nature, the various creatures of the world, the progenitor on his lotus throne, the sages and the shining angels. I see Thee infinite in form, with as it were faces, eyes and limbs everywhere; no beginning, no middle, no end; O Thou Lord of the Universe, *whose form is Universal* ! If the Avatara is so great, how much more must the MAHA-AVATARA be !"

But what is the use of discussing all this for it could be treated by the present undeveloped race of man as so much fiction. Man, 'wise' as he is or as he thinks he is needs to unlearn all that he knows and like a child should begin his studies once again, this time using the proper way to learn whatever Mighty Nature and God has to teach him. But let us end at that.

Take this thought for serious thinking, "What other conscious forms could there be in creation ? Of the total number of forms on earth there is no counting, surely Nature is not so bankrupt as to be 'empty' in the mighty space around us."

In our days of the inter-planetary rocket, the satellite and interplanetary travel, we find that the purpose of all this experimentation is urged or motivated by man's inherent drive to be free from bondage, whatever the bondage may be. Certain nations have tried and have achieved their freedom, and other nations more free, find themselves in bondage to this earth and so we see their repeated attempts show how very determined they are to be free.

Today, most nations are trying to be free from the domination of another nation. Other nations struggle to maintain that freedom. There will come a stage when political freedom will not be in danger and man will struggle to be free from emotional bondage. At a much later stage will come a time when people everywhere will struggle for freedom from sex bondage and finally in a very distant future people will struggle to be free from intellectual bondage. In short, they will, over a very long period of time, succeed in creating the inside harmony of the centres of Section 1 of brain and mind.

Now, what is the actual purpose behind this urge ? There are many and mixed motives (many honest and some perverted) behind this urge to reach outer space. One of the many is research, the natural curiosity of man to know what are the contents on the surface and under the surface of other planets. On the data collected, the decision could be taken to land space-ships for further research and to return safely to Earth. When that stage is reached then only will a human go with the space-ship and the crew will be highly trained and specialised.

Men will depend on sensitive instruments for recording many things. These instruments will record besides other things, pressure, temperature, atmospheric conditions, gravitational pull, contents within planets of certain metals and chemicals. These sensitive instruments will react to chemicals, metals, magnetic, cosmic, and radio-active rays, etc.

Suppose, we were to say, "Oh, the poor instruments, how excited they are and how they react !" Such a statement will be viewed as coming from a mind that is not sane ! Each human being contains within his body substances which emit chemical, metallic, magnetic, cosmic and radio-active rays ! These rays emitting from one human being fall on another human being when they come in proximity just as a space-ship comes in proximity to a certain planet for study and research. Further, the human body has extremely sensitive instruments, a few of the gross ones being our senses and our centres besides others. Our sensitive instruments, therefore, react and the readings recorded by human sensitive instruments are not interpreted as 'readings' but are called *emotions* or human behaviour patterns.

Such readings (i.e. human behaviour patterns) give vital information as in the case of the sensitive instruments within a space-ship but in the case of a human being we come to the conclusion that the behaviour of a particular human being is good or bad and from such data we theorise as to what is good and what is evil. If only human reactions could be treated as readings of certain instruments within the human body and traced to these instruments for study then we would very easily be able to solve most of our psychological problems.

The rays which are given out by planets or stars or suns and which our future space-ships will record on their sensitive instruments carried by them are capable of being recorded and will record even on some sensitive instrument on our planet without being confined to a space-ship. It is also possible for a human being, who is equipped by God and Nature with super sensitive perception within the human frame, to record accordingly !

Astrology (and/or palmistry) as practised all over the world today is incomplete. Not that we infer that the sciences of palmistry and astrology by themselves are incomplete. Yet we find that some events do occur in keeping with the readings of these sciences as practiced today. From this has arisen an erroneous conception and interpretation of predestination.

We have noted that an average person is below that Critical-Certain-Stage and is more like man the machine, than like man the human being. In cases of such people the rays emanating from the few planets of our Solar system (as known and practised by present astrology and palmistry) have a certain effect and give us the idea of each planet having its own minus or plus resultant intensity due to the same coding and decoding methods as in man.

These effects impinge on the super sensitive instruments within a human being. These coded impulses, in a person below the Critical-Certain-Stage, enter into a very mismanaged and chaotic inner state when a 'disinfection chamber' or the three-step rhythmic breathing or corrective methods and other disciplines are missing. In that case they evoke certain reactions automatically and so create a set kind of thought-decoding which makes man only a machine or makes him act in a particular manner only with certain defects attendant thereto; and this can be correctly and mathematically worked out.

Arjuna said, "My Lord ! verily, the mind is fickle and turbulent, obstinate and strong, yea extremely difficult to control" The Almighty replied, "Doubtless, O Arjuna the mind is fickle and exceedingly difficult to restrain, but O Arjuna *with practice* and renunciation it can be done. It is not possible to attain Self-Realisation if a man does not know how to control himself but for him who, *striving by proper means*, learns such control, it is possible."

The more a man is in the 'machine' state, the more are even trifling acts influenced by 'Fate' and so the theory of predestination gains further momentum. All average (or below that Critical-Certain-Stage) persons have either a low plus (or worse, even minus) resultant intensity and so they are within the range of the law of the rhythm of Numbers. Such persons cannot but be affected by the astrological influences of the heavens, caused by the individual intensities of the planets concerned. There are only a few planets whose resultant intensity is equivalent to that of the Critical-Certain-Stage and there are certainly no planets in our Solar system whose resultant intensity is above that of the Critical-Certain-Stage and, therefore, for those persons in the higher spiritual stage and beyond, these planets seem to have no effect on them because such beings, like rockets, are free from the 'gravitational' pull of the flow of life. They are also free from the pull of the planets in the Solar system but are in bondage to and are affected by other Stars or Suns or Solar systems just beyond our Solar system and these Stars and Suns have a range of intensity up to two Zenoga-Units (plus or minus) and over. Thus we shall find that there are Stars and Suns in creation with all grades of intensity.

The difference between our planets and these Stars and Suns and Solar systems outside our Solar system is that such Stars and Suns sweep enormous distances and re-appear at enormous intervals and so predestination occurs in a very few instances and, that too, only because such persons deliberately work out and create their own destiny. (E.g. Avataras).

To be more precise and to summarise what we have said:

1. Most of our planets are below half (plus or minus) a Zenoga-Unit of resultant intensity and have a corresponding minimum to maximum range.
2. Persons below that Critical-Certain-Stage fall within a mini-or Maximum range that is equivalent to below half a (plus or minus) Zenoga-Unit.
3. The law of harmony of Numbers, therefore, brings about a certain interplay between planetary influence and such people on Earth.
4. The planets singly and in conjunction have many combinations of effects resulting in various actions and reactions on persons below the Critical-Certain-Stage.
5. The chaos within an average person causes, in the absence of any method or technique of internal discipline, a situation which amounts to feeding certain data into a computer and getting a preset result at will.
6. An average person has not reached a stage where, of his own free-will and choice, he would like to create certain unpleasant conditions with a view to equalise some minor or major past (pre-natal) minus resultant intensity, i.e. causes brought over from the past awaiting karmic fulfilment in this life.
7. In such a case it is, therefore, left to God or karma (=Nature, or Natural laws) to see that these are imposed.
8. This means, therefore, that predestination *has* to be so in

the case of persons below that Critical-Certain-Stage and is less and less applicable till the person crosses over to higher spiritual states. After that the consciously *self-evolving human being* has evolved sufficiently to take care of himself or herself. Free will as ever, is possible in all matters big and small yet will be as wisely, judiciously and consciously as far as *this* world is concerned.

9. It is not true, therefore, that (i) *all* human beings are machines and that there is *no* free will but only predestination. (ii) It is not true that those not above a certain stage cannot come up to that stage to be free from bondage. (iii) It is also not true that once free from the Earth or human limitations there is no further limitation in varying grades. (iv) It is true that, like truth (which is relative or varying and depends on the enlightened or otherwise state of a person), the exercise of free will is relative or in direct proportion to the rate of resultant intensity.

Exercise :

Make a chart of all the known planets in our Solar system. Then try to imagine these planets going round in their orbits with you sitting on top of this planet Earth. Then visualise the same movement from a point away and below our Solar system and see our Solar system also recede away; and now try to visualise from a point away and *above* our Solar system and see our Solar system also approach nearer. Repeat for many, many days and then try to put on paper in words or pictures whatever you see.

APPENDIX IV

WHAT HAPPENS TO THE RESULTANT INTENSITY FINALLY

(Or the Rhythm of Reincarnation)

That space is full of forces which are unknown to us, and that living beings emit radiations or effluvia of which we are not aware, are facts which science must soon accept. Today, modern science knows that everything—even a cabbage—*both* receives and gives off waves of resultant energy and so it would be far more fantastic to disregard this observable phenomena in our study of mental influences than to accept the magnetic fluid theory of Mesmer. We have seen that 'resultant intensity' can be either high or low plus, or zero, or high or low minus.

What happens to the resultant intensity at the time of death? What happens to hundreds of thousands of thought patterns? If it is so far proved that Nature destroys nothing but changes one form of energy into another. Can we not expect this of the accumulation of resultant intensity and resultant patterns? The resultant minus or plus intensity is at times equal to some Zenoga units (or a fraction of it) while maintaining the needed ratio of balance between the five centres : I., E., S., M. On the other hand, it may be only I. or E. or M. or S. (minus or plus) intensity *without* the needed ratio between them.

Whatever it is, whether plus or minus, this intensity is energy. As energy, it cannot be destroyed and so it must change form or re-appear again somewhere in some form or it may be projected to somewhere on our planet or in some form away from our planet or may be projected to some distant planet and recalled. If it remains on earth it must remain in some form or another.

"There was never a time when I was not, nor thou, (O Arjuna) nor these princes were not! There will never be a time when we shall cease to be. As the soul experiences, in this body, infancy, youth and old age, so finally it passes into another. The wise have no delusion about this. Those external relations that come and go, they are not permanent; the hero whose soul is unmoved by circumstances, who accepts pleasure and pain with equanimity, only he is fit for immortality. The spirit which pervades all that we see, is imperishable. The material bodies which this Eternal, Indestructible, Immeasurable Spirit inhabits are all finite. I have been born again and again, from time to time; thou too, O Arjuna ! My births are known to me, but thou knowest not thine !"

In the same way the hundreds of thousands of thought patterns are also very minute energy impulses; 10,38,800 impulses is the smallest possible quotient in a normal man. These patterns, according to the state of the person's resultant intensity, form a fraction of the total sum of energy flowing from the I., E., or S. centres. Energy cannot be destroyed and the same process holds good as in the case of resultant intensity viz. that this energy if it should remain on Earth must change its form, or be projected, or after being projected, be recalled. In the meantime what happens to the body ? It returns to its elements. Can, in the same way, the resultant intensity and the resultant thought-patterns be said to return to their elements ? What are *their* elements ? We have seen that the planets of the Solar system, sun, or moon and the other Suns in our galaxy have a certain minus or plus inherent resultant intensity and also a range 'maximum-to-minimum' for such resultant intensity whether minus or plus.

Now in comparison to the life of a man these suns and planets exist for a very long duration and they can be considered as both the source and recipients of those minus or plus resultant intensities. We may thus very well expect that the resultant intensity as well as the resultant patterns, both together, go to their respective sources. As the resultant (plus or minus) intensity is composed of the same energy, as the thought-patterns, both go together at first !

The accumulated plethora of thought-patterns keep on revolving at a particular rate, within a certain range, and differ only a little in their rate of vibration from that of the accompanying Resultant-Intensity. Once outside the body (or corpse) of an individual, and thus free from the restricting influences of psycho-spiritual cohesion and adhesion, they so to say spread out a little. This is what is called the 'desire body' of the individual. The thought-patterns can function on the cellular-molecular plane; on the other hand, the Resultant (minus or plus)-Intensity is but a 'speck' of no significance unless a certain minimum of power has been gained. Once over this minimum it gains momentum in geometric-ratio rapidity (=2, 4, 16, etc.). High plus intensity of any type magnifies this speck however insignificant and once over half a Zenoga unit the Resultant-Intensity reaches very big proportions. *This enlargement is known as the Mental body*, which is not a very correct description. It is actually the 'wisdom body' of the individual which can function on the electronic plane.

We have seen that even a high *minus* resultant intensity has a personality and power of its own but even though the minus resultant intensity be as high as one or two Zenoga units it will have no 'Mental' body because the Resultant-Intensity remains a mere speck, for it has not the required minimum over which alone begins the increase in geometric rapidity; and therefore, such a minus or negative force is not able to function on the electronic plane but is only able to function on the cellular-molecular or molecular planes along with its respective thought-patterns.

Now all the while it is possible to locate, trace and find out by various methods both scientific and para-scientific that every 'planet' (sun, moon or star) sends out rays not necessarily known as light but could be magnetic, radioactive, cosmic, or undetectable. What are these rays if not the receiving and sending forth of the above mentioned Resultant-Intensity and accompanying thought-patterns back to earth i.e. maintaining a harmonious and inter-dependent traffic between all the planets (moon, suns, and stars) in our Solar system as also in 'the whole' galaxy !

This is in ratio dependent on :

1) The distance of the planet from the Earth;
2) Its speed of rotation on its own axis;
3) The speed of its revolutions round its centre point;
4) Its mass (and satellites);
5) Its own total of (plus or minus) resultant intensity.

Based on this particular formula, known only to Avataras and Masters, we can arrive at the calculations of the period of cycles i.e., the time required for released Resultant-Intensity and karmic Bardo thought-patterns to go and return to Earth.

Dependent on these cycles, which can be short or long, is the time required for the Resultant (plus or minus) Intensity of the individual to reach the respective sun, moon, star or planet and return to Earth in the form of re-birth called Sidpa-Bardo. When the Resultant-Intensity together with the thought-patterns of the individual returns to Earth, it gathers the necessary 'earth' or physical elements to function once again on this planet.

The fluid of life is everywhere in all creation and is not only peculiar to earth but greatly varying for each planet or sun in intensity; basically it remains the same as one great ocean in all creation. Whenever the Resultant-Intensity (along with total karma = called thought-patterns) returns to earth and gathers the necessary physical elements the 'life-fluid' soaks in, because for hundreds of miles around each 'planet' (sun, moon or star) it is potentially there.

The essence, gross or fine, of each individual at the time of so-called death returns to the respective Centre Point of revolutions of the 'planet' concerned. In the case of our Solar system it is the Sun. Each of these i.e. moon, planets, sun, stars, follow fixed and immutable laws; and so also the Resultant-Intensity and karmic patterns of each individual and so also the gross or fine essences which are together at the time of birth and death.

When any two of the three factors are missing, there is no life or movement as life. (1) Resultant-Intensity, (1a) Thought-Patterns, (2) Life (3) Gross or Fine Essence.

Derivation of the Zenoga-Reincarnation Formula :

To recapitulate the notation let us suppose an individual called Mr. Smith died at the age of 100 (years) and let X be the number of years after which he could be reborn (X can never be less than one). Further :

g = actual rate of GROWTH of Smith's Resultant-Intensity

K = Karma of the world where Smith lived (= Earth's total karma)

W = Propensity of Smith's thought-patterns

L = Smith's Lifespan (= e.g. : 100 years)

S = the distance of the planet to which Smith's R-I and T-P must go.

r = the above planet's speed of rotation on its own axis.

p = the speed of the above planet's revolutions round it's centre point

gs = the square-root of its mass (including that of its satellites)

v = the planet's own R-I.

RI = the Resultant-Intensity of the (deceased) Smith.

TP = Smith's thought-patterns.

We state first, the basic equation

$$gK = wLK \div s(1-r)\ pk-(1-s)\ (g-gs)\ kv\ rpK$$

If we now work it out all through to obtain 'g' we might get :

$$g = wL\ sp\ (1-S)\ (rp\ gsv-gv).$$

$$R\text{-}I = wL\ sp; \quad TP = (RI + gL)w.$$

$$V = \frac{s/r-s}{1-S}$$

$$X = \frac{v(gk-p) + v(gk-RI)s\ p(w-TP)si + (TP-gs)^2-(K\ L)^2}{\sqrt{\frac{S}{1-S} \cdot \frac{g}{pv-gL}}}$$

∴ X = 50 f (rotations of the Earth around its own centre point, the Sun =) years.

Thus the ex-carnating Smith will be re-incarnated no earlier than 50 f, not later than 1014, years after his demise.

The planet to which his R-I and T-P had to go was then Pluto (about 5 Light-hours away from here). All figures approximately only.

Life and essence have their own intensity also ! From this we see that the meaning of Heaven, Judgment, Hell and various Bardos, i.e. states or planes, will take a different meaning. When all the three, i.e. (1) Resultant-Intensity & thought-patterns, (2) Life and (3) Gross or Fine Essence of the individual are together present inside the earthly or physical elements which form the shape of the human body (or any other conscio-body, down and along the line) there is a particular type of limitation and pain consciousness, experienced. Pain especially is registered by earth or physical elements when gross or fine essence along with life enters and draws the first breath to start the mechanism.

So what does happen to the Resultant-Intensity ? No one knows perhaps ! Perhaps it all dies with the body and is no more ! But it is different from the body. It is distinct from the body. It is composed of a substance much rarer than ether. It is in fact much more important than anything else for it is able by its resultant to influence the incoming coded impulses and translate them into decoded thoughts. It is not thinking itself but the medium of influence on thinking.

What will happen to the accumulated, hard-earned *plus* intensities ? It is not part of an earthly estate which one can bequeath to children and depart.

The Resultant is cardexed and filed in God's wonderful filing and cardexing system. If this is filed somewhere by Nature it cannot be filed for all time to come, for then it would be better to destroy it earlier.

But what are we assuming ? Who is this person about whom we are talking ? Is he not dead ? What part of that man exists which we call that person ? That part of a person we call the Resultant-Intensity is not the same as the gross essence and both do not or cannot die with the body on earth. This gross essence cannot be destroyed by anyone, save itself. This gross essence was created by Nature not to be destroyed for it was created as a self-evolving substance with a very great amount of consciousness and with a potential for very great growth. This gross essence can only destroy itself by transforming itself into the subtle or fine essence and so becoming dead to itself and its state of gross essence !

This gross essence is a kind of 'Junior Managing Director' and the whole mechanism is under his jurisdiction till four plus Zenoga units are gathered as the Resultant-Intensity. After that the gross essence becomes the subtle or fine essence and comes under the jurisdiction of the Senior Managing Director. This evolving, conscious essence, and its Resultant-Intensity in man, therefore, go on evolving from one stage to another ! All Evolution is God-Ideation.

It follows, therefore, that if one body is dead the essence and its Resultant-Intensity seek another body to proceed with the work. It follows, therefore, that, to proceed with the work, they must take several bodies one after the other. This they do by obeying (though in early stages being forced to obey) certain laws. This presupposes that every time they take a body the beginning Resultant-Intensity is the same as the Resultant-Intensity when passing out of the body on the previous occasion. This also works out therefore, that the Resultant takes up the same symptoms, circumstances, environment, achievement, growth, emotions, intellect, sex (according to sex control) habits, corrective or non-corrective methods of the previous occasion or incarnation.

It would, therefore, take a body that is possible of this combination from a parent anywhere on this planet of two or more billion human beings. If it has to select this beginning commensurate with the Resultant-Intensity which is the same as the previous ending Resultant-Intensity, the question of heredity and unnatural inequality imposed by another power on human beings does not arise for the gross essence and the Resultant-Intensity are constantly evolving. The gross essence is on the way, through many such lives to become subtle essence.

If this is so, the whole process of repetitions till the purpose is achieved is free and governed by the proper use of the free will of man. It is also the use of free will of man whether he decides to remain like a machine. If the analysis is not done daily, if the corrective methods are not applied, if the coded impulses are not subjected to the disinfection chamber and if free will is not exercised in the basic functions of eating, breathing, sleep and sex etc. then neither God nor Nature is able to force their will on him; for then it would immediately mean the denial of free-will even though it may be in his own interests.

No destiny, just or unjust, is forced on man. Let man honestly ask God or Nature to take away this prerogative of free-will that is given him, and God or Nature would immediately take such a man in hand and see that he progresses. This is called resignation to the Divine Will and in fact even though such a person be amidst normal life, it amounts to real renunciation of action : this is Right Surrender.

Once the Resultant-Intensity goes beyond the required plus range it cannot return to this planet. This is termed *Moksha* or freedom from the gravitational pull of the flow of life as known on this planet ! As long as this resultant intensity is between a certain maximum-minimum the Resultant-Intensity together with thought patterns will karma-bound return to our planet in set cycles. This is termed reincarnation. The last departing Resultant Intensity and the karmic patterns of the incoming or the next life are always in a specific ratio to their parallel qualities (=*vāsanās*) and Constitution (=Vāsanā) of psychospiritual forces.

When the Resultant-Intensity goes beyond the earth's measure, we have seen that it cannot return. This is freedom from life and birth as is understood on our planet. The ocean of life is present in all creation and as such there can be no absolute *Moksha* or freedom from the 'gravitation-life' pull of the flow of Universal Life, though from life as it is known on this planet.

We have also noted how a rocket can escape from this planet to be caught or held by another planet, or go beyond our Solar system to be caught or held in the next Solar system or it might go out and beyond but then there are millions of Solar systems all around us in our galaxy and there are millions of other galaxies. So *Moksha* like the freedom of the rocket is a relative term for the individual. By all means the gradual creeping in of the stage of Cosmic Consciousness is far too grand as compared to the self-consciousness of the normal state. When this happens, the Resultant-Intensity accumulates the elements of other planets *which may be radically* different to the shape and size and texture of a *physical human body.* It may, therefore, even be replaced by a molecular body and later on, in more advanced states, may be replaced by an electronic body. But there is seldom, a sort of "no-existence" or merging with the Infinite and no annihilation as we have been accustomed to think so far. There are very many intermediate stages and stages of existence and freedoms or 'lesser bondages'. Only a Mahā-Avatāra is beyond all bondage.

Life in its intensity is varying for each planet but basically it is one great ocean and is present in all creation. If the Resultant-Intensity and thought-patterns are able to *deviate consciously* (gross or fine) to their Source before they return to earth, i.e. to the life peculiar to any planet which could be the source of such Resultant Intensity and thought-patterns then even such Source could be experienced by the individual in the interval between death and rebirth. *This is an extremely advanced* stage of the individual and beyond the four (plus) Zenoga units stage. When this happens it is possible to deviate the essence towards any lower form of life; even when lower than a human being that particular form of life is experienced consciously as a human ! It is incorrect to call such an experience *which is consciously experienced*, a retrograde movement in consciousness.

Consciousness, thought-patterns, Resultant Intensity, gross essence or fine, and Life in the form of creation are peculiar and inherent in all *matter*. The ocean of life is everywhere and in all creation, varying greatly for each planet but present everywhere and so certain elements are peculiar to certain planets. *If the resulting intensity* and resultant patterns can consciously deviate essence anywhere, they can accumulate elements peculiar to that planet, to take a required body in keeping with that planet, and acquire valuable new experience.

Naturally such movements require very great speed. The speed of light (relatively speaking) is great, being about 300,000 kilometres per second. The speed of the thought-patterns along with the Resultant-Intensity is 1,16 million kilometres per second; sufficient to escape from this planet yet it reaches a maximum speed nearly hundred times more viz. 160 million kilometres per second depending on its (plus or minus) Intensity. *But a point in time comes when* (plus or minus) Resultant Intensity separates from the thought-patterns because the latter cannot keep up in speed with that of the Resultant-Intensity and then the karmic patterns loose the force of momentum and just drift for some time and spread out more and more and are absorbed in bits or fragments by other thought-patterns and karmic entities more in keeping with *their speed.* These patterns have only an inherent, simple, mechanical consciousness of the animal kingdom *when separate from the Resultant-Intensity.* The plus or minus Resultant-Intensity alone has Self-Consciousness of the higher human kind.

The essence, gross or fine, has Cosmic-Consciousness and Universal Life, all-prevailing, has proceeded from Cosmic-Consciousness to Super Cosmic Consciousness to near Absolute Consciousness; only Unmanifest Spirit has absolute consciousness.

The planets and suns and stars according to their intensity

have a consciousness, ranging between simple to super cosmic consciousness. At the infinitely advanced stage of super consciousness, movements take place in the entire galaxy and even beyond. At that stage the speed of light is too slow to be of any use. At that stage even cosmic consciousness becomes a great limitation and so the *super-cosmic consciousness functions* at the absolute speed of the galaxy and not at the absolute speed of the solar system which is the *speed of light*! This point is to be well understood. Light takes 60,000 years to cross the diameter of our galaxy; a speed (analogically) slower than that of a bullock-cart on earth!

This in our earthly language amounts to being present instantaneously and simultaneously everywhere in our galaxy. This is known as the spirit underlying the whole creation. *This is actually* spirit manifest. Even this speed of spirit manifest is slow and is not of much use for the inter-galaxy travel between millions upon millions of galaxies. So the super cosmic consciousness state then becomes a great limitation in its turn. So even this state has its own absolute speed and its own super galaxial consciousness which is called "seed manifest" being beyond the manifest state of spirit. This Seed is underlying the whole of creation even underlying the spirit manifest, yet yet beyond this Seed manifest is the Unmanifested Spirit-in-itself.

It is true also that in the Self-consciousness or ego-state the number of patterns are maximum, they are much less in the simple conscious state of animals and diminish further again in the Cosmic Consciousness and Super Cosmic state and so forth. The small number in the former is due to lack of thoughts for the patterns and in the latter case it is the *discarding* or outgrowing of thoughts which accounts for the diminishing number of patterns.

In the lower, earlier state it is like the mind of a child with limited patterns that are simple and several complex and crooked patterns have not yet been accumulated as in the adult stage. In the Cosmic Consciousness stage it is again like the child stage for the patterns are few and simple; *but here the complex and the crooked have been deliberately laid aside.*

The rhythmic breathing, the subjecting of all coding and decoding to the disinfection chamber, the use of corrective methods, bring about slowly an intensity of 2 (plus) Zenoga units which slowly take self-consciousness across the stages of concentration and meditation with the result that the coding and decoding rate drops very appreciably. The patterns now do not accumulate but remain very limited. The stored-up patterns are in turn also subjected to the same process and corrected with the result that a great reduction of the number of patterns takes place. Great amount of mental, emotional, sex and physical energy is saved and the Resultant-Intensity increases greatly. *This diminishing of patterns* (=*karma*) *reaches a point* in time when the Resultant-Intensity separates from the thought-patterns and the cast-off patterns 'in bits and piece' are absorbed by other karma-bound entities on their way to progress through spiritual evolution.

It is, therefore, not possible for the elementary consciousness to understand what is simple consciousness and for simple consciousness to understand what is self-consciousness and for self-consciousness to understand what is cosmic-consciousness and for cosmic-consciousness to understand what is super cosmic-consciousness and for super-cosmic-consciousness to understand the galacical consciousness and for galaxical consciousness to understand the super galaxial consciousness, and this in turn the absolute consciousness.

When the lower or more limited consciousness (by a continuous process of increasing or progressing consciousness) reaches the next stage higher up, *there is a sudden blending* of the two states of consciousness and none of the normal calculating processes of the self-consciousness stage are of use or can help as can reason etc. and so the blending appears to be very sudden or as if in a flash, like lightning between the two clouds due to the electrical energy of the resultants.

It is, therefore, not possible for any state of simple consciousness to understand super-galaxical consciousness and beyond *directly by any methods known*; but the super cosmic state of consciousness by slow progress, can reach the next higher state i.e. galaxial consciousness. When this happens, the purpose of creation is understood. When the stage beyond is reached the purpose of creation is even fulfilled. But what actually happens in between is that, during the same duration, the elementary consciousness reaches the self-consciousness state and the self-consciousness state reaches the cosmic consciousness state and the cosmic-conscious state reaches the super-cosmic state and so forth in all creation.

Though each higher or less limited state is much more wonderful, the gap or gulf becomes progressively greater and greater with the result that the gap or gulf between galaxical and super-galaxical consciousness is greater still than that between our usual consciousness and cosmic consciousness. The gap between super-galaxical consciousness and near-absolute Consciousness is the greatest even in proportion to the 'speed of super cosmic consciousness ! Like the difference between the speed of an animal-drawn carriage and a motor car and between a motor car and a jet plane, a jet and a rocket and between an ordinary rocket and a rocket that can leave the solar System, the difference in speed and progress at each stage is comparatively faster and greater !

From this it is apparent that it is no use crying about destiny. Let us make proper use of the free-will given to us to earn yet more. Let us use corrective methods and make constant progress. Let us increase consciously the plus resultant intensity. Let us increase the harmony between the inter-play of all the centres and create plus Zenoga units and continue the onward march. At the end of the tunnel is the Light, at the end of the struggle is the Victory.

APPENDIX V

EXTRA NOTE
to Chapter XVI

The Neuro-physiological Basis of our Mind

My esteemed friend Florin Laubenthal became famous through his book on the interconnection between brain and soul; also worthy of mention is Sir John ECCLES book (Oxford 1953).

However even these authorities underestimated the anatomy of the brain as a clue to the secrets of the Soul. Zarathustra explains these secrets guardedly in his Gathas and if you will open the Bible at the Revelation of St. John you will find an exact description of the anatomy of the brain in the light of *Kundalini* and Zen-Yoga. The 7 Stars, 7 golden candlesticks etc. are but centres of brain anatomy as would be seen by the *Kundalini* when entering the brain through the spinal cord:—

1. Medulla-Oblongata
2. Cerebellum
3. Corpora-Quadrigemina
4. Thalamus et Hypophysis
5. Truncus-Corporis-Callosi
6. Pallium
7. Septum-Pellucidum.

The spinal cord is like a magnet with the brain as its north pole and the reproductive organ as its other pole. Along this magnet flows the electromagnetism of *Kundalini*. And the *Kundalini* has junctions along the line: the plexuses: sacralis, prostaticus, cardiacus, laryngens etc. etc. terminating in cavernosus and Hypophysis. The so-called "rainbow" of St. Johns Revelations is but the corpora striatii of brain anatomy, both the "lions"=pallium, the "bull"=brachia pontis and so on; the whole of the Revelations being but a tortuous and tentative attempt to explain *Kundalini* Yoga to culturally less advanced civilizations.

Now as far as centre 5 of our book is concerned we know that it has 2 Sub-sections (a) and (b). Now where, anatomically, is the Sub-section (a) of the In. or 5 centre? It is situated more or less between the Thalamus and Hypothalamus and is called the:

Reticular Activating System

or RAS for short.

It is this RAS which determines what sensory information (if at all) be brought to Sec. 1. and, therefore, to 'awareness' in the popular sense. It, therefore, is the agent which determines whether we be able to concentrate or not, for it alone can enable us to focus our thoughts on a specific point in spite of the constant and disconnected barrage of impulses from the five senses of perception.

Without the RAS man would be anatomically incapable to pay full attention to any one specific thing at a time. The RAS diverts incoming messages which can be automatically dealt with thus permitting only that which demands special attention to reach 'awareness'. It is (anatomically) centered in a cone-shaped maze of nerves in the brain stem in such a way that its fibers intercept the inflow of sense-data coming up from the body before such messages hit the thalamus for re-distribution to the decision-making points in the Neo-cortex. As sensory information coming in from eyes, ears, tongue etc. is also intercepted by the RAS, it can heighten or reduce the subjective effect of any impulse it chooses. It can block out the physical pains of a toothache if we wish to go deep in meditation or instantly alert us if an intruder suddenly breaks into the room. It can heal a person without his even knowing it for through its direct connection with the Hypothalmus it can get corrective action done without even bothering the (so-called) 'conscious' mind. The RAS relieves us of the bother of such activities as breathing and digestion —until something goes seriously wrong. In addition to screening sense information the RAS regulates consciousness (in the popular sense of 'awareness') itself. Should neural activity in the RAS drop below the sleep-export-point we fall into stupor; if it rises above the anxiety-import-point we toss about all night and go through the hells of insomnia. In fact, the RAS can close down the 'conscious' mind altogether for the purpose of a temporary transfer from Sec. 1 to Sec. 2 of the mind.

If all that can be done even by sub-section (a) of the In. Centre—this sub-section (a) being the RAS of anatomy—it is idle to speculate on what cannot be achieved by sub-section (b) of the same centre. Further, we should not fail to note that the achievements of RAS are not 'speculations on Yoga' but the tried and tested facts of Physiology which no critic can deny. The RAS enables you to keep your awarness sharply focussed on what you consider 'important' by blocking out such sense messages which you (for the time being) consider 'unimportant'. While the RAS in kybernetic feed-back enables the Neo-cortex to make computations as to activities, the limbic system in the brain (the I. Centre of Sec. 1.) evaluates the pros and contras or the 'risks' of the activity being planned. But alas the limbic system lies in the sphere of influence of the E. Centre. By constantly colouring our thoughts with emotions the E. Centre joins forces with the S. Centre to corner the I. Centre as a common rival. The anatomical counterparts of these centres are:

1. Thalamus
2. Limbic Lobe
3. Hippocampus
4. Amygdala
5. Septal region
6. Hypothalamic nuclei
7. Olfactory bulbs

The limbic system taken as a whole is itself a counterpart to the Neo-cortex. Just as the Neo-cortex is *predominantly* the seat of the I. centre and in its sphere of influence, so is the limbic system predominantly the seat of E. and S. Centres and in their venue of jurisdiction.

Properly speaking, the limbic system is not the *real* brain of *man* at all but a leftover from infra-human planes of evolution. The child in the womb develops at first a brain similar to that during the Age of Reptiles—that is to say, a crocodile's brain. When the pregnancy of its mother progresses, then comes a higher brain structure like that of a horse. With the coming of the Neo-cortex the two forgoing and obsolete brain structures are not eliminated but combined (the crocodile-like brain with the horse-like brain) and put into a 'stocking' (=limbic system) which then forms a loop around the thalamus, linking to-gether several of the brains key centres. The tragic part of it all is that the two almost entirely different "brains": Neo-cortex (really human) and limbic system (crocodile+horse conglomerate) are not functionally separable from each other. Vitality for instance is an attribute of the limbic side etc. Man's brain therefore resembles a wrongly programmed computer. Or in other words: scratch even the most intelligent person in the world and there lurks (the brain of) a crocodile or a horse under the surface of sophistication. For example, the brain of a shark or crocodile predominantly consists of the sense of smell so that such creatures can smell a unit of blood even when diluted with a million units of water. Man's limbic system still includes the ordour transmitting olfactory bulbs. That is why certain expensive perfumes are called "tempting" or "irresistible". For through these odours the one perfumed arouses the vital-activity in the animal brain of the other person (his "passion" so to say) a split-second before his "reason" (the I. centre in the Neo-cortex) has resumed sway. Thus the immediate promptings of the limbic system (Centres E. and S.) clash more often than not with the carefully thought out long-range strategy of the I. Centre. Inhibitions, psycho-hysterical denial and other variations of emotional conflict such as excessive eating or drinking sets in as a defense mechanism making the price of rational behaviour inflationary.

Man is thus *not* a rational being. He has but a tiny raft of reason (I Centre) in a rather stormy sea of emotions (E. Centre) and passions (S. Centre). The limbic system can fool "reason" in any number of ways. A physiological turbulence or even an upset can be tarnished to appear "pleasant" such as the increased hormonal flow during sexual infatuation. Our emotions distort our perception almost in initio and there would be no hope of progress to higher planes of evolution were it not for Yoga.

Anatomically it is like this: the Hippocampus along with

the limbic lobe picks up signals from the already mentioned RAS and cortex to send them on a tour of the *inner* brain. The Hippocampus being the seat of memory can evaluate events in terms of previous experience, even the experience gathered in prenatal incarnations. But very close at hand lies the AMYGDALA, the favourite locus of the E. Centre and thus capable of amplifying the intensity of *any* expression to an explosive outburst. Its activity is heightened wherever we come across new or unexpected things. This could play havoc were it not for the Viceroy of the I. Centre in the limbic system. That is the Septal region and as agent an ally of the I. Centre it dampens (in contrast to the Amygdala) the emotional outbursts and reactions of the E. Centre. Excessive emotional stress releases Noradrenaline in the brain and excessive amounts of it can cause such inner turmoil as to drive a person catatonic. The catatonic's hypervigilance, itself a characteristic of paranoia, is also the result of excessive Noradrenaline release. Thus evolutionary outgrowths in the physiological construction of the brain hamper man's further growth on the evolutionary ladder. Luckily we have in Yoga and Zen a way out of this sorry state.

APPENDIX VI

PRACTICAL EXERCISES

1—*To develop expanding Consciousness.*

Take up a suitable position for meditation.

Establish rhythmic breathing. Now imagine the Universe as a great globe with yourself in the centre of the globe. Now imagine your mind as a fluid which you can emit, like a bubble, and visualise that you are sending out this bubble, that it grows larger and larger, until it completely fills the globe that is the Universe.

Feel your Consciousness expanding.

2—*To develop Perception and Awareness.*

Take up a suitable position for meditation. Establish rhythmic breathing.

Sit perfectly still, close your eyes, and concentrate all your attention on listening.

Let the mind pass from one sound to another as a bee passes from flower to flower, alighting on each for only a few seconds. Pause, and recall as much of the character of each sound as you can from memory.

3—Concentrate on sonnds as before, but this time make an effort to penetrate more deeply into it.

Try to analyse its origin, its effect, its character.

4—Repeat exercise 2, but this time look instead of listening.

5—Repeat exercise 3, using the eyes instead of the ears.

Try to consider colour, texture, form, purpose, character, and relationship to environment.

6—Practice listening to music played by a good orchestra.

(1) listen only to the principle melody.
(2) listen for a counter-melody and isolate this.
(3) choose one instrument and isolate it, hearing this only.
(4) analyse how the harmony is built up.

7—Practice looking at Paintings.

(1) seek out the key colour and decide whether the other colours are in contrast or in harmony.

(2) seek out forms and decide whether there exists a common key, (e.g. square, circle, angles etc.)

(3) analyse the dynamics (direction of movement, lines of action and structure).

8—Whenever you take a walk, either in town or country, apply listening as in Exercise 6, and seeing as in Exercise 7.

NOTE that SEEING means more than just LOOKING
LISTENING means more than just HEARING.

BIBLIOGRAPHY

AL-GHAZZALI. *Confessions.* Translated by Claud Field (London, 1909).

ANSARI OF HERAT. *The Invocations of Sheikh Abdullah Ansari of Herat.* Translated by Sardar Sir Jogendra Singh (London, 1939).

ATTAR. *Selections.* Translated by Margaret Smith (London, 1932).

AUGUSTINE, ST. *Confessions* (numerous editions).

AUROBINDO, SRI. *The Life Divine,* 3 vols. (Calcutta, 1939)+ Complete works.

ABEGG, EMIL, *Indische Psychologie.* Zürich 1945.

Archiv für indische *Philosophie*—siehe Zeitschrift.

AVALON, ARTHUR (= Sir John Woodroffe) u.a., *The Principles of Tantra,* 2 Bde., 1941/1946.

—*The Great Liberation,* Mahānirvāṇa Tantra, 2. Aufl. Madras 1927.

—*Die Schlangenkraft.* München 1960.

—*Shakti und Shākta.* München 1961.

—*Introduction to Tantra Shāstra,* 2. Aufl. Madras 1952.

—*The Garland of Letters* (Varṇamālā). Studies in the Mantra-Shāstra. London, 1922.

BENZ, ERNST (s.a. Wolff, Otto), *Indische Einflüsse auf die frühchristliche Theologie.* Wiesbaden 1951.

Bhagavadgītā siehe Garbe, Glasenapp, Krämer, Schroeder, Radhakrishnan.

BHATTACHARYA, J.N., *Hindu Castes and Sects.* Calcutta 1896.

BHATTACHARYYA, Benoytosh, *The Indian Buddhist Iconography.* Oxford 1924.

—*An Introduction to Buddhist Esoterism.* Oxford 1932.

BLYTH, R. H., *Zen in English Literature and Oriental Classics.* Tokyo 1948.

BLOOMFIELD, MAURICE, *The Life and Stories of the Jaina Savior Pārśvanātha.* Baltimore 1919.

—[Ubers.], *Hymns of the Atharva Veda*, Sacred Books of the East, Vol. XLII. Oxford 1897.

BROWN, W. NORMAN, *The Story of Kālaka*, Texts, History, Legends and Miniature Paintings of the Śvetāmbara Jain Hagiographical Work: The Kālakācāryakathā. Washington 1933.

—*Miniature Paintings of the Jaina Kalpasūtra as executed in the Early Western Indian Style.* Washington 1934.

—*Manuscript Illustrations of the Uttarādhyayana Sūtra.* New Haven 1941.

BRUNTON, PAUL, Complete Works.

BAKER, AUGUSTINE. *Holy Wisdom* (London, 1876).

BEAUSOBRE, JULIA DE. *The Woman Who Could Not Die* (London and New York, 1938).

BERNARD OF CLAIRVAUX, ST. *The Steps of Humility* (Cambridge, Mass., 1940).

On the Love of God (New York, 1937).

Selected Letters (London, 1904). An admirably lucid account of St. Bernard's thought may be found in *The Mystical Doctrine of Saint Bernard*, by Professor Etienne Gilson (London and New York, 1940).

BERTOCCI, PETER A. *The Empirical Arguments for God in Late British Philcsophy* (Cambridge, Mass., 1938).

BINYON, L. *The Flight of the Dragon* (London, 1911).

BUHLER, G. (Ubers.), *The Laws of Manu*, Sacred Books of the East, Vol. XXV. Oxford 1886.

—*The Sacred Laws of the Aryas*, Sacred Books of the East, Vol. II und XIV. Oxford 1879/1882.

BURLINGAME, E. W., *Buddhist Parables.* New Haven 1922.

Cambridge History of India, The.

CHAKRAVARTI, Appāsvāmī (Hrsg. u. Übers.), *Kundakundācārya's Pañcāstikāyasāra*, Sacred Books of the Jaina. Allahabad 1920.

COHN, WILLIAM, *Indische Plastik*, Die Kunst des Ostens, Bd. I. Berlin 1920.

COLEBROOKE, H. T. u. Wilson, H. H. (Hrsg. u. Übers.), —*Sāṅkhya-Kārikā.* Bombay 1887 Oxford 1937.

CONZE, EDWARD, Complete Works.

COOMARASWAMY, ANANDA K.,
—*Spiritual Authority and Temporal Power in the Indian Theory of Government.* New Haven 1942.
—*The Transformation of Nature in Art,* Cambridge, Mass 1934.
—*Why Exhibit Works of Art?* London 1946.
—*Figures of Speech or Figures of Thought.* London 1946.
—*The Dance of Śiva.* New York 1918 (franz. Paris 1922).
—*Religious Basis of the Forms of Indian Society.* New York 1946.
—*A New Approach to the Vedas,* An Essay in Translation and Exegesis. London 1933.
—*The Rg Veda as Land-nama-book,* London 1935.
—*Recollection, Indian and Platonic* und *The One and only Transmigrant.* New Haven 1944.
—*Yakshas.* Washington 1928-1931.
—*Buddha and the Gospel of Buddhism,* New York 1916.
—*Hinduism and Buddhism.* New York.
—*Elements of Buddhist Iconography.,* Cambridge Mass. 1935.

COWELL, E. B. (Hrsg. u. Ubers.), *The Jātaka, or Stories of the Buddha's Former Birth,* 6 Bde. Cambridge 1895-1907.

COWELL, E. B., MULLER, F. Max u. Takakusu, Junjire,
—*Buddhist Mahīyāna Sūtras* (Buddha-carita of Aśvaghosha; grössere und kleinere Sukhāvatī-vyūhas; Vajracchedikā; grössere und kleinere Prajñā-pāramitā-Sūtras; Amitāyur-dhyāna Sūtra), Sacred Books of the East, Vol. XLIX. Oxford 1894.

COWELL, E.B. u. Gough, A. E. *Sarvadarshanasaṅgraha* (engl.), 1894.

DASGUPTA, SURENDRA NATH, *A History of Indian Philosophy,* 5 Bde. Cambridge 1932-1955.
—*Yoga as Philosophy and Religion,* London 1924.
—*Yoga Philosophy in Relation to the other Systems of Indian Thought.* Calcutta 1930.

BOEHME, JACOB. Some good introduction is needed to the work of this important but difficult mystic. On the theological and devotional side the Danish Bishop H. L. Martensen's *Jacob Boehme* (trans., London, 1885) is recommended; or from a more philosophical viewpoint A. Koyré's splendid volume *La Philosophie de Jacob Boehme* (not yet translated, Paris, 1929) or H. H. Brinton's *The Mystic Will* (New York, 1930).

BRAHMANANDA, SWAMI. Records of his teaching and a biography by Swami Prabhavananda are contained in *The Eternal Companion* (Los Angeles, 1944).

CAMUS, JEAN PIERRE. *The Spirit of St. Francois de Sales* (London, n.d.).

CAUSSADE, J. P. DE. *Abandonment* (New York, 1887).
Spiritual Letters, 3 vols. (London, 1937).

CHANTAL, ST. JEANNE FRANCOISE. *Selected Letters* (London and New York, 1918).

CHAPMAN, ABBOT JOHN. *Spiritual Letters* (London, 1935).

CHUANG TZU. *Chuang Tzu, Mystic, Moralist and Social Reformer.* Translated by Herbert Giles (Shanghai, 1936).
Musings of a Chinese Mystic (London, 1920).

Chinese Philosophy in Classical Times. Translated by E.R. Hughes (London, 1943).

The Cloud of Unknowing (with commentary by Augustine Baker). Edited with an introduction by Justice McCann (London, 1924).

CURTIS, A. M. *The Way of Silence* (Burton Bradstock, Dorset, 1937).

DIONYSIUS THE AREOPAGITE. *On the Divine Names and the Mystical Theology.* Translated with an introduction by C. E. Rolt (London, 1920).

DANIELOU, ALAIN, *Yoga, méthode de réintégration.* Paris 1951.
—*Catalogue de la musique indienne classique et traditionnelle enregistrée.* Paris (Unesco) 1952.

DAVIDS—siehe Rhys Davids, C.A.F. und T.W.

DEUSSEN, PAUL, *Allgemeine Geschichte der Philosophie.* I. Bd., 1. Abt. : *Philosophie des Veda*, 4. Aufl. Leipzig 1920.
—*Die Philosophie der Upanishad's*, 3. Aufl. Leipzig 1919.
—*Sechzig Upanishad's des Veda*, 3. Aufl. Leipzig 1921.
—*Das System des Vedanta*, 3. Aufl. Leipzig 1920.
—*Die Geheimlehre des Veda*, Ausgew. Texte der Upanishad's, 6. Aufl. Leipzig 1921.

DUNBAR, SIR GEORGE, *Geschichte Indiens von den ältesten Zeiten bis zur Gegenwart.* Vom Verfasser überarbeitet und übersetzt v. Heinrich Zimmer. München/Berlin 1937.

DUTT, MANMAṬHA NATH, *Kāmandakīya Nītisāra,* Wealth of India Series. Calcutta 1896.

EGGELING, J. (Übers.), *Śatapatha Brāhmaṇa,* Sacred Books of the East, Vol. XII, XXVI, XLI, XLII, XLIV. Oxford 1882—1900.

EIDLITZ, WALTHER, *Der Glaube und die heiligen schriften de Inder.* Olten u. Freiburg 1957.

ELIADE, MIRCEA, *Yoga, Unsterblichkeit und Freiheit.* Übers. v. Inge Köck. Zürich 1960.

—*Le Temps et l'Eternité dans la Pensée Indienne.* In : Eranos-Jahrbuch XX/1951. Zürich 1952.

Eranos—Index der Jahrbucher I—XXV. Bearbeitet von Magda Kerényi, Zürich 1961.

Eranos-Jahrbuch. Die Vorträge der Eranos-Tagungen in Ascona. Hrsg. v. Olga Fröbe-Kapteyn. Zürich, seit 1933 ff.

FADDEGON, BAREND, *The Pravacana-sāra of Kundakunda Ācārya,* Jain Literature Society Series. Cambridge 1935.

—*The Vaiśeṣika-System.* Amsterdam 1918.

FARQUHAR, J. N., *An Outline of the Religious Literature of India* Oxford 1920.

FRAUWALLNER, ERICH, *Geschichte der indischen Philosophie,* 2 Bde. Salzburg 1953 bis 1956.

—*Die Philosophie des Buddhismus,* Berlin 1956.

GANDHI, M. K., *The Story of My Experiments with Truth.* Ahmedabad 1927-1929.

—siehe Kraus, F.

GARBE, RICHARD, *Die Sāṅkhya-Philosophie,* 2, Aufl. Leipzig 1917.

—*Die Bhagavadgītā,* Leipzig 1921.

(In : Hastings, *Encyclopaedia of Religion and Ethics*) :

—*Lokāyata* (Vol. VIII, p. 138).

ECKHART, MEISTER. *Works,* translated by C. B. Evans (London, 1924).

Meister Eckhart, A Modern Translation. By R. B. Blakney (New York, 1941).

EVANS-WENTZ, W. Y. *The Tibetan Book of the Dead* (New York, 1927). and *Of the Great Liberation*
Tibet's Great Yogi, Milarepa (New York, 1928).
Tibetan Yoga and Secret Doctrines (New York, 1935).
The Following of Christ. Unknown author, but mistakenly attributed to Tauler in the first English edition (London, (1886).

FOX, GEORGE. *Journal* (London, 1911).

FROST, BEDE. *The Art of Mental Prayer* (London, 1940).
Saint John of the Cross (London, 1937).

GARBE, Essays on :— *Mīmāṁsā* (Vol. VIII, p . 648).
— —*Nyāya* (Vol. IX, p. 422-424).
— —*Sāṅkhya* (Vol. XI, p. 189-192).
— —*Vaiśeṣika* (Vol. XII. 568—570).
-- -- *Vedānta* (Vol. XII, p. 597—598).
— —*Yoga* (Vol. XII, p. 831-833).
— —*Sāṅkhya und Yoga.* Strassburg 1896.

GELDNER, KARL FRIEDRICH (Übers), *Der Rig-Veda* (kommentiert). Wiesbaden 1951 (Harvard Oriental Series 33-35).

GLASENAPP, HELMUTH VON, *Der Jainismus*, Eine indische Erlösungsreligion. Leipzig 1925 (Kultur und Weltanschauung, Bd. 1).

—*Buddhismus und Gottesidee.* Wiesbaden 1954.

—*Die Religionen Indiens*, 2, Aufl. Stuttgart 1955.

—(Hrsg. u. Übers.), *Der Pfad zur Erleuchtung*, Grundtexte zur buddhistischen Heilslehre. Dusseldorf 1956.

—(Hrsg.), *Indische Geisteswelt* Eine Textauswahl. Gütersloh 1958.

—*Indien*, Munchen 1925.

—*Die Philosophie der Inder*, 2, Aufl. Stuttgart 1956.

—*Der Hinduismus, Religion und Gesellschaft im heutigen Indien.*, München 1922.

—*Madhva's Philosophie des Vishnu-Glaubens. Ein Beitrag zur Sektengeschichte des Hinduismus.* Bonn 1923 (Geistesströmungen d. Ostens, Bd. 2).

—*Der Buddhismus in Indien u.i. Fernen Osten.* Berlin 1936.

—*Entwicklungsstufen des indischen Denkens. Untersuchungen über die Philosophie der Brahmanen und Buddhisten.* Halle 1940.

—*Bhagavadgītā. Das Lied der Gottheit. Übers*, v. R. Boxberger. Stuttgart 1955 (Reclams UB 7874/75).

—*Die fünf grossen Religionen*, Bd. I (*Brahmanismus, Buddhismus, Chinesischer* Universismus), 8, Tsd. Düsseldorf 1958.

—*Buddhistische Mysterien.* Die geheimen Lehren und *Riten des Diamantfahrzeugs.* Stuttgart 1940.

Gough, A. siehe Cowell.

Griffith, R.T.H. (Übers), *Ṛgveda, Sāmaveda, White Yajur veda, Atharvaveda.* Benares 1895—1907.

Guenon, Rene, *L'homme et son devenir selon le Vedānta,* Nouv. édit. Paris 1948.

—*La Métaphysique orientale*, Nouv. édit. Paris 1951.

—*Introduction générale `a l'étude des doctrines hindoues.* Paris 1952.

Guenther, Herbert, *Der Buddha und seine Lehre.* Nach der Uberli eferung der Theravadins. Zürich 1956.

Guerinot, Armand Albert, *La religion d jaina.* Paris 1926.

Hass, George C.O., *The Daśarūpa of Dhanañjaya, a treatise on Hindu Dramaturgy.* (Ubersetzung). Columbia University, Indo-Irian Series, New York 1912.

Hacker, Paul, *Vivarta, Studien zur Geschichte der illusionistischen Kosmologie und Erkenntnistheorie der Inder.* Wiesbaden 1951.

Garrigou-Lagrange, R. *Christian Perfection and Contemplation* (London and St. Louis, 1937).

Goddard, Dwight. *A Buddhist Bible* (published by the editor, Thetford, Maine, 1938). This volume contains translations of several Mahāyāna texts not to be found, or to be found only with much difficulty, elsewhere. Among these are 'The Diamond Sūtra', 'The Suraṅgama Sūtra' 'The Laṅkāvatāra Sūtra', 'The Awakening of Faith' and "The Sūtra of the Sixth Patriarch.'

Guenon, Rene. *Man and His Becoming according to the Vedānta* (London, n.d.).

East and West (London, 1941).
The Crisis of the Modern World (London, 1942).

HEARD, GERALD. *The Creed of Christ* (New York, 1940).
The Code of Christ (New York, 1941).
Preface to Prayer (New York, 1944).

HILTON, WALTER. *The Scale of Perfection* (London, 1927).

HUEGEL, FRIEDRICH VON. *The Mystical Element in Religion as Studied in Saint Catherine of Genoa and Her Friends* (London, 1923).

HARE, E. M. Woodward.

HASTINGS, JAMES (Hrsg), *Encyclopaedia of Religion and Ethics.* 13 vols. New York 1928.

HAUER, J. W., *Der Yoga. Ein indischer Weg zum Selbst.* Mit Übers. v. Texten. Stuttgart 1958.

HAVELL, E.B., *The History of Aryan Rule in India, from the Earliest Times to the Death of Akbar.* London 1918.

HARRIGEL, EUGEN, *Zen in der Kunst des Bogenschiessens.* Munchen 1957.

HILLEBRANDT, ALFRED (Übers.), *Upanishaden—Altindische Weisheit,* Brāhmaṇas und Upanishaden in Auswahl. Nachwort von H. V. Glasenapp. Düsseldorf 1958.

ISHERWOOD, CHRISTOPHER (Hrsg.) *Vedānta Isherwood, Aldous Huxley.*

JACOBI, HERMANN, *Jainism.* In : Hastings, *Encyclopaedia of Religion and Ethics,* Vol. VII, p. 465-474.)
—*Zur Frühgeschichte der indischen Philosophie.* Berlin 1911. (Hrsg. u. Ubers.), *Eine Jaina-Dogmatik* (Umāsvāti's Tattvārthādhigama Sūtra). Leipzig 1906.
—*Jaina Sūtras,* Sacred Books of the East, Vol. XXII u. XLV. Oxford 1884 u. 1895.

JAINI, JAGMANDAR LAL, *Outlines of Jainism.* Cambridge 1916. (Hrsg. u. Ubers.). *Tattvārthādhigama Sūtra,* Sacred Books of the Jainas. Arrah o.).

KEITH, ARTHUR BERRIEDALE, *The Sāṁkhya System.* New York 1918.
—*Indian Logic and Atomism.* Oxford 1921.
—*The Karma-Mīmāṁsā,* The Heritage of India Series, London/Calcutta 1921.

—*The Religion and Philosophy of the Veda and Upanishads.* Cambridge, Mass. 1925.

KOPPERS, WILHELM, *Probleme der indischen Religionsgeschichte.* Fribourg 1941.

—*Zum Ursprung des Mysterienwesens im lichte von Völkerkunde und Indologie.* In: Eranos-Jahrbuch XI 1944. Zurich 1945.

KRAMER, ILSE (Ubers), *Bhagavadgītā, Gesang des Erhabenen.* Zürich 1954.

KRAMRISCH, STELLA, *The Hindu Temple,* Photographs by R. Bürnier, 2 Bde. Calcutta 1946.

—*Indische Kunst.* Köln 1956.

KRAUS, FRITZ, *Vom Geiste des Mahatma. Ein Gandhi-Brevier.* Baden-Baden 1957.

LANMAN, CH. R. Whitney.

LAUFER, BERTHOLD, *Mīlarappa* (Rje btsun la ras pai ruam thar rgyas par phye ba mgur 'bum). Munchen 1922.

LOMMEL, HERMANN (Ubers.) *Gedichte des Rig-Veda* (Auswahl). München 1955.

MACDONELL, A. A., *Vedic Mythology* Strassburg 1897.

—*Vedic Religion.* (In : Hastings, *Encyclopaedia of Religion and Ethics,* Vol. XII, p. 601-618).

MACKEY, ERNEST, *Indus Culture Mohenjo-daro und Harappa.*

MARSHALL, SIR JOHN, *Mohenjo-daro and the Indus Civilisation,* 3 Bde. London 1931.

IBN TUFAIL. *The Awakening of the Soul.* Translated by Paul Bronnle (London, 1910).

The Imitation of Christ. Whitford's translation, edited by E. J. Klein (New York, 1941).

INGE, W. R. *Christian Mysticism* (London, 1899).

Studies of English Mystics—including William Law (London, 1906).

JOHN OF THE CROSS, ST. *Works,* 3 vols. (London, 1934-1935).

JONES, RUFUS. *Studies in Mystical Religion.*

The Spiritual Reformers in the 16th and 17th Centuries (New York, 1914).

The Flowering of Mysticism (New York, 1939).

JORGENSEN, JOHANNES. *Saint Catherine of Siena* (London, 1938).

JULIANA OF NORWICH. *Revelations of Divine Love* (London, 1917).

LAO TZU. There are many translations of the Tao Teh King. Consult and compare those of Arthur Waley in *The Way and Its Power* (London, 1933), of F. R. Hughes in *Chinese Philosophy in Classical Times* (Everyman's Library) and of Ch'u Ta-Kao (London, 1927) reprinted in *The Bible of the World* (New York, 1939).

MCGOVERN, WILLIAM, *Introduction to Mahāyāna Buddhism.* London 1922.

MEYER, J. J. (Hrsg. u. Übers.), *Das Arthashastra des Kautilya. Das altindische Buch vom Welt-und Staatsleben.* Leipzig 1926.

MULLER, F. MAX (s.a. Cowell), *The Dhammapada,* sacred, Books of the East, Vol. X, I. Teil. Oxford 1881.

—*Indien in seiner weltgeschichtlichen Bedeutung.* Leipzig 1884 (u. i. *Ausgew. Werke,* 1900).

—*Six Systems of Indian Philosophy,* London 1899.

u. OLDENBERG, H. (Übers.) *Rg. Veda Hymns,* Sacred Books of the East, Vol. XXXII.u. XLVI. Oxford 1897.

MUIR, J., *Original Sanskrit Texts on the Origin and History of the People of India, their Religion and Institutions,* 5 Bde. London 1868—1874.

NANJIO, BUNYIU, *A Short History of the Twelve Japanese Buddhist Sects,* Tokyo 1886.

NAWRATH, ALFRED, *Unsterbliches Indien. Landschaft, Volksleben, Meisterwerke der Baukunst und Plastik,* Wien-München 1959.

NEUMANN, KARL EUGEN (Übers), *Die Reden Gotamo Buddhos,* Gesamtausgabe in 3 Bdn. mit Anmerkungen. Zürich 1958.

NIKHILĀNANDA, SWAMI, *Self-Knowledge* Der Ātma-bodha des Śaṅkara. Engl. Ubers, New York 1946.

—*The Vedāntasāra of Sadānanda* (Sanskr. u. engl.) Mayavati, Almoras, Himalayas 1931.

NYANAPONIKA, Complete Works.

OHASAMA, SCHUEJ, *Zen, der lebendige Buddhismus in Japan.* Mit übers. Stücken des Zen-Texts. Hrsg. v. August Faust, Geleitwort von Rudolf Otto. Gotha-Stuttgart 1925.

OLDENBERG, H. (s. a. Müller), *Religion der Vedas.* Berlin 1884.

OLSCHAK, BLANCHE CHRISTINE, *Tibet ; Erde der Götter . Vergessene Geschichte, Mythos und Saga.* Mit einem Vorwort von H. Harrer und Thubten Norbu. Zürich 1960.

LEEN, EDWARD. *Progress through Mental Prayer* (London, 1940).

McKEON, RICHARD. Selections from Medieval Philosophers, 2 Vols. (New York, 1929).

The Mirror of Simple Souls. Author unknown (London, 1927).

NICHOLAS OF CUSA. *The Idiot* (San Francisco, 1940).
The Vision of God (London and New York, 1928).

NICHOLSON, R. *The Mystics of Islam* (London, 1914).

OMAN, JOHN. *The Natural and the Supernatural* (London, 1938).

OTTO, RUDOLF. *India's Religion of Grace* (London, 1930).
Mysticism East and West (London, 1932).
—*Siddhānta Des Rāmānuja.* Jena 1917.

PALLIS, MARCO, *Peaks and Lamas.* New York 1949.

PIGGOTT, STUART, *Prehistoric India.* Harmondsworth (Penguin Books) 1950.

POUSSIN, LOUIS DE LA VALLÈE, *The Way to Nirvāṇa.* Cambridge 1917.
—*Bouddhisme,* 3. Aufl. Paris 1925.

PRATT, JAMES BISSETT, *The Pilgrimage of Buddhism.* New York 1928.

PRZYLUSKI, JEAN, *Die Erlösung nach dem Tode in den Upanishaden und im ursprünglichen Buddhismus.* In: Eranos-Jahrbuch V/1937. Zürich 1938.
—*Der Lebendig-Erlöste in dem entwickelten Buddhismus* (ebenda).

RADHAKRISHNAN, SARVAPALLI. Complete Works.
U. CH. A. MOORE, *A Source Book in Indian Philosophy.* Princeton, Bombay, Oxford 1957.

RAFSON, E. J., (Hrsg.), *The Cambridge History of India.* Cambridge and New York 1922.

RAMAKRISHNA, SRI, *Ewige Botschaft.* Nach der engl. Ausgabe v. Swāmi Nikhilānanda übers, v. Franz Dispeker. Zürich 1955.

RAU, HEIMO, *Die Kunst Indiens bis zum Islam.* Stuttgart 1958.

Rhys Davids, Caroline Augusta Foley, *Psalms of the Early Buddhists.* London 1913. *The Book of the Kindred Sayings,* London 1922.
Visuddhi-Magga. London 1921.
—*Indian Religion and Survival,* London 1934.
In den Eranos-Jahrbüchern, Zürich 1933 ff. :
—*Religiöse Übungen in Indien und der religiöse Mensch* (Bd I/1933).
—*Zur Geschichte des Rad-Symbols* (Bd. II/1934).
—*Der Mensch, die Suche und Nirvāṇa* (Bd. III/1935).
—*Erlösung in Indiens Vergangenheit und in unserer Gegenwart* (Bd. IV/1936).

Patanjali. *Yoga Aphorisms.* Translated with a commentary by Swami Vivekananda (New York, 1899).

Plotinus. *The Essence of Plotinus* (G. H. Tumbull, New York, 1934). A good anthology of this very important and voluminous mystic.

Ponnelle, L. and L. Bordet. *St. Philip Neri and the Roman Society of His Time* (London, 1932).

Poulain, A. *The Graces of Interior Prayer* (London, 1910).

Pourrat, P. *Christian Spirituality,* 3 Vols. (London, 1922).

Pratt, J. B. *The Pilgrimage of Buddhism* (New York, 1928).

Quakers. *The Beginnings of Quakerism,* by W. P. Braithwaite (London, 1912). See also George Fox, p. 348.

Rumi, Jalal-uddin. *Masnavi.* Translated by E. H. Whinfield (London, 1898).

Rolland, Romain, *Der Götter-Mensch Ramakrishna u. d. universale Evangelium d. Vivekananda.* Übertr. v. Paul Amann. Erlenbach 1931.

Ruben, Walt, *Die Philosophen der Upanishaden.* Bern 1947.
—*Einführung in die Indienkunde.* Berlin 1954.
—*Geschichte der indischen Philosophie.* Berlin 1954.

Ruysbroeck, Jan van. *The Adornment of the Spiritual Marriage* (London, 1916). Consult also the studies by Evelyn Underhill (London, 1915) and Wautier d'Aygalliers (London, 1925).

Sales, St. Francois de. *Introduction to the Devout Life* (numerous editions).

Treatise on the Love of God (new edition, Westminster, Md., 1942).
Spiritual Conferences (London, 1868).
See also J. P. Camus.

SAHER
Complete Works
in German 14 Volumes
in English 5 „

The Secret of the Golden Flower. Translated from the Chinese by Richard Wilhelm. Commentary by Dr. C. G. Jung (London and New York, 1931).

SPURGEON, CAROLINE. *Mysticism in English Literature* (Cambridge, 1913).

STOCKS, J. L. *Time, Cause and Eternity* (London, 1938).

STOUT, G. F. *Mind and Matter* (London, 1931).

Sūtra Spoken by the Sixth Patriarch, Hui Neng. Translated by Wung Mou-lam (Shanghai, 1930). Reprinted in *A Buddhist Bible* (Thetford, 1938).

SUZUKI, B. L. *Mahāyāna Buddhism* (London, 1938).

SUZUKI, D. T. *Studies in Zen Buddhism* (London, 1927).
Studies in the Laṅkāvatāra Sūtra (Kyoto and London, 1935).
Manual of Zen Buddhism (Kyoto, 1935).

SUZUKI, DAISETZ TEITARO, *Die grosse Befreiung. Einführung i.d. Zen-Buddhismus.* Geleitwort v. C. G. Jung, Bearbeitet nach dem engl. Original text v. Heinrich Zimmer. 4. Aufl. Zürich 1958.
—*Die Zen-Lehre vom Nicht-Bewusstsein. Die Bedeutung des Sūtra von Hui-neng (Wei-long)* München 1957.
—*Studies in the Laṅkāvatāra Sūtra.* London 1930.
—*Outlines of Mahāyāna Buddhism.* Chicago 1908.
—*A Manual of Zen-Buddhism.* London 1950.
—*Essays in Zen-Buddhism*, 3 Bde. Kyoto/London 1927, 1950, 1953.
—*Leben aus Zen. München* 1955.
—*Der Weg zur Erleuchtung.* Baden-Baden, 1957.
—*Zen und die Kultur Japans. Übers.* v. Otto Fischer.

Stuttgart 1941. Leicht gekürzte Ausgabe in *rowohlt's deutsche enzyklopadie* (Nr. 66). Hamburg 1958.

In den Eranos-Jahrbüchern, Zürich 1933 ff. :

—*The Role of Nature in Zen-Buddhism* (Bd. XXII/1953).

—*The Awakening of a new Consciousness in Zen* (Bd. XXIII/1954).

SCHROEDER, LEOPOLD VON, *Bhagavadgītā, des Erhabenen Sang.* 28-30. Tsd. Köln 1955.

SEIDENSTUCKER, KARL, *Pāli-Buddhismus.* Texte aus dem buddhistischen Pālikanon und dem Kammavāca, 2. Aufl. München 1923.

SINHA, NANDLAL (Sanskrit). *The Sāṁkhya-pravacana-sūtram Sacred Books of the Hindus*, Vol. XI. Allahabad 1915.

SMITH, VINCENT A., *Aśoka, the Buddhist Emperor of India*, 3. durchges. u. erw. Auflage. Oxford 1920.

SOKEI-AN, *Cat's Yawn.* New York (Erstes Zen-Institut von America) 1947.

SPEYER. J. S. *The Jātakamālā*, Sacred Books of the Buddhists, Vol. I. London 1895.

SPRINGMANN, THEODOR, *Bhagavad-Gītā—Der Gesang des Erhabenen* 8, Büdingen Gettebbach 1952.

STCHERBATSKY, TH., *The Conception of Buddhist Nirvāṇa.* Leningrad 1927.

STERN, PH.—Siehe Masson-Oursel, Paul.

STEVENSON, MRS. S., *The Heart of Jainism.* Cambridge 1916.

—*Without the Pale. The Life Story of an Outcaste.* Calcutta 1930.

—*The Rites of the Twice-born.* Oxford, 1920.

TAGORE, RABINDRANATH. *One Hundred Poems of Kabir* (London, 1915).

TAULER, JOHANN. *Life and Sermons* (London, 1907).

The Inner Way (London, 1909).

Consult Inge's *Christian Mysticism*, Rufus Jones's *Studies in Mystical Religion* and Pourrat's *Christian Spirituality.*

TENNANT, F. R. *Philosophical Theology* (Cambridge, 1923).

Theologia Germanica. Winkworth's translation (new edition London, 1937).

TILLYARD, AELFRIDA. *Spiritual Exercises* (London, 1927).

TAKAKUSU, JUNJIRO (s. a. Cowell), *The Essentials of Buddhist Philosophy*, 2 Aufl. Honolulu 1949.

Tempelanlagen, buddhistische in Siam. 1. Abt. v. *Der indische Kulturkreis in Einzeldarstellungen.* Hrsg. v. A. Grünwedel, H. Stönner, K. Döring. Bangkok-Berlin, 1920.

THIBAUT, G. (Übers.) *The Vedānta Sūtra, with Śaṅkara's Commentary* (2 Bde.), Sacred Books of the East, Vol. XXXIV u. XXXVIII. Oxford 1904.

—*The Vedānta Sūtra, with Rāmānuja's Commentary,* Sacred Books of the East, Vol. XLVIII. Oxford, 1904.

THOMAS, E. J., *The Life of Buddha as Legend and History.* New York 1927.

THOMAS, FREDERICK WILLIAM, *Bṛihaspati Sūtra,* Punjab Sanskrit Series, Lahore 1921.

TUCCI, GIUSEPPE, *Il Buddhismo,* Foligno 1926 (engl. 1930).

—*Indo-Tibetica.* Roma 1932-1936.

—*Indian Paintings in western Tibetan Temples.* Leipzig 1937.

—*L'Oriente nella cultura contemporanea.* Firenze 1943.

—*Ramakrishna paramahaṁsa.* Roma 1952.

—*Earth in India and Tibet.* In : Eranos-Jahrbuch XXII/ 1953. Zürich 1954.

Vātsyāyana, Kāmasūtra. Pandit Durgāprasāda, Bombay 1891. Sanskrit (Jayamangala) Yashodhara v. Richard Schmidt, 6. Berlin, 1920.

VĪRESHVARĀNANDA, SWĀMĪ, *Brahma-Sūtras* (Sanskr. u. engl). Mayavati/Almoras/Himalayas 1936.

VIVEKANANDA, SWĀMI, Complete works.

WATTS, ALLAN W., *Zen.* Stanford, Calif, 1948. and complete works.

WESTHEIM, PAUL, *Indische Baukunst.* Orbis Pictus, Bd. 1, Berlin 1920.

WHITNEY, WILLIAM DWIGHT u. Lanman, Charles Rockwell (Übers)., *Atharva Veda* Harvard Oriental Series, Vol. VII u. XIII. Cambridge, Mass. 1905.

WILMAN-GRABOWSKA, H. de—siehe Masson-Oursel, Paul.

WILSON, H. H.—siehe Collebrooke.,

WINTERNITZ, MORITZ, *Geschichte der indischen Literature.* 3, Bde. Leipzig 1905-1922.

—*Die Frau i.d. ind. Religionen.* Leipzig 1920.

WOLFF, OTTO, *Indiens Beitrag zum neuen Menschenbild, rowohlt's deutsche enzyklopadie* (Nr. 56). Hamburg 1957.

—*Der Supramentale Übermensch nach Shrī Aurobindos, Integralem Yoga.* In : *Der Ubermensch.* Eine Diskussion (mit 9 wissensch. Beitragen), hrsg. v. Ernst Benz, Zürich, 1961.

WOODROFFE, SIR JOHN—Avalon, Arthur.

WOODS, JAMES HOUGHTON (Übers), *The Yoga-System of Patañjali.* Harvard Oriental Series. Cambridge/Mass. 1927.

WOODWARD, F. L. u. Hare, E. M., *The Book of the Gradual* Sayings" (Aṅguttura-Nikāya), 5 Bde. London 1932-1936.

YATISWARANANDA, SWAMI, *Religiöse Hindu-Symbolik in ihrer Beziehung zu geistigen Übungen und zur Höherentwicklung.* In : Eranos-Jahrbuch II 1934. Zürich 1935.

ZEITSCHRIFT, WIENER, für die Kunde Süd-u. Ostasiens und Archiv f. indische. Philosophie. Hrsg. v. Erich Frauwallner, Wien 1957 ff.

ZIMMER, HEINRICH s. a. Dunbar u. Suzuki.

—*Ges. Werke* (Rascher-V.)., Bd. 1 : *Mythen und Symbo le in indischer Kunst und Kultur.* Hrsg. v. Joseph Campbell Übers. v. E(rnst) W(ilhelm) Eschmann. Zürich 1951.

—*Ges. Werke,* Bd. 2 : *Maya, der indische Mythos,* Neuaus gabe. Zürich 1952.

—*Ges. Werke,* Bd. 3 : *Der Weg zum Selbst : Leben und Lehre des indischen Heiligen Shri Ramana Maharshi aus Tiruvanna malei.* Mit einem Vorwort hrsg. v. C. G. Jung u.-Nachruf v. Emil Abegg. Neuausgabe Zürich 1954.

—*Ges. Werke,* Bd. 4 : *König und Leichnam* (*The King and the Corpse*). Ubers. v. Joh. Piron, überarb v. Lucy Heyer-Grote.Zürich 1961..

—*Ges, Werke* (inhalt der späteren Bände) :

—*Indische Spharen* (Erstausg. München-Zürich 1935. Schriften d. Corona 12).

—*Spiel um den Elefanten. Ein Buch v. indischer Natur* (München 1929).

Anbetung Mir. Indische Offenbarungsworte nach ā. Aṣṭāvakragitā (Erstausg. München 1929).

—*Karman* (*Divyāvadāna* (*Teilserie*). *Ein buddhistischer Legendenkranz.*

Ubertr. u. hrsg. v. Heinrich Zimmer (Erstausg. München 1925).

—*Hindu-Medizin.* Ubertr. a. d. Englischen.

Ewiges Indien. Leitmotive indischen Daseins (Erstausg Potsdam 1930., Das Weltbild, Bd. 14).

—*Weisheit Indiens. Märchen und Sinnbilder* (2. Aufl. d. Erstausg. Darmstadt 1941).

—*Kunstform und Yoga im indischen Kultbild* (Erstausg. Berlin 1926).

—*Studien zur Geschichte der Gotras* (Diss.), Leipzig 1914.
—In den Eranos-Jahrbüchern (Rhein-Verlag):

—*Zur Bedeutung des indischen Tantra-Yoga* (Bd.I/1933, Zürich 1934).

—*Indische Mythen als Symbole* (Bd. II/1934, Zürich 1935).
—*Die indische Weltmutter* (Bd./VI 1938, Zürich 1939).
—*Tod und Wiedergeburt im indischen Licht* (Bd. VII/1939, Zürich 1940).

—(*Rudrabhaṭṭa*) : *Zeichen der Liebe. Wie man lieben und in Liebe dichten soll* (Schtingara-Tilaka). Ubers. v. Heinrich Zimmer. Calw-Wien 1948.

—*The Art of Indian Asia. Its Mythology and Transformations.* Completed and edited by Joseph Campbell. With photographs by Eliot Elisofon, Dimitri Kessel and others. Text-und Tafelbd. Bollingen-Series XXXIX, New York 1955.

Z. JOHN TAYLOR : *Black Holes : End of the Universe?* London 1974.

ZENSKI, SHIBAYAMA : *A Flower does not talk* Tokyo 1974 (All about ZEN with Foreword by D. T. Suzuki).

INDEX

C

F

G

H

I

J

K

L

M

T

1.

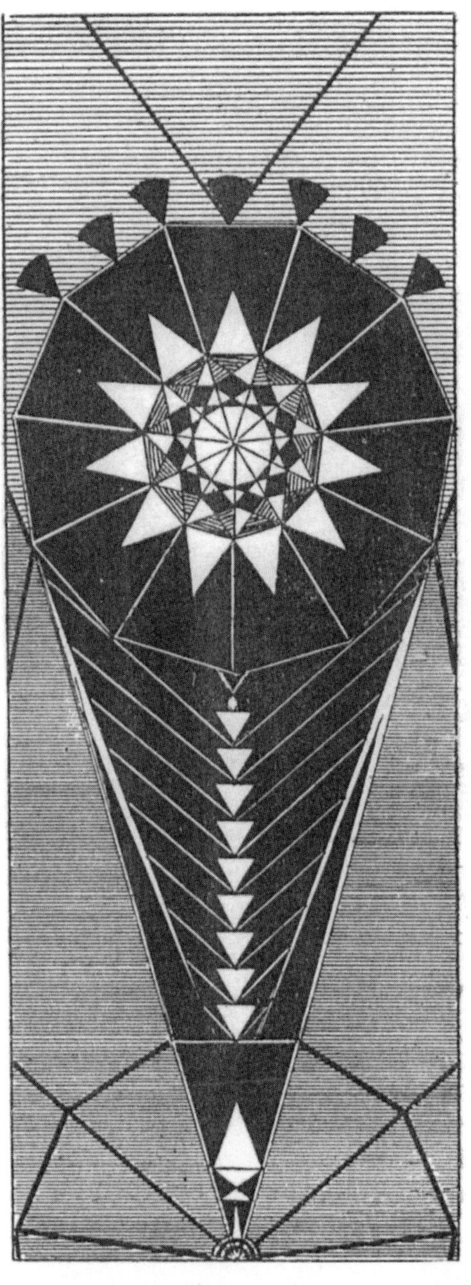

The rising of the Kundalini in the Spinal Cord (as seen through esoteric X-Rays of Röntgen Laboratories) during deep meditation as explained in this book.

2

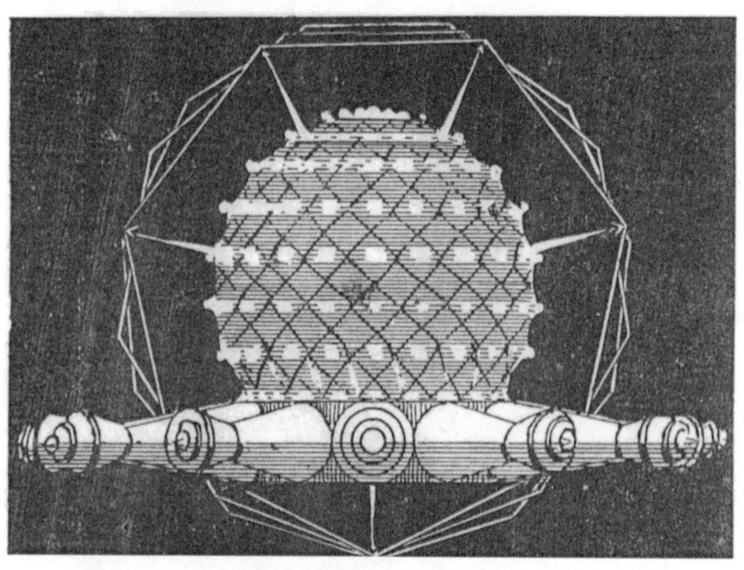

The anatomical brain reconstructed as a Computer kybernetically co-ordinating the Centres.

Wabe 16×
0 250 500 750 1000 1250 1500

$(3528+1 \times \text{Wabe}) = 961^3 \times \pi^{18}$ $y = 33\,5544\ 4851$

A Centre seen as a Mandala of anatomical re-constructs.

4.

0 100 200 300 400 500 600 700 800 900 1000

V-8.4851.4851 F- 1.4851.4851

The brain as pivot of the seven channels leading to it from the Centres.—Mandala of the Esoteric Sciences.

5.

0 25 50 75 100

The ancient Temple of Aloma—Alomanaris in Lemuria where this secret science was first practised.

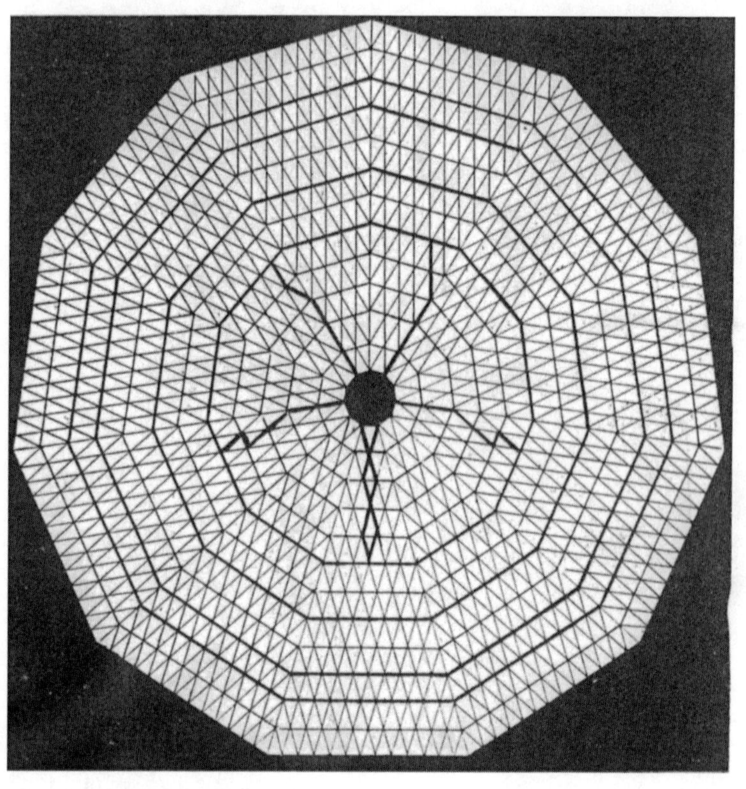

Mandala meditation practice for beginners.

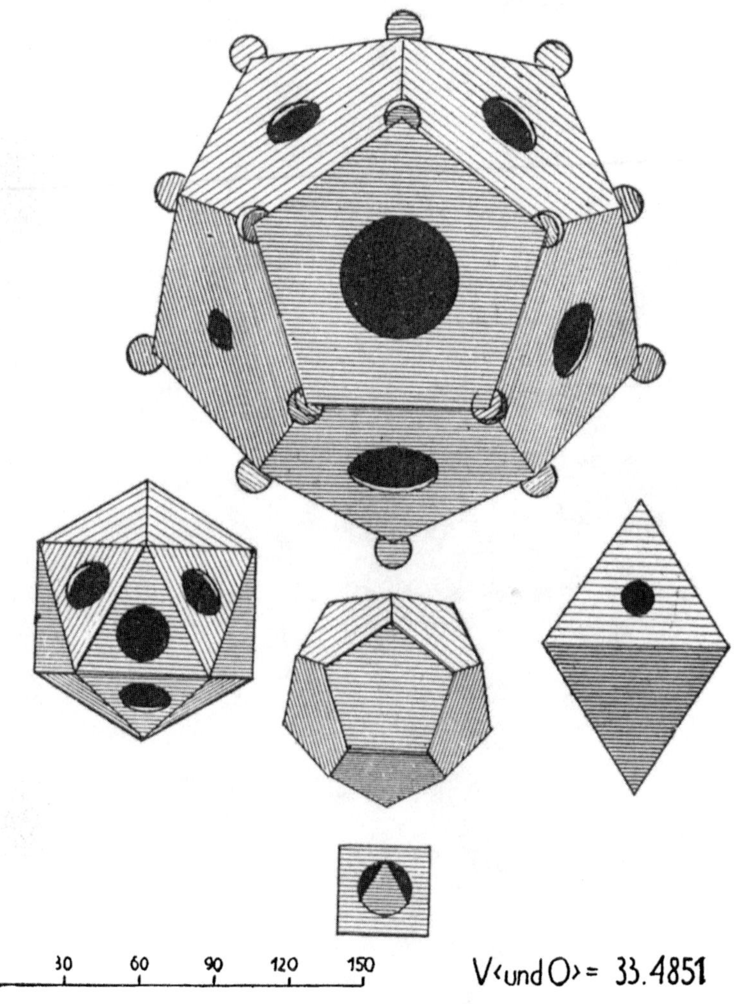

The Centres—and how they fit inside the anatomical brain.

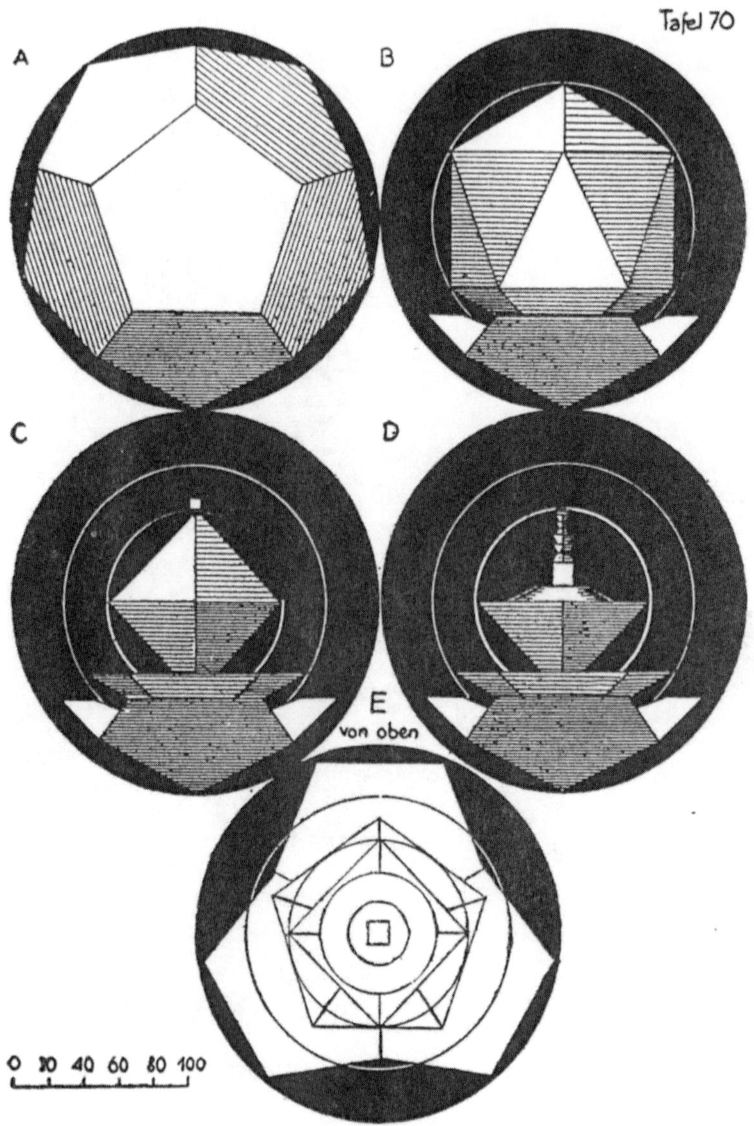

Anatomy of the first 5 Centres.

9.

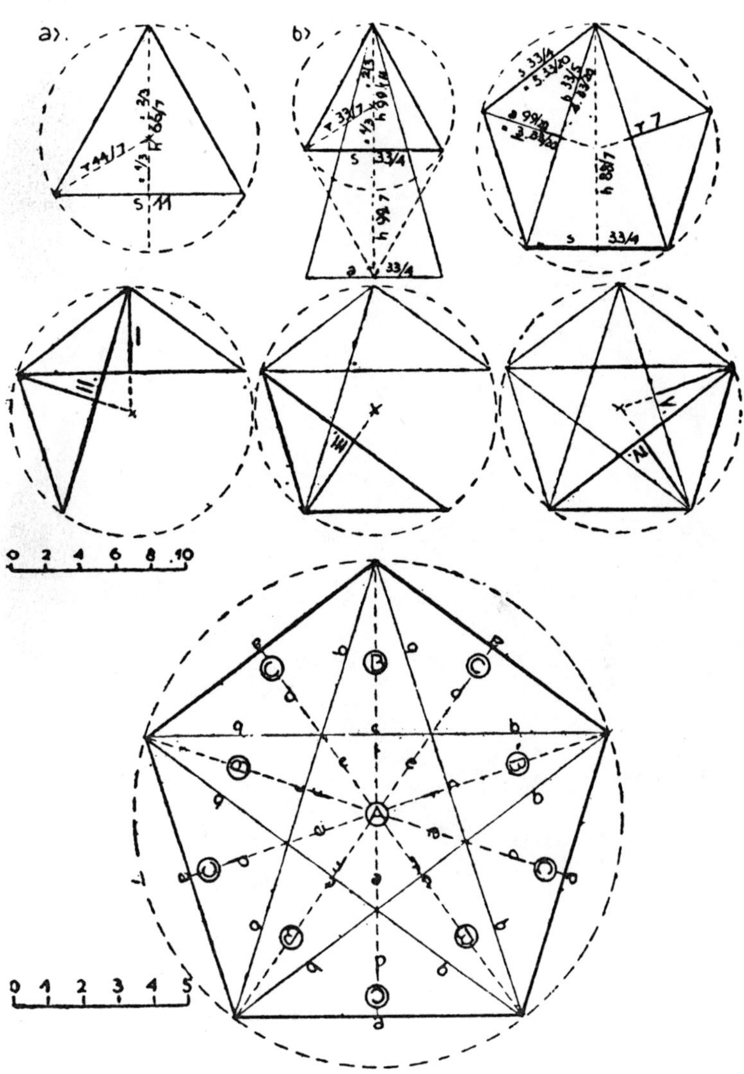

Psychocybernetics of the seven Centres.

10.

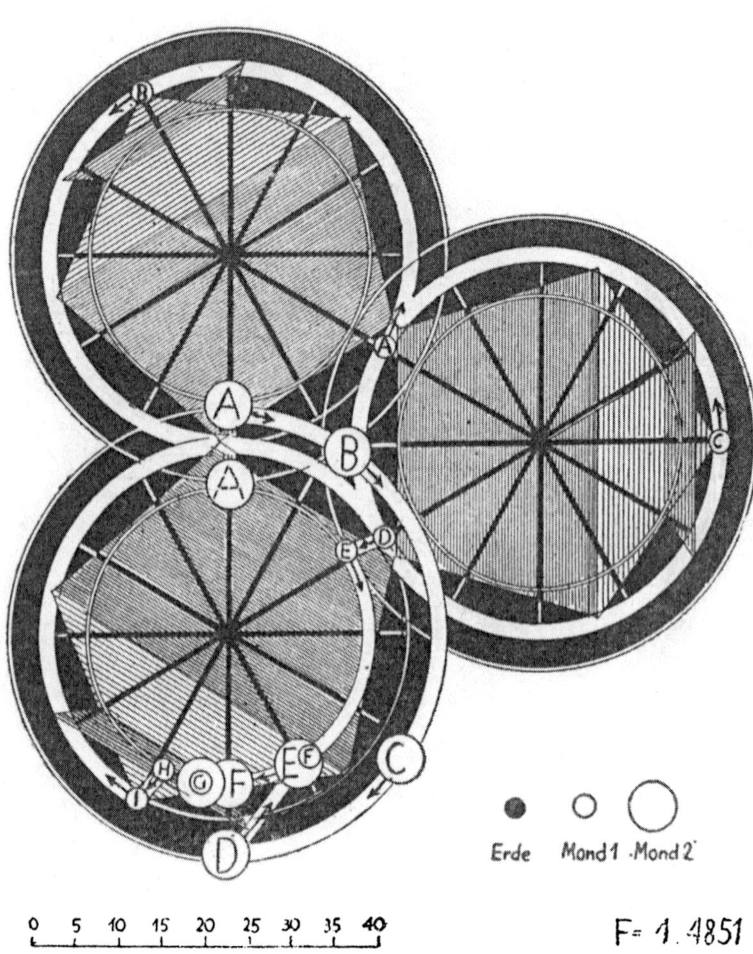

The principal Three Centres working in cosmic harmony with the Phases of the MOON.

11.

Travels with the Astral Body to other Galaxies.

12.

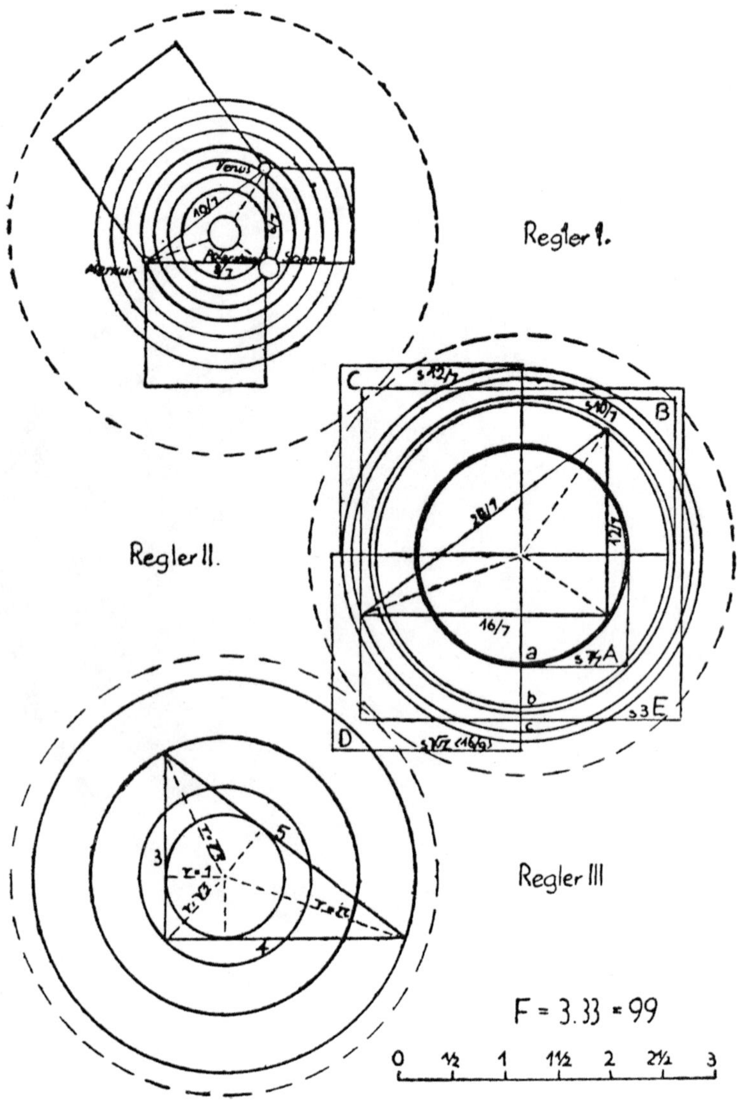

The three principal Centres in psycho-cybernetic Regulation with each other.

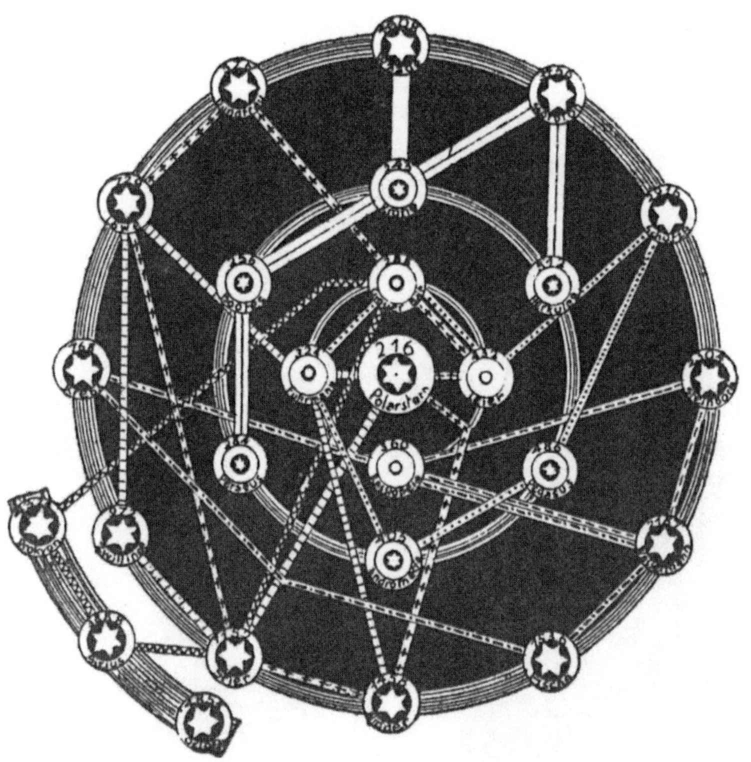

The "Milky Way" seen as an exact Replica of psycho-astrological Meridian Points in the brain.

A Centre converging with a Chakra of the Kundalini.

The third Chakra of the Kundalini as seen in an Astral Body.

16.

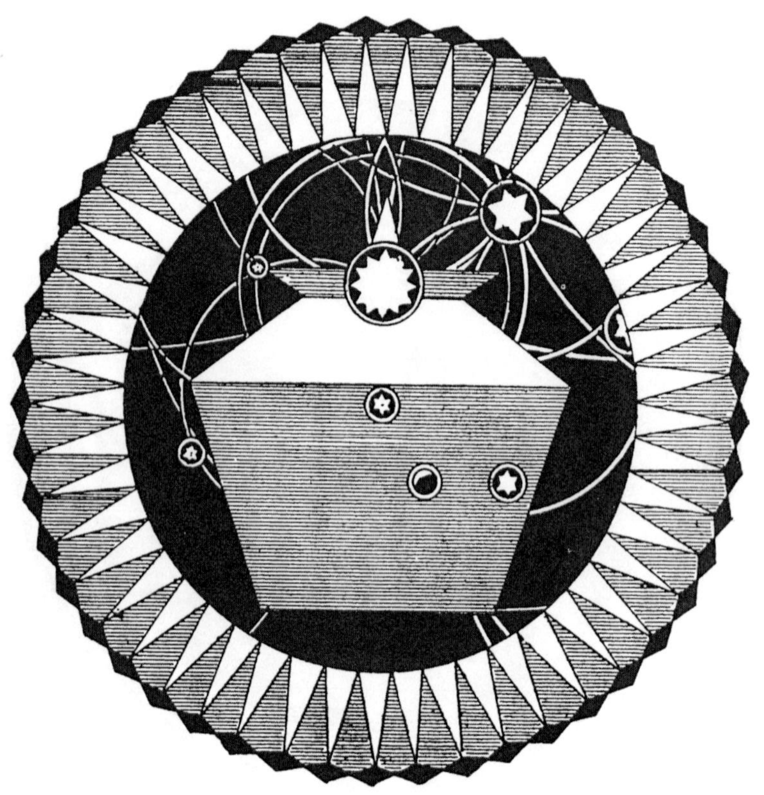

The same third Chakra as seen in a Mental or Causal Body.

17.

The complete astral body as seen during a Zenoga meditation as described in this book.

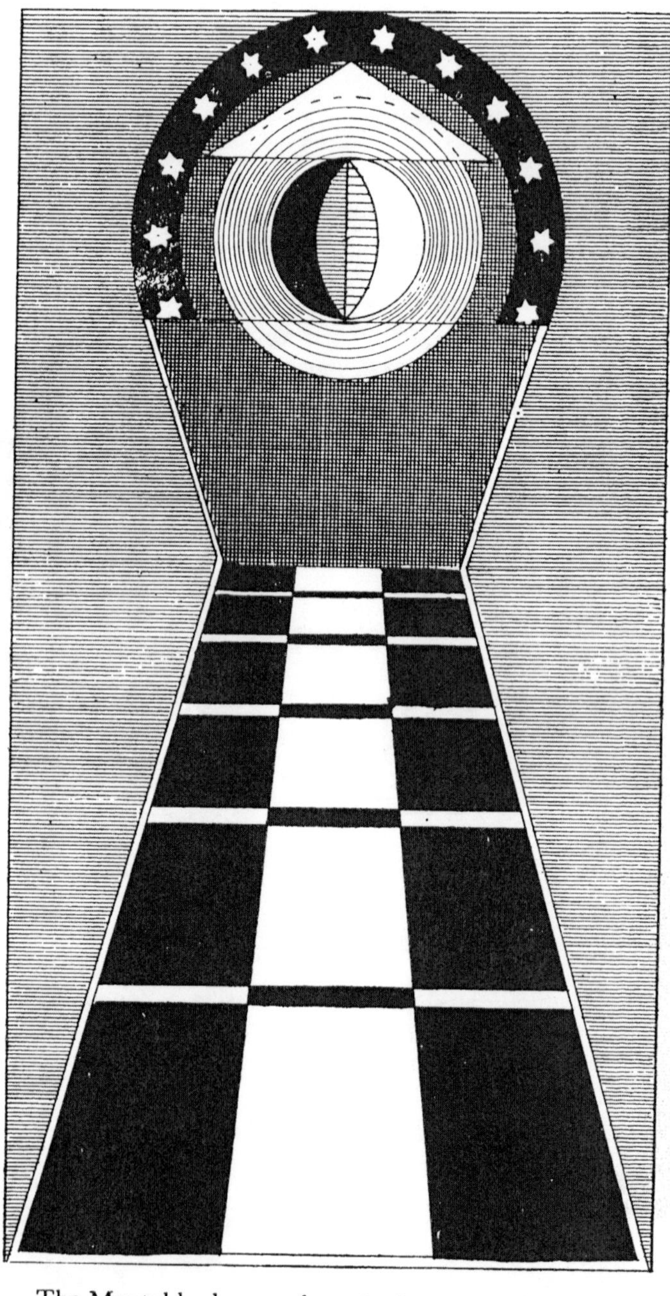

The Mental body—as above in foregoing illustration.

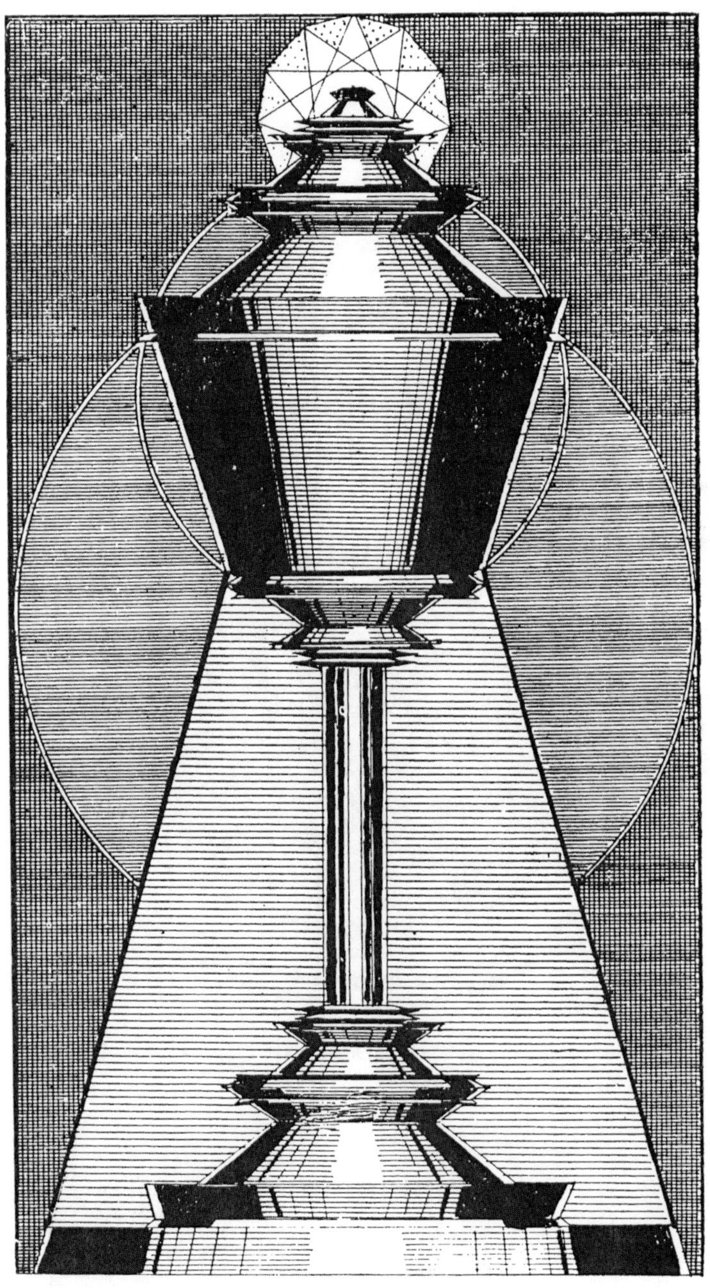

All three bodies combined—DHARMAKAYA—seen as in previous illustration.

20.

The central Star as the macrocosmic Centre co-ordinating the micro-cosmic Centres.

21.

Man in Cosmos : seen as middle-point of co-ordinated astral influences—the Most Primary Horoscope of Man's History on this Planet.

22.

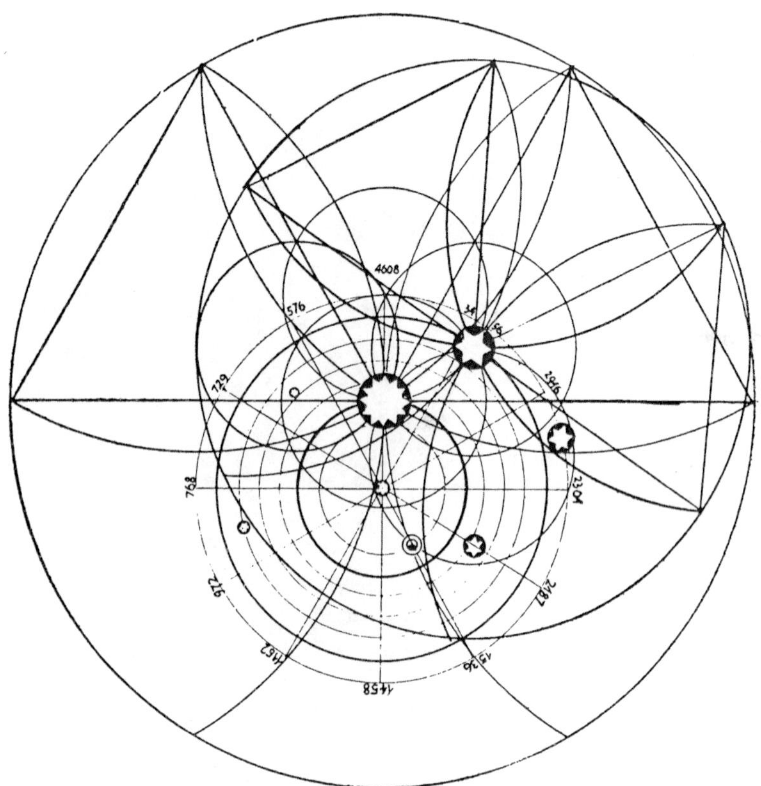

The internal astro-geometric construction of a Chakra.

23.

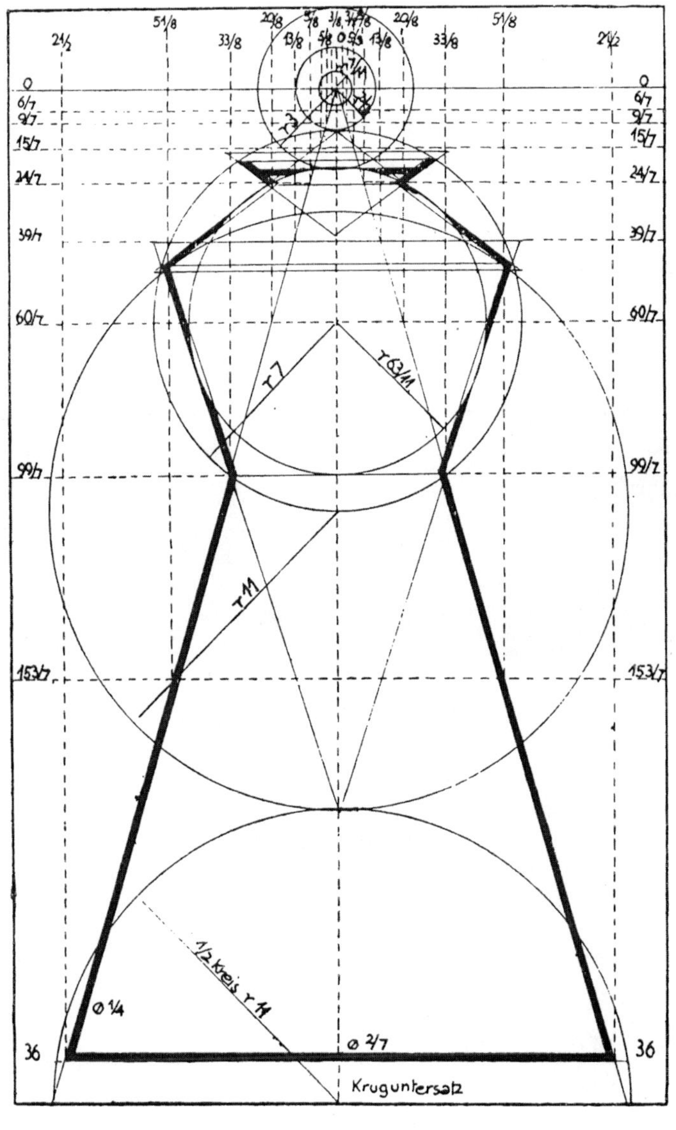

0 2 4 6 8 10 12 14

Kreise U 216

Geometrical proportions of the Astral Body and its Chakras.

24.

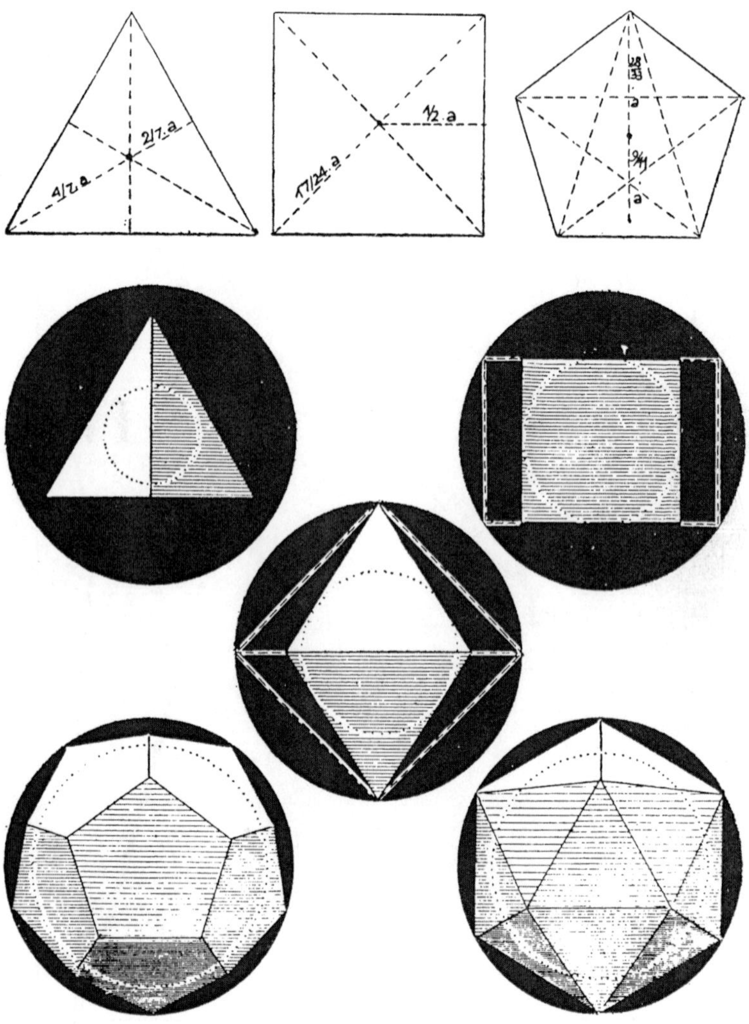

The First Five Centres in their geometric Ratios of an esoteric Mathematics.

25.

The Mandala of the Expanding Universe.